ON THE OFFENSIVE

The Americans were attacking from 19,000 feet. Ashore and on the ships the antiaircraft guns began to open fire and puffs of smoke surrounded the American planes as they came whistling down. But the Japanese gunners were new to the job and no plane was hit. Next came the torpedo planes. Three of the torpedo bombers went after the transports. Seven went after two small minesweepers and one destroyer. The torpedo bombers did a good job. They sank two minesweepers and hurt one destroyer so badly she beached herself.

That day the Americans launched three air strikes. They had done a good deal of damage but not as much as they believed. In fact, the battle had scarcely begun . . .

The Jungles of New Guinea

EDWIN P. HOYT

AVON BOOKS ◆ NEW YORK

CONTENTS

CHAPTER ONE

Retreat Down Under

February 1942. On Bataan, after nearly three months of fighting the Japanese invaders of the Philippines, the American military forces were hoping to go on the offensive. From the attitude of the Japanese troops of Lt. Gen. Masaharu Homma's 14th Imperial Japanese Army, the Americans gathered that Japanese morale was very low. American intelligence officers believed that an offensive at this time would be successful. On February 11, an American naval observer noted that American army morale had not been higher at any time since December 7, 1941, the day the Japanese attacked Pearl Harbor.

But the suggestions of the troops in the line for an American attack were ignored by higher headquarters. What the line troops did not understand was that, since the first days of the war, the Japanese had controlled the sea and the air. Possibly the Americans could win a victory and drive the Japanese back off Bataan Peninsula. Perhaps, as General Homma later testified, a strong American attack might have taken the Americans all the way back to Manila. But that made no difference at all. The real difference was that the Japanese could reinforce their Philippine operations any time they needed to do so. The Americans could not reinforce their positions. Or, at least, looking at the war from the viewpoint of the Joint Chiefs of Staff in Washington, the Americans were not going to reinforce the Philippines. The battering of the U.S. Pacific Fleet at Pearl Harbor and the piecemeal destruction of the U.S. Asiatic Fleet in the Philippines, China, and the Dutch East Indies was part of the reason. The American navy was in no condition at this time to contest the Japanese navy in open battle. As for reinforcements for the

1

Philippines, in Washington the political decision had been made at the highest level that the major American military and naval effort must be against Adolf Hitler in Europe.

Although most Americans expected a vigorous prosecution of the Pacific War, it was going to have to wait. The decision made in Washington was that the Americans in the Philippines were to hold out as long as possible against the Japanese. Something might break in the interim to make the situation better. But the fact was that no one in Washington really believed that.

Early in February, the Joint Chiefs of Staff were considering the situation of Gen. Douglas MacArthur, American commander in the Philippines and former U.S. Army Chief of Staff. What was to be done about him? The bearer of a distinguished name, particularly distinguished in Asia, MacArthur was again regarded in Washington as a valuable man. That had not always been so; he had gone to the Philippines as chief of the Philippine armed forces when he had apparently run out his string in Washington in the early 1930s. But times had changed. The war had brought a new perspective to the military men in Washington. The problem in February, according to Former Secretary of War Patrick J. Hurley, was to extricate MacArthur from the Philippines without soiling his reputation.

Gen. George C. Marshall, the U.S. Army Chief of Staff, was turning over a plan in his mind. There had to be some basic line of defense in the Pacific so that the Americans could begin planning for an offensive war. Just now, in February, the Japanese were reaching a high watermark. Their victories had been swift and simple; the Western Allies had been totally unprepared for the sort of offensive the Japanese had unleashed. They had also shown themselves to be soft and undertrained for warfare. The Japanese troops were tough as leather; they could march forty miles a day and live on a ball of rice and a pickled plum. The American, British, and Dutch soldiers in the Far East were used to soft garrison life. In the Philippines, the American and Filipino soldiers were just now becoming effective. Elsewhere, the Japanese were triumphant. On February 15, Singapore surrendered to Gen. Tomoyuki Yamashita. In the Dutch East Indies, the Japanese were forging ahead, and Gen. Archibald Wavell's American-

British-Dutch-Australian (ABDA) defenses were crumbling fast. As General Marshall knew, there was simply not time to save what was being lost in the Pacific. The new line had to be established, and the Americans had to fight their way back to victory.

Marshall and the others in Washington were still pretty fuzzy about what was actually going on in the Philippines. Marshall suggested to MacArthur that he might want to go down to Mindanao and hold out with a guerilla operation until Washington could bring help. But MacArthur told Washington that the condition of the American forces on Bataan was so bad that they could not hold out long. He seconded a suggestion by President Manuel Quezon of the Philippines that the United States immediately grant the Filipinos the freedom promised them—but promised a few years hence—and also declare the Philippines a neutral in the Pacific War. Thus, American and Japanese forces would both be withdrawn.

It seems most unlikely that the Japanese in their euphoria of victory would have accepted such a solution, but the point is moot because the Americans did not accept it.

As February came to an end, events were moving so rapidly that the Americans and British could scarcely keep up with them. At the outbreak of the Pacific War, the two nations had adopted a Combined Chiefs of Staff system that covered all fronts. The Combined Chiefs of Staff surveyed the Pacific War situation, saw that it was becoming desperate, and told General Wavell to dissolve his ABDA command in Java and turn the local fighting over to the Dutch. The Dutch East Indies, then, were seen as lost.

Although the situation looked completely negative at the moment, the plan for the Allied war in the Pacific was beginning to take shape.

The Japanese had moved south into the Bismarck Archipelago and into Dutch New Guinea, and they were casting their eyes at Port Moresby and Australian New Guinea, which the Australians had taken over from the Germans after World War I. The Japanese might capture New Guinea. But they would certainly hesitate before launching a major offensive against New Zealand or Australia until they had a much larger landing force and naval support force available than they had at the moment in that area. They also needed some time to build up their forces at Truk and at Rabaul, respectively, the new major military and air base they had occupied. Therefore, the Joint Chiefs of Staff decided that Australia was the place from which the American comeback would have to be staged, and the Combined Chiefs of Staff agreed. Starting anew in Australia would give the Americans a little breathing space. The Washington leaders had decided what was gone was gone, and that meant the Philippines.

President Franklin Delano Roosevelt talked of defending the American flag in the Philippines "to the death" and of marshaling forces outside the Philippines to come in and drive the Japanese out.

It was a pious but not a very practical hope, given the commitment of the United States to the European war and the paucity of American forces at that moment.

MacArthur accepted the no surrender policy and decided that he and his family would remain on Corregidor and share the fate of the American garrison, which at that moment appeared to be annihilation.

When General Marshall learned of that decision, he suggested that MacArthur really should come out and take a new command. The American need for military genius was enormous at the moment.

For a brief time, on February 21, it appeared that MacArthur might move down to Mindanao and undertake to fight from there. But if that were to be effective, he would need the support of major air and naval attacks from the Dutch East Indies by Allied forces to support an invasion of Luzon Island. And hour by hour, the impossibility of such a project was becoming clearer, as the Japanese rolled up victory upon victory.

The problem in Washington was lack of accurate information. Nobody knew what was happening in the Dutch East Indies. President Roosevelt then showed a considerable degree of prescience. Without information, he acted. On February 22, he personally directed MacArthur to leave the Philippines. First, he said, MacArthur would go to Mindanao and organize the resistance to the Japanese. Then, he would leave for Australia where he would assume command of Allied forces and begin the struggle to defeat the Japanese.

* * *

First, there was talk about taking MacArthur and his party out of Corregidor by submarine. But the submarines were heavily occupied in fruitless attacks on the Japanese. For one thing, their torpedoes were defective. In the end, the decision was made to go out by patrol torpedo (PT) boat, and a flotilla of four PT boats was put together under Lt. J. D. Bulkeley. MacArthur along with his wife, his son, the boy's Chinese amah, and seventeen staff officers were chosen to be saved. These last included Maj. Gen. Richard K. Sutherland, MacArthur's chief of staff; Brig. Gen. Richard J. Marshall, assistant chief of staff; Gen. Charles A. Willoughby, intelligence officer; Brig. Gen. Spencer B. Akin, signal officer; Brig. Gen. Hugh J. Casey, engineering officer; Brig. Gen. William F. Marquat, antiaircraft officer; Brig. Gen. Harold H. George, air officer; and a number of aides—Maj. C. H. Morhouse, a medical officer, and Rear Adm. Francis W. Rockwell of the U.S. Asiatic Fleet. The latter had remained in the Philippines when his command moved to Java.

On March 12, the party left Corregidor as darkness settled down over Manila Bay. At 9:15 P.M., the PT boats edged out of the minefield and went south at top speed. In the night, the flotilla got separated, and one PT boat, mistaking another for an enemy, dumped its spare fuel and speeded up to evade. The next morning, Bulkeley had a problem. One boat was going to run out of fuel before they got to Mindanao. He rounded up the flotilla by radio, and they put in at an uninhabited island in the Cuyo group. The fuel-short PT boat was abandoned and its passengers were split up among the other three boats. They hurried on toward Mindanao Island. At dawn on March 14, they reached the north shore of that island. There, they were met by Brig. Gen. William F. Sharp, commander of American forces in the southern Philippines. Sharp took the party to Del Monte Airfield where they were supposed to be met by four B-17s sent up from Australia. But it is a measure of the lack of American military competence and preparedness of the period that two of the B-17s had gotten lost and failed to arrive. A third had crashed. The fourth was in such poor shape that when MacArthur looked it over, he declared it unfit to carry passengers.

There was a reason for this problem. Since December, the

6 THE JUNGLES OF NEW GUINEA

B-17s in the Pacific had been overworked. Day after day they had been sent out on bombing missions without respite. The crews were tired, and the relief crews were not very well trained. So, it was problem upon problem.

Three more B-17s were sent up from Australia and two of them made it, reaching Del Monte at midnight on March 16. MacArthur was satisfied that these planes and crews were an improvement, and the party boarded. At 9:00 A.M. on March 17, they reached Darwin. After a little heroics,* MacArthur settled down to assess his situation.

At this point, General MacArthur was still thinking about mounting an offensive in Mindanao against the Japanese. He had so told General Sharp and Brig. Gen. B. G. Chynoweth, whom he put in command of the American forces in the Visayan Islands. As he left Corregidor, he had told the defenders that he would return. It was the precursor to his famous "I shall return . . ." speech, and he meant every word of it. But what MacArthur did not know at the time was that Washington and London had agreed to take their lumps in the Pacific for the moment and to concentrate on defeating Hitler. A holding action would be fought in the Pacific, with such limited offensives as might be possible with minimal resources. Then, once Hitler was defeated, the total power of the Allies would be turned against Japan. That thinking, of course, was more London than Washington, but it prevailed because President Roosevelt saw the logic of it and the greater danger to humanity posed by Hitler's depredations.

In all innocence, then, MacArthur expected to be given the resources to reconquer the Philippines in short order. His last instructions to the commander of the Corregidor garrison were to hold Corregidor until he returned.

* * *

* MacArthur's message to General Marshall on safe arrival: "[T]his hazardous trip by a commanding general and key members of his staff through enemy controlled territory undoubtedly is unique in military annals. I wish to commend the courage and coolness of the officers and men who were engaged in this hazardous enterprise. It was entirely due to their invincible resolution and determination that the mission was successfully accomplished."

Only after General MacArthur arrived in Australia did he learn the true state of affairs in the Pacific. There would be no relief of Corregidor. Washington would give him only two divisions of American troops. Even these were not regulars, but National Guardsmen—still in training—of the 32nd and 41st divisions. The Australians were going to have trouble helping: their four trained divisions were all involved in Britain's war effort elsewhere; the 8th Division was largely lost in the fall of Malaya. The 6th, 7th and 9th Australian Infantry divisions were fighting the Germans in the Middle East. What was left in Australia was around 250,000 militia, the equivalent to the U.S. National Guard, with just about as much training and experience.

Equally difficult, from MacArthur's point of view, the Joint Chiefs of Staff had chosen to split the Pacific command. President Roosevelt had talked about making MacArthur supreme commander of American forces in the Pacific. But when it came down to the actual designation, it was a bit different.

MacArthur was to be supreme commander all right. The command would include Australia, New Zealand, Timor, Amboina, and New Guinea. But, in reality, the Pacific was divided into two commands. One area was the Pacific Ocean, which included the North, Central, and South Pacific. This was under the command of Adm. Chester W. Nimitz of the U.S. Navy. His deputy was Rear Adm. Robert L. Ghormley, who was setting up headquarters in New Zealand. The second area was the Southwest Pacific. It included Australia, the Philippines, a part of the Dutch East Indies, and the land and sea approaches to Australia. General MacArthur would hold that command. So, in the interim period between the time he left the Philippines and the time he arrived in Australia, the entire command situation had changed. In addition to all his other problems, MacArthur now discovered that he was not going to be the kingpin in the Pacific and that he was not going to be given the resources to counterattack the Japanese in the Philippines.

CHAPTER TWO

Japan's Drive South

In 1906, the Imperial Japanese Government of Emperor Meiji, surveying the Pacific scene, established the United States as the successor to Russia as Japan's number one potential enemy in the Pacific. Japan had defeated the Russians in the Russo-Japanese War of 1904–1905. The Americans, offering to act as peacemakers, had forced upon Japan at the Treaty of Portsmouth a peace that did not include any financial reparations. The treaty was unacceptable to the Japanese military, but it was not in control of the government at that time. Its attitudes, however, did help shape policy then and for the future.

It is more than coincidental that smarting from the peace treaty, the military was infuriated by President Teddy Roosevelt's naked show of force in sending the Great White Fleet on a round-the-world voyage. His major reason was to make a show of force in Japanese waters. It all happened in 1908, the dispatch of the Great White Fleet and the basic change in Japan's defense orientation.

Theodore Roosevelt's real intent in sending the Great White Fleet out was admittedly to impress the Japanese. Although the fleet was half fake (with false armor and plating on some ships), it did impress the Japanese, and they assembled their own considerably larger fleet to make their own show of force. The whole enterprise was a dreadful failure in American foreign policy, and the results are obvious: Japan decided that America was the natural enemy.

Thereafter, the basic Japanese defense policy was founded on that assumption. In World War I, Japan found herself allied with the United States through her alliance with Britain. Japan's eagerness to enter that war was occasioned by her desire for territorial aggrandizement, which was achieved, at first, by the takeover of the old German Kiaochaw colony in China's Shantung Province (now Chiao Hsien, Shandong Province). But the territory had to be relinquished on the assumption of most of Germany's Pacific colonies as a League of Nations' mandate, one that Japan had no intention of honoring.

Only in 1934, when the British had improved the fortifications of Singapore, did the Japanese add Britain to the list of potential enemies and begin planning for military and naval operations against the British, the Australians, and the New Zealanders. All this was an indirect result of the military takeover of Japan by the army–navy oligarchy that had become firmly established in 1930 and the invasion and capture of Manchuria in 1931. Britain then showed her concern over events in Asia. Thus, the long alliance that had led Japan into World War I at the side of Britain came to an end. From the point of view of the militarists, Britain became just another of the "oppressive powers" that were trying to box Japan in.

So, the Japanese planning began. In case of war, Australia and New Zealand as well as the British colonies in Hong Kong and Malaya would have to be dealt with.

Since 1938, the Imperial Japanese Navy had been reconnoitering the South Pacific area with spies, submarines, and every other device they knew. By 1941, they had a thorough knowledge of the area and its defenses. In December, the Australian defenders of Rabaul and Papua became accustomed to the Japanese overflights with big four-engined Kawanishi flying boats that were both long-range reconnaissance aircraft and bombers.

In Tokyo in December 1941, the Imperial General Headquarters (IGH) watched in a sort of awe the results of the chain of events it had set in motion with the move southward into Malaya, the Philippines, and the Dutch East Indies. The victories came very rapidly. By New Year's Day it was apparent that the Japanese could go farther if they wished. They decided to capture Rabaul, the strategic port on New Britain Island and from that major base to undertake the capture of New Guinea. Their eye was now turned to Australia and New

Zealand, although they were not prepared to commit so far at the moment. There was a feeling in the Tokyo air that the whole Pacific was Japan's oyster.

The Combined Fleet's striking force, the Japanese carriers, had returned from the Pearl Harbor operation unscathed and could easily and usefully be employed in a new adventure. Therefore, IGH speeded up their planning, which had not envisaged so swift a movement, and ordered the softening and then the capture of Rabaul. That would be followed, said IGH, by the invasion of southern New Guinea and by the capture of Port Moresby as a base for further operations against Australia.

The action began on January 4, 1942, with an air raid on Rabaul. Then, on January 20 Adm. Isoroku Yamamoto sent the carriers down. A hundred planes blasted Rabaul, destroying the Australian air force contingent based there and the air installations. The next day the Japanese were back, and their dive-bombers headed straight for the two six-inch naval guns—discarded by the navy but picked up by the shore defenders—that protected the harbor. Both were destroyed, along with two smaller antiaircraft guns, and the way was cleared for a swift invasion of Rabaul.

The Japanese chose the best shock troops they had in the South Pacific to make the attack on Rabaul. The unit was the *Nankai Shitai* (South Seas Detachment). This unit had been organized out of the Imperial Army's 55th Infantry Division, which was stationed on Shikoku Island. It was, in reality, a reinforced regiment, the 144th Infantry, but it was nearly double the strength of an ordinary regiment and its troops were highly trained in jungle warfare, highly disciplined, and highly motivated. They were five thousand strong, with double weaponry. They were something like the U.S. Marines in esprit de corps. Their leader had left command of the 55th Infantry Division to take over this special unit. That tells something: he was a major general, the normal rank for commander of a division, and he was heading up a unit that would normally be under a colonel. He was Maj. Gen. Tomitaro Horii, considered to be one of Japan's best fighting generals. The *Nankai Shitai*'s first military adventure had been a piece of cake: the invasion of Guam, an American colony ruled by the U.S. Navy but manned by only a handful of troops who had promptly surrendered. The *Nankai Shitai* had stood poised for the invasion of Wake Island. They were also scheduled, later, to undertake the invasion of Port Moresby and, still later, Midway Island if Admiral Yamamoto's Midway Plan was finally approved.

In the meantime, Admiral Yamamoto was ordered to support Vice Adm. Shigeyoshi Inoue's 4th Fleet, which would, in turn, support the army landings on Rabaul. At the same time, Admiral Inoue's naval troops would capture Kavieng on the long tip of New Ireland Island northeast of New Britain. The two captures would give the Japanese command of the seas around southeastern New Guinea.

D day was January 23.

On January 16, the invasion fleet left Guam. It consisted of eight army transports, carrying the *Nankai Shitai* and the 4th Fleet units, which were supported by two Combined Fleet carriers, *Kaga* and *Akagi*.

The Japanese army always supplied its own transports, which were manned by army personnel. Ultimately, this practice would lead to one of the great Japanese tragedies of the South and Southwest Pacific campaigns—but the Japanese separation of army and navy was total. In the months to come, the Japanese operations in New Guinea would be managed by the army, whereas those in the Solomon Islands would be a mixed operation. The navy's prime role in the area would be to seek out the American fleet and destroy it as well as to provide air support to army operations. Later, the navy would be charged with the resupply of army forces.

But in January 1942, none of this seemed important or even very difficult. Japan was winning everywhere—not only winning, but doing so with ridiculous ease.

The first port of call was Kavieng. As the Japanese convoy went by, the naval troops stopped and captured the town without opposition. The very small Australian garrison tried to escape in a sloop; but when a destroyer pulled alongside, there was nothing for the sloop skipper to do but surrender.

The main body of the Rabaul invasion force arrived off New Britain Island on the night of January 22 just after midnight. Thus, it was early on January 23 that the invasion began. Troops landed at Karavia and at Simpson Harbour. Others landed at Raluana Point and Vulcan Island. The Australian garrison consisted of fourteen hundred officers and men. By dawn, the Japanese had surrounded them. The Australians continued to fight. Their weapons were not imposing—mortars, machine guns, and rifles. The Japanese had all these plus the naval artillery of the fleet to support them. By 10 o'clock on the morning of January 23, it was painfully apparent that the game was up, and the Australian order was given to disband and try to escape in small groups. Some of the troops insisted on fighting to the death. Most of them were either captured or killed in their ragged retreat. But about four hundred of them managed to elude the Japanese in the jungle and ultimately to march to the south and northern coasts of New Britain. In miniature then, this was an Australian Dunkirk, with brave sailors in small boats moving into waters that were controlled by the Japanese navy and taking off the survivors to safety.

From the Japanese point of view, the Rabaul–Kavieng operation was totally successful, of a piece with everything else that was going on these days. With an absolutely minimal loss of life, they had taken Rabaul. With no loss at all, they had taken Kavieng.

The next step for the Japanese, then, would be to take Port Moresby. After that, they could clear out the few remaining troops in the Bulolo Valley of New Guinea, a three-thousand-foot-high area notable for its Wau Airfield. There were no Australian troops at Lae or Salamaua. So, it would not be much of a job, it seemed, to take all of Papua, the Australian half of New Guinea Island. Except for Port Moresby and Balolo, there was only a handful of Australian commandos in the Solomons, but they were ready to disappear at a moment's notice and become guerillas or coast watchers. With a few airfields, including the two very good ones at Rabaul, the Japanese would be able to dominate the Australian shipping lanes and prevent any trouble from this area. This was their aim as they rolled up the Allied forces in the Dutch East Indies.

The Malayan campaign ended on February 15 with British surrender. The Japanese invaded Celebes and Borneo. They captured Amboina. They invaded Sumatra.

On February 19, they bombed Darwin, Australia, severely; on February 20, they landed on Timor.

The plans were already issued by IGH for the occupation of Lae and Salamaua, preparatory to taking Port Moresby. Tulagi Island, across the strait from Guadalcanal in the Solomons, was also to be occupied at that same general time in order to build a seaplane base at that spot.

Admiral Inoue and General Horii agreed that the navy would occupy Lae and the army would occupy Salamaua. The navy would then undertake to supply both new garrisons.

The IGH had called for the invasion to begin before the end of February, but the American navy threw a monkey wrench into the plans. Rear Adm. Aubrey W. Fitch's carrier task force, built around the USS *Lexington*, was sent out by Admiral Nimitz to break up the Japanese operations in the Rabaul area. *Lexington*'s planes were soon buzzing around Rabaul and creating a certain amount of surprise and confusion. From Rabaul, the Japanese sent out a strong force of bombers. Intercepted by the *Lexington*'s carrier fighters, eighteen of the Japanese bombers were shot down. This was really the first defeat of any sort that the Japanese had suffered, but it did not deserve to be called a battle. The Japanese were surprised by the fury and efficiency of the Americans. Unfortunately, American carrier admirals had not yet learned how to refuel efficiently except on the calmest of seas, and Admiral Fitch had not seen many calm seas recently. The force ran short of oil and withdrew beyond the range of Rabaul's bombers. Thus, the day of reckoning was postponed. Admiral Fitch was not really aware of it, but he was the first American commander to put a hitch in the plans of IGH: the Lae–Salamaua invasion was postponed until March. Beginning on March 2, planes of Japan's 10th Air Fleet, now stationed at Rabaul, began hitting all the Australian communities on New Guinea. They bombed Port Moresby, Lae, Salamaua, Bulolo, and Wau. Meanwhile, the invasion force was assembled.

The attack would be made by a strike force of battalion strength from the *Nankai Shitai*. The Japanese would go in with naval and air support, capture Salamaua, wipe out all resistance, and then return to Rabaul. A naval-base command and some construction troops to build an airfield would go ashore. They would remain as garrison.

Lae would be captured by navy troops of the Maizuru 2nd

Special Landing Force, a unit roughly comparable to the U.S. Marines. That unit, too, would wipe up the opposition, and then the base would be occupied by construction troops and a garrison force.

The Japanese had been surprised by the appearance of Admiral Fitch's task force in the area. Admiral Yamamoto had detailed no carriers to work there. With the two major airfields at Rabaul and another under construction at Kavieng, no one at IGH thought it necessary to worry too much about Admiral Fitch's evanescent task force once it showed up. So, they did not. Besides, there was still another reason for the absence of Japanese carriers in the south: the Combined Fleet's big carrier task force was off on other business, attacking the British fleet at Ceylon (now Sri Lanka). Other carriers might have been dragooned into service, but no particular need was seen because the naval air units on Rabaul and at Truk were so strong.

The Japanese invasion convoy consisted of eight transports and cargo ships protected by three cruisers, eight destroyers, and a seaplane tender. At this stage of the war, the Japanese put great store by their seaplane flotillas, which were particularly useful for short-range observation. The beauty of a seaplane base in the front line was the speed with which it could be put together. No field to build, no hangars to worry about. A protected cove, a launching ramp, and all was complete for operations.

At Lae and Salamaua, the Japanese once again had ho-hum landings. The convoy reached the Huon Gulf on the night of March 7. Right on schedule at 1:00 A.M. on March 8, the Japanese army troops went ashore at Salamaua. Within an hour, the shock troops had wiped out all opposition and were ready to go back aboard their ships.

Eighteen miles north, the navy troops landed at Lae with the same ease. The Australian garrisons of both towns moved up into the Balolo Valley. The only enemy the Japanese met for the next few days were members of a few patrols.

On land, it all looked simple.

But at sea, Admiral Inoue's convoy got into trouble.

On the morning of March 9, a flight of ANZAC (Australian Strategic Command) B-17s from Townsville, Queensland, appeared over the Japanese convoy. From high altitude, they bombed, but they did not hit anything. This was not unusual; indeed, the Japanese naval commanders by this time had developed such a contempt for the bombing of B-17s that they accused the Americans of being unable to hit anything at all. The problem, as the Allies would learn in this campaign, was altitude; it was a problem that would be solved. A bomber cannot hit maneuvering ships with a Norden bombsight. An entirely different technique was needed.

But the B-17s were not the only enemy aircraft in the area. Admiral Nimitz had sent Adm. Frank Jack Fletcher on the carrier *Yorktown* down to the South Pacific to help Admiral Fitch break up the Japanese operations. As senior commander, Fletcher was in charge of the combined operations of the two carrier forces. This day, March 9, the carriers, very nicely situated in the Gulf of Papua, put out 104 planes from their decks. They flew across a pass in the Owen Stanley Mountains and burst out upon the Japanese task force in the Huon Gulf. Later, along came six Royal Australian Air Force Hudson bombers and more of the B-17s. In this unheralded naval battle, the Allied airmen sank three ships and damaged four. That meant the Japanese troops were ashore, but they were already suffering from short supply. The next day, the B-17s were back and they did something they were prepared to do: they bombed the shore and air installations at Lae and Salamaua.

The Japanese were not seriously disturbed, however. Confidence was a useful weapon. They knew that they could not expect to go totally unscathed. They had already brought in fighter planes from Rabaul; by nightfall on March 10, the construction battalions had repaired the damage done to the runways and buildings at both Lae and Salamaua. Three days later, the area was declared by Admiral Inoue to be secure; his task force took aboard all the shock troops and carried them back to Rabaul. They arrived safely on March 15 and began to prepare for the next operation: the capture of Port Moresby.

CHAPTER THREE

Port Moresby

General MacArthur faced the problems of organizing a whole new command with extremely limited resources. In April, he put together a command staff:

Land Forces: Gen. Sir Thomas Blamey, Australian Army
Air Forces: Lt. Gen. George H. Brett, U.S. Army
Naval Forces: Vice Adm. Herbert F. Leary, U.S. Navy

The first problem that MacArthur faced in terms of Allied relationships was the feeling among the Australians that their defense had to be conducted on the shores of Australia, not on its approaches. Thus, the Australians had failed to reinforce Rabaul, Salamaua, Lae, and Port Moresby. Now, the last-named seaport was directly under threat of Japanese occupation.

But MacArthur had hardly arrived when, on looking at his maps, he saw that the real key to Australia's defense lay in New Guinea. The battle, he said, would have to be waged on the outer-perimeter territories.

In the first week of April, the Australian military authorities and MacArthur's staff prepared a joint estimate of the military situation. They noted the impending Port Moresby attack, which could come at any time. They needed aircraft and land forces. Fortunately, the 7th Australian Infantry Division had been sent back from the Middle East to help meet this threat. Also, the 41st U.S. Infantry Division—untried to be sure—was just docking at Melbourne. The 32nd U.S. Division was under orders for Australia, although still in the United States.

In April, the greatest help came from the build-up of the air forces. MacArthur said he needed about seven hundred aircraft, and by the end of the month he had most of them, with more promised. The sea force provided a greater problem. Admiral Leary managed to put together three heavy cruisers, three light cruisers, fifteen destroyers, thirty-one submarines, and some smaller ships. They were a combination of Australian and American vessels, with one Dutch light cruiser. Two heavy cruisers, one light cruiser, and four destroyers were Australian. The rest of the major ships were American, including all the submarines.

MacArthur did not pause to argue the question of perimeter versus far-reaches defense. Immediately in April, he began the reinforcement of Port Moresby. The submarines began working from Brisbane and Fremantle, Australia.

One of the saving graces for MacArthur was the availability of merchant shipping—Dutch, Australian, and New Zealand—an enormous boon in terms of resupplying the islands north of Australia. The great difficulty was that the Japanese had undisputed control of the air in both the Southwest Pacific and the South Pacific. That factor would have to be turned around before any sort of victory could be expected.

The Japanese air control made it difficult to reinforce Port Moresby because the normal sea route was across the Gulf of Papua. Further, the port facilities of Port Moresby were old fashioned and had not been improved. The two airfields were totally inadequate for military operations. There was only one intermediate airfield at Horn Island in Torres Strait. Otherwise, the planes came from the Townsville area, seven hundred miles away in Australia.

So, as all else was being done, MacArthur's engineering officers were working on the rebuilding of the airfields and the rebuilding of Port Moresby's harbor facilities. American engineers and labor troops were brought in to do the job. Also, MacArthur ordered the reinforcement of the Australians in the Bulolo Valley.

Late in April, the Port Moresby fields were militarily operational. Medium and heavy bombers, using them regularly, began attacking Lae, Salamaua, and Rabaul. The bombers were B-17s, B-25 Mitchells, Hudsons, and B-26s. The fighters were a mixed bag of P-39s and P-40s. The air force also included some Catalina flying boats, excellent for medium-range reconnaissance and as night fighters. Of course, Mac-Arthur was not satisfied with the resources allocated, and he immediately asked for more. Then he ran into the overall Allied plan: the Pacific was going to have to give way to the Atlantic. Until Hitler was defeated, the Combined Chiefs of Staff had agreed that Pacific operations would be primarily defensive in nature.

This decision rankled MacArthur no less than it did Adm. Ernest J. King and Adm. Chester W. Nimitz. As it turned out, however, it was going to be a decision they would have to live with to a point. The navy did manage to secure enough ships to begin thinking about offensive operations, but it was going to be very difficult for the next two years.

This meant that MacArthur was not going to get any more divisions right away. He was not going to get the aircraft carrier he wanted for his navy. That was the word from Washington. MacArthur tried to go a different route, to appeal through Prime Minister John Curtin of Australia to Prime Minister Winston Churchill in London. He ran into a buzz saw. Churchill was the prime architect of the Hitler-first policy. He saw what MacArthur was trying to do and sent a quizzical note to FDR, who called General Marshall on the carpet, and Marshall called MacArthur on the carpet. The latter blamed it all on Curtin, which was less than candid. But out of it all came one clarification: the Pacific area was going to have to wait while the Americans and British dealt with Hitler, just as Churchill had wanted it to be.

The war of words went on, however. MacArthur kept asking: he wanted two aircraft carriers, a thousand aircraft, and three American divisions.

He was, as time showed, barking up the wrong tree. General Marshall put it down on paper, "The directive to General MacArthur definitely assigns a defensive mission with the task of preparing an offensive." If it sounded like "Mission Impossible," given the forces at hand, there were a lot of Australian officers just then who would have agreed with such an analysis. But MacArthur had one great quality: no matter how much he disliked his orders and no matter how much he tried to finagle around them, he was a fighting man.

There were Japanese to be fought and he was going to fight them.

Even as the messages streamed back and forth to Washington and London, MacArthur was preparing his defenses with what he had.

Port Moresby was just a sleepy little copra port before the war, not even that in the spring of 1942. The native population had largely fled to the hills and the civilian whites had been evacuated. Its garrison wandered about among the splintered huts and bombed-out warehouses. Its only visible protection was a pair of antique coastal guns that faced the harbor.

On the land side, however, Port Moresby had a natural protection: the Owen Stanley Range, a barrier of jungled mountains that rose six thousand feet above the coastal plain and ran the length of this tail of New Guinea. The map showed a road over the mountain from Port Moresby to Buna. In fact, part of this "road" did not exist at all. Part of it was the Kokoda Track, a narrow trail from Port Moresby through the rain forest and mountain jungle to a hill station in the foothills on the Solomon Sea side of the peninsula. It had to be kept open by the occasional missionary or native tracker who came along with a machete to clear away the creepers that constantly threatened to close the trail off altogether. There was, then, part of a road, part of a route, and part of a trail; together they connected Port Moresby with Buna, a government post on the other side of the Owen Stanley Mountains. Buna was on the Solomon Sea that faces Rabaul. It was a government station located near a native village. A few miles to the north was Gona, where the Anglican Church had a mission. Other than that, the whole area was trackless jungle right down to the beach. That, then, was the condition of transportation facilities on land. The Australians came closest to understanding the situation than anyone else. The Japanese were still under the impression that they had a road to contend with; the Americans agreed. It was hard to yield, however, to the concept that this almost nonexistent route could be used by one side or the other to stage an attack across the Owen Stanley Range. But the Australian high command was sure of it. The planning took that into consideration.

One thing was certain in April, the Australian high command learned from its coast watchers spread out as far as New Britain Island itself. The Japanese were up to something. They were massing troops and transports at Rabaul, and those soldiers and ships had to be going somewhere. It was the guess of the Australians that the somewhere was going to be Port Moresby.

CHAPTER FOUR

The Battle of the Coral Sea—I

Admiral Yamamoto had been very displeased with the performance of Adm. Chuichi Nagumo in the Pearl Harbor attack. Admiral Nagumo had gone to the Hawaiian islands with the mission of destroying the American Pacific Fleet. As he knew very well, and so did everyone else, the heart of that fleet as far as the Japanese were concerned was in the three or four carriers the Americans had in the Pacific. Most of the American battleships were very old and were not regarded by the Japanese as a serious menace in case of a fleet battle. But the American carriers were another story, and the Japanese were wary of them. What a disappointment it was, then, when Nagumo failed to find a single one of the American carriers and left the scene just as two of them were coming back to Pearl Harbor. If he had stayed another day, and there was no reason that he should not have, he would have had a chance to knock out Adm. William F. Halsey's carrier *Enterprise* and Adm. Wilson Brown's *Saratoga,* which were just coming back from the West Coast.

After that, in mid-February 1942, Admiral Nagumo had been sent down to make some strikes at Darwin, the Dutch East Indies, and Rabaul. He had performed perfectly satisfactorily there because there was no fleet danger. Admiral Yamamoto had become convinced that Admiral Nagumo was a very timid man. And that conviction had been reinforced by Nagumo's performance in early April off Colombo, Ceylon. Nagumo had been sent down to challenge the British fleet in the Indian Ocean and had caught the cruisers *Dorsetshire* and *Cornwall* in Colombo on April 4. Both ships were sunk by planes from the carriers *Akagi* and *Kaga*. Then on April 9, the task force hit the British naval base at Trincomalee and sank several more ships, including the aircraft carrier *Hermes*. Yet the other capital ships of the British fleet escaped and the shore installations were not seriously damaged. Once again, Admiral Nagumo had been sent to do a thorough job and had pulled out in a hurry leaving it undone. True, he did sink the carrier *Hermes,* but it was an ancient weapon dating back to World War I, and Nagumo had not stayed around long enough, once more, to wreak the vengeance he could have against the other heavy ships of the British force. Any way one looks at it, from a naval commander's standpoint, Nagumo's performance had been miserable.

But then, how does one argue with "success"? Imperial General Headquarters' propaganda machine was telling the world how great the Japanese carriers were and how they had won stunning victories. A few more such victories, said Yamamoto, and the war would be lost. There was, he continued, only one chance to solve the problem of the war created by Gen. Hideki Tōjō and his war hawks. It was for Yamamoto to find and engage the American fleet and wipe out the carrier force so that the Americans would have to come to the peace table and accept as inevitable the conquests of the Imperial Japanese Forces made in the early months of 1942. A long war was going to be fatal to Japan, Yamamoto concluded.

His chance to smoke out the American fleet was before him. He had made it himself in his plan for the simultaneous invasion of Midway Island in the Pacific and the Aleutian Islands off the Alaskan shore. The Midway invasion would give the Japanese a new submarine base in the heart of the Pacific, and a striking point from which Hawaii could be attacked. The plan for the invasion of Hawaii was already in motion: the invasion money had been printed up. The IGH expected great things from Hawaii. After all, the population there was about thirty percent Japanese or second-generation Japanese, and these people could be expected to welcome the troops. Knock out the American fleet when it came to defend Hawaii; put troops ashore on the edge of the North American

Continent; take Midway; take Hawaii; then the Americans would have to give up. Yamamoto would have done his very best, solving an almost insoluble problem that Tojo (whom he considered to be a boor and not very bright) had posed for Japan.

The Midway invasion was uppermost in Yamamoto's mind. He was not particularly favorable to, or impressed by, the Imperial General Staff's new decision to extend the southern perimeter farther south. The navy, which was responsible for sea defense and air defense of all this region, had quite enough to do as it was. Every mile south the army pushed meant another mile that supplies had to be carried and escorted in the hot spots. Now IGH had announced a new program to isolate Australia, with an eye to extending the empire even down under. It was, to Yamamoto's mind, madness; but again, there was no quarreling with success. Every time the navy won some sort of a victory Radio Tokyo began playing the "Battleship March," much to Yamamoto's annoyance. One of these days, he knew, Japan was going to suffer some defeats. How would the propagandists act then?

No one paid any attention to the minor debacle that had beset the Lae–Salamaua striking force. The troops had gotten ashore all right. The ships that had been sunk and damaged were cargo and transport ships. Only 132 men had been killed in the Allied air attacks. On balance, it had been successful, and if Yamamoto's staff had a report on the action, which it certainly did, the admiral was not even interested enough to study it.

What he was studying were orders from IGH to supply carrier protection to Admiral Inoue's 4th Fleet in a new South Seas adventure. This would be the simultaneous invasion of Port Moresby, thus sealing off Australian New Guinea, and Tulagi Island in the Solomons, where a seaplane base was to be built for further observation of the Australian north shore. After softening up Rabaul, the carriers had withdrawn. No carriers had been used, nor apparently were needed, for the invasions of Lae and Salamaua. That was just the problem, said IGH. The Americans had two carriers in South Pacific waters now; therefore, the Inoue invasion fleet must have carrier protection.

By a little juggling, Admiral Yamamoto was able to free

up the 5th Carrier Division for support of this South Pacific action by the 4th Fleet. But by doing this to meet IGH's timetable, which had been speeded up so much in the national euphoria, Yamamoto may have deprived Nagumo of the extra force he needed to complete the job on the British Asiatic Fleet. For the two fleet carriers of the 5th Division could very easily have gone along to Trincomalee. That meant the fleet carriers *Shokaku* and *Zuikaku* would be on hand. Yamamoto could also provide the old small carrier *Shoho,* which was not part of the Combined Fleet in the regular sense. She was too old and slow for that.

On March 24, the *Shokaku* and the *Zuikaku* reached the Celebes Islands, where Admiral Inoue's 4th Fleet was anchored.

Following the Indian Ocean raids, the Japanese carrier striking force went to Truk. The next military action seemed to be heading for this area. First would be the Port Moresby landing. Then, IGH warned General Horii he would be expected to take New Caledonia. The Japanese had their eyes on the whole area, including Samoa and Fiji, which were to be seized after New Caledonia.

The Japanese navy was running it close these days. Immediately after Port Moresby, Admiral Yamamoto would invade Midway and the Aleutians. That accomplished, the Combined Fleet was to prepare to undertake the New Caledonia, Samoa, and Fiji operations. It promised to be a busy spring and summer.

Horii's orders called for the South Seas Detachment *(Nankai Shitai)* to leave Rabaul on May 4 and land on a beach seven-and-a-half miles northwest of Port Moresby. The unit would be supported by the 3rd Special Naval Landing Force and the 1st Battalion of the 14th Infantry. So, three landing units were staged. They would attack in a converging pattern north and south of the town and capture Kila Kila Airfield as quickly as possible. Then the 10th Air Fleet would send planes to Port Moresby and the setup for the next operation would begin.

The Port Moresby invasion was called Operation MO. From the Japanese point of view, it was simple and direct with no particular opposition expected. Admiral Inoue was a careful man, and he came to Rabaul from Truk to supervise the preparations. The troops would be carried and protected by seven destroyers, five troop transports, and several seaplane tenders.

Supporting the whole operation was a task force that consisted of the *Zuikaku,* the *Shokaku,* four heavy cruisers, two light cruisers, and a squadron of submarines. The task force would conduct a raid on Townsville, Australia, the site of Allied air force concentration, to stop the Allies from sending air strikes to interfere with the Japanese landings.

On May 3, a small detachment of Japanese naval construction engineers landed at Tulagi in the Solomon Islands. It was to prepare the way for the seaplane tenders that would create the seaplane base there. Forewarned, the Australian detachment left a few hours earlier. The enemies did not meet.

Meanwhile, the South Seas Detachment was boarding its ships at Rabaul. Rear Adm. Aritomo Goto commanded the invasion force. His flagship was the cruiser *Aoba.* Five hundred ten planes were coming down to Rabaul under Rear Adm. Sadayoshi Yamada in order to serve as land-based air support of Operation MO. On May 4, the convoy set out and met the *Shoho* and its protective ships off Buin on Bougainville. Vice Adm. Takeo Takagi took his *Shokaku–Zuikaku* task force off to the Solomons prepared for a fight. On May 7, the attack convoy was moving through the Louisiade Archipelago and into the reef waters toward Port Moresby.

On they came, not really expecting much trouble, although they had been warned by the excellent Japanese Naval Intelligence Service that there were two American carrier task forces "somewhere" in the region. "Somewhere" was the best that could be said because the American forces were in motion. The Japanese were firmly aware of their own superiority on land and sea, and they expected to search out the Americans before any trouble could start—if they were anywhere in the vicinity. No trouble was expected at Tulagi; the landing force with its supplies was carried in one transport and was covered only by two destroyers and two minelayers.

The chances of trouble at Port Moresby were much greater. Rear Adm. Sadamichi Kajioka had six destroyers to protect the eleven transports, several converted minesweepers that were now anti-submarine patrol ships and gunboats, three ordinary gunboats, a minelayer, two oilers, and a minesweeper. Goto's force protected all these, too. So, the *Shoho* was almost the least of it, an old carrier of only 12,000 tons that could make only twenty-five knots. That is why she could not travel with the sleek *Shokaku* and *Zuikaku*—20,000 tons and thirty knots.

The Australians had known since May 1 that something was up, but they were not going to contest it at Tulagi. At Pearl Harbor, Admiral Nimitz also knew. He had sent Admiral William F. Halsey with his carrier *Enterprise* toward the South Pacific to take over operations of all three American carriers. That would give the United States a good strong force with which to contend any action the Japanese proposed to start. The reason Halsey had been sent was not primarily to get a third carrier into the area but to get a fighting admiral down there. Admiral Fitch was a fighting admiral and a real airman, a flier. But he was not the senior officer. Admiral Fletcher, who was really a converted-battleship admiral, was in command of the carriers, and he was not very good at using them. He worried interminably about logistics and the risking of the carriers. Halsey and Fitch, on the other hand, had the Horatio Nelson approach: if a captain put his ship into contact with the enemy, he could not be all bad.

In fact, the whole MO Operation could have been stopped in the first days of May by a powerful air attack on Rabaul. Fletcher was in position to make it with his two carriers, but he was afraid that if he did so he would reveal the existence of his carriers in the area. He did not realize that he had been spotted by Japanese reconnaissance plancs the moment he entered the seas and that there was no surprise in store for the Japanese. So, the chance was missed.

Fletcher had been fumbling around the area for a month without doing anything. Every time he was ready to make an attack, the Japanese moved somewhere else or his oil situation was bad or he had to transfer ammunition. Or, or, or. Admiral Nimitz was becoming quite vexed with Fletcher's nonperformance and from Washington came mumbling that perhaps he ought to be put out to pasture and a younger man given the job.

What Nimitz could do and did, was radio Fletcher an attack plan and ask him to follow it. Fletcher was to take Admiral Fitch's task force and Australian Rear Adm. J. G. Crace's cruiser force into the Coral Sea and look for a chance for battle. Nimitz was certain he would find it.

Admiral Fletcher moved his task force to the middle of the Coral Sea on May 3. He was fueling as the Japanese landed on Tulagi Island in the Solomons. The success of that Japanese landing made Admiral Inoue relax. The Americans were not much on the alert, he decided. But just then Fletcher had learned about the Japanese Tulagi landings and prepared to attack. Having landed, the Japanese unloaded their transports and moved them back out to sea.

Now the Japanese attention shifted to the Port Moresby operation, which was by far the more important of the two assaults. But the Tulagi landing put Admiral Fletcher into a flap because he knew how Admiral King felt about having the Japanese moving up on Australia. So, he steamed all night to launch planes the next day for an attack on Tulagi. Ten minutes before sunrise, the *Yorktown* began launching her planes. Fighters, bombers, and torpedo bombers all got off that day.

That morning of May 4 found the Japanese happily ensconced at Tulagi. Admiral Shima, the officer in charge, was preparing to set up the seaplane base. A number of antiaircraft guns and machine guns had been landed the day before from the transports. Two destroyers and the admiral's flagship, the *Okinoshima*, stood off the island, riding easily at anchor among the destroyers and transports. Several gunboats and other service craft were also in the fleet.

The work was just beginning at a leisurely pace. It was 8:30 in the morning. Suddenly, up above came the screaming of dive-bombers. The Americans were attacking from 19,000 feet. Ashore and on the ships the antiaircraft guns began to open fire and puffs of black-and-white smoke surrounded the American planes as they came whistling down. But the Japanese gunners were new to the job and no planes were hit. The dive-bombers attacked and turned to go back to their carrier. They reported four hits.

Next came the torpedo planes. Three of the torpedo bombers went after the transports. Seven went after the two small minesweepers and one destroyer. The Americans thought they were two destroyers and a cruiser—such errors were common in the early part of the war.

The torpedo bombers did a good job. They sank two mine-sweepers and damaged one destroyer so badly she beached herself. Then the torpedo planes were gone, but along came a second wave of American dive-bombers. By this time, the Japanese had recovered from the surprise of the attack and all the ships in the area were maneuvering. The second wave of bombers did not make any hits. They did, however, get one Japanese floatplane. The pilot had swum out to the plane, climbed up on the float, and gotten aboard. He started the engine and took off. But just as he was clearing the water, down came the frustrated bomber pilots looking for something to strafe—and there was the seaplane.

Less than an hour after the fight began, the attack force was back aboard the *Yorktown* refueling and rearming.

That day the Americans launched three air strikes against Tulagi. They had done a good deal of damage but not as much as they believed. The base was still viable, even if several of the seaplanes had been destroyed and half-a-dozen ships of various sizes had been sunk. In fact, the battle had scarcely begun.

CHAPTER FIVE

The Battle of the Coral Sea—II

Vice Adm. Takeo Takagi came steaming up to Tulagi on the morning of May 5, shortly after the Americans left the scene. There was not much to see except some sunken hulks. He had arrived too late—in response to frantic messages—to do any good for the Japanese builders of the seaplane base. They were gone, ordered to join up with the MO Operation forces for safety's sake.

He looked around for the Americans but did not find them.

Closer to New Guinea, the Port Moresby invasion force steamed along. It was a task force of twenty-eight ships guarded from air attack by the carrier *Shoho*. Twice during May 5, the convoy was attacked by American bombers from Australia. Both times the planes were driven off by the *Shoho*'s combat air patrol. Late in the day, the convoy pulled into the harbor at Shortland Island to refuel and spend the night.

Admiral Fletcher spent most of May 5 refueling his ships. He seemed to spend most of each day refueling his ships. He was a very nervous admiral, and his view of carriers was the reason for it. To Admiral Fletcher the carrier was so precarious a weapon that surprise was its only real safety. Once the carrier was spooked by an enemy, to Fletcher it was always in trouble. He did not have much confidence in combat air patrols or in antisubmarine patrols. He really should never have gotten out of the heavy-surface-ship class, but in the years between the two World Wars, seniority in the American navy was everything; ability was strictly a secondary matter.

Fletcher was searching for the Japanese, but not very diligently. The Japanese, on the other hand, were searching for him with a definite plan in mind. They hoped to put the American carrier force into a pincers, with the small carrier *Shoho* and the seaplane carrier *Kamikawa Maru* on one side, the *Shokaku* and *Zuikaku* on the other. In addition to their air force, the Japanese could use their heavy cruisers and destroyers if it came to surface action.

On May 6 at 8:00 A.M., a Japanese scout seaplane found the Americans. The Japanese turned toward them. Admiral Inoue was nervous about the fate of his relatively unarmed Port Moresby attack force, so he turned them northward to keep them out of trouble until the issue was decided.

On the night of May 6, the pilots aboard the carriers *Lexington* and *Yorktown* were issued maps and instructions regarding the plane fight that would occur the next day. They were eager to go and have a crack at the Japanese. Aboard the *Shokaku* and *Zuikaku*, the Japanese pilots felt precisely the same way. They, too, were getting maps and instructions; they, too, wanted to go out and destroy the American carriers.

That night the forces were primed.

On the morning of May 7, the Japanese struck the first blow. They found the oiler *Neosho* and the destroyer USS *Sims*. Ironically, the rendezvous position chosen by Admiral Fletcher's staff was right in the middle of the Japanese carrier force's search pattern. The Japanese identified them as a carrier and a cruiser, which was not very well done. But that did not stop them from making an attack. Adm. Tadaichi Hara, the carrier division commander, believed what his pilots had said, so they made a strong effort to sink these two ships. The determination was very real, one of the Japanese dive-bomber pilots, his plane in flames from accurate antiaircraft fire, crashed onto the deck of the *Neosho* and created a dreadful fire in the Number 4 gun enclosure. In a very few minutes, the *Sims* was sinking and the *Neosho* was a hulk.

The American planes were not far behind. At a few minutes before dawn that morning, Admiral Fletcher's intelligence officers came in with news that the Japanese invasion force for Port Moresby had been spotted heading towards

Jomard Passage from the Rabaul area. The intelligence was a little old, but valuable nonetheless. Admiral Fletcher ordered Admiral Crace to take the cruiser force around to head the Japanese off at the pass. They would move in between Port Moresby and the China Strait and wait.

Admiral Crace uttered no word of complaint. But below decks there was some concern: here they were in Japanese carrier waters and Admiral Fletcher was dividing his force and sending the surface ships off without any air cover.

The concern became real a few hours later when the cruiser force was picked up by a Japanese floatplane that began tailing them, staying just out of range and reporting their movement to somebody.

Just before 7 o'clock that morning of May 7, Admiral Fletcher's *Yorktown* launched ten dive-bombers to move out like spokes of a wheel to search for the enemy carriers. About two hours out, a pilot suddenly reported that he had found two carriers and four heavy cruisers 175 miles from the American force on the northeast side of the Louisiade group of islands. But the searchers made so many mathematical miscalculations that, although they found some element of the Japanese force, no one else could follow up. No one could even figure out what the searchers had seen that morning. They missed Admiral Takagi's big carriers altogether.

It was later discovered that what the Americans had seen was a force of two old light cruisers, a seaplane carrier, and three gunboats that had been laid on as extra protection.

Although the Americans could not find the Japanese, they had to do something, so at 9:25 A.M., the carrier *Lexington* began to launch her planes into an attack pattern. In a few minutes, ten fighter planes, twenty-eight dive-bombers, and a dozen torpedo bombers were in the air heading for that reported sighting of the enemy fleet over at the Louisiades.

Then came the word that the *Yorktown* search pilots had made some serious errors. What to do? Captain Frederick Sherman, a hotheaded young man, wanted to bring the planes back immediately and start all over again. But Admiral Fitch, an old hand at the game, said no, let them stay out. There was something out there, maybe they would find it.

At 6:30 that morning of May 7, Admiral Goto's flagship, the cruiser *Aoba,* reported that the Americans were 140 miles away and 160° off Deboyne Island. The report was completely correct. Even so, the Americans got the luck of the draw, that time.

Comdr. W. B. Ault was leading the U.S. air strike from the *Lexington*, and he was not quite sure what to do after he heard that the report from the *Yorktown* search plane was not verifiable. But he learned quickly enough by passing over Tagula Island in the Louisiades without seeing anything. He began looking down through the cloud cover. And then, Lt. Cmdr. W. I. Hamilton spotted a carrier, two cruisers, and several other ships off to starboard. This was no mirage. It was the carrier *Shoho* and part of her support force.

It was an unexpected pleasure. There the American strike force was, courtesy of their admiral's hunch, in the right place at the right time with the right weapons.

In a moment, the Americans were attacking, and the Japanese fighter cover was attacking the Americans. A Zero fighter shot down the plane of the executive officer of the scouting squadron. The bombers began to bomb. At first, there were misses, although the second near miss was close enough to blow five aircraft off the deck of the *Shoho*. More planes were hit and more Americans headed for neutral territory to bail out and hope that they would be rescued.

Suddenly, the pressure was off the *Lexington*'s planes because the strike planes from the *Yorktown* had just joined up, thus putting ninety-three planes in the air over the Japanese squadron. Down below, the captain of the *Shoho* was maneuvering very skillfully, but there were just too many enemy bombers converging on him and not enough sea to hide in.

He stopped for a few moments, holding steady into the wind, to launch more fighters that might save him from attack. But as he did so, the Americans flew in, and he saw two torpedo wakes off to starboard. He ordered the helm pushed to starboard and managed to miss those two torpedoes. But two minutes later the *Yorktown*'s bombers were on top of him, dropping thousand-pound, armor-piercing bombs. One bomb struck the forward part of the rear elevator on the flight deck, smashing it inward, so that the metal hung high above the deck. Another bomb came along and changed the angles of the wreckage. The bombs set fires in the gasoline supply on the hanger deck, and the fires surged toward the torpedo stowage compartment.

Up above, the odds were ten to one in favor of the Americans. Even the Japanese Zero fighter, with its marvelous turning capacity and speed, could not change the ratio. And what the Americans learned that day was that the Zero fighter and its seaplane counterpart had no armor. Therefore, a well-placed burst into the back of the seat would take care of the pilot.

Bombs and torpedoes smashed the *Shoho* from one end to the other. Soon, the issue was no longer in doubt. The carrier was going to sink if she did not blow sky-high first. The ship was in flames, the smoke was so thick that the attacking Americans could not take proper photographs of the stricken vessel; all they could get was the bow of the ship, everything else was smoke and flame.

The ship took an enormous beating, some said twenty torpedoes and fifty bombs hit her. Whatever the number, it was more than enough. At 9:20 A.M., thirty minutes after the raiders had first appeared in the sky over the carrier, she was sinking. So definite was her fate that the last American bomber pilot, looking for a target, turned away from the stricken carrier and devoted his attention to a "cruiser" that he said he sank. However, no cruiser was sunk in that position that day, but a gunboat was. The excitement of the moment made it easy to escalate the size of the target.

The Americans made the first score of the day in terms of carriers.

But when the planes reached their own carriers and the pilots clamored for gas and ammunition to go back and sink the rest of the ships in the *Shoho* entourage, their admirals quieted them down. No, said Admiral Fletcher. There was a naval force out there somewhere with two big fleet carriers, and they were going to have to devote their attention to that group.

At the same time, the Japanese had now gotten a very good idea of where the American carriers were located. Admiral Takagi decided that he would launch a strike in the middle of the afternoon so that his planes would reach the American ships just at sundown, the time that he estimated they would be least on the lookout and most vulnerable to attack. At 2:30 in the afternoon, fifteen torpedo planes and a dozen level bombers took off from the Japanese ships and headed for the Americans.

But the weather had suddenly turned squally in the American operating zone; consequently, the Japanese carrier planes missed the American task force entirely. They flew out past it and searched and searched. In the flypast, radar picked them up and the Americans began launching more fighter planes to attack the Japanese planes and to protect their carriers. They did so, too. The planes of the *Lexington* found nine Zeros heading for the carrier and went out after them. They shot down all nine Japanese fighters, with a loss of two of the American planes.

Then came one of those strange accidents of war. The Japanese planes, trying to get home to their carriers, made the mistake of identifying the *Lexington* as one of their own, and they tried to land on her. In the gathering darkness, the ships in the group opened up with every gun they had. The Japanese discovered their mistake and moved out of the landing pattern and headed as quickly as they could for their own carriers.

The last the Americans saw that night was a bunch of blips orbiting something, and the radar men knew that it was Japanese planes not far away landing on their own carrier. Fletcher finally got the word but decided it was too late to launch a night attack. Besides, he was not sure how a night attack would go. It was not one of the specialties of the American carrier admirals at that stage of the war.

Nor did the Japanese make a night attack because Admiral Koso Abe, commander of the Port Moresby attack force, asked that the two big carriers come in close to protect his invasion force. That was the purpose of the operation; so, Admiral Takagi ordered the carriers to head north to cover Admiral Abe's force. Meanwhile, Admiral Fletcher's American carriers headed southeast to await the coming of daylight. Thus, the two carrier admirals broadened the gap between them and made sure that a whole new search pattern would have to take place the next day. That threw the outcome of the battle back into the sphere of luck. The best guess was likely to find the enemy fleet, and finding that enemy fleet was the first step.

Long before dawn, the pilots of the *Lexington* were up and briefed on their mission for the day. Admiral Fitch wanted them to go out two hundred miles to the north, but only twenty-five miles to the south. It was Fitch's hunch that the Japanese had gone north during the night. Fletcher yielded to Fitch; it was a matter of airmanship, and he knew that Fitch was the better man, although not senior. And with the search planes a little more than two hours out from the *Lexington,* the admiral's hunch proved to be correct. At a little after 8:00 A.M. Lt. Joseph Smith radioed back from his Scout 2-S-2 that he had seen two carriers, four cruisers, and three destroyers. The problem was that his position was garbled. The *Lexington* began trying frantically to reach him.

The *Yorktown* picked up the message first. Smith was over the Japanese force, 120 miles to the northeast.

Three minutes after Admiral Fletcher learned that, he also learned that the American task force had been sighted by the Japanese.

Before sunrise Admiral Hara had launched his search planes, and they had gone south on his hunch, which was just as good as that of Admiral Fitch.

The odds were even. Each force had spotted the other. But the odds were tilted a bit by the weather. The Japanese had moved into the protection of a cold front, which meant squalls and clouds for the Japanese ships to hide under. The Americans had moved into broad sunlight, which was good for getting a tan, but not for safety. Admiral Hara then took a bold action that was to pay off for him. While his planes were still out on search, he launched his air strike. This could mean an enormous confusion of landings and a general slowup in readying a second strike. But if his first strike succeeded, he might not need a second strike, and that is the chance he was taking.

The Americans were slower to get into action. Lieutenant Smith's radio seemed to be cracking up, and he could not be raised again to confirm his findings. Another pilot, Lt. Comdr. Robert Dixon, crossed over into that sector to take a look and flew around for a while before spotting the Japanese ships hiding below the heavy clouds, moving in and out of squalls.

So, it was after 8:30 A.M. before Admiral Fitch ordered the planes to take off and strike the Japanese.

Up above the Japanese fleet, Commander Dixon dodged in and out of the cloud cover, hiding from Zero fighters of the Japanese combat air patrol that were out to get him if they could. For two hours Dixon held position, waiting for the air strike to arrive. The Zeroes kept after him all the time, but the rear gun of the scout plane kept them at bay.

The *Yorktown* launched first, but not until 9:24 A.M. Soon, the fighters were in the air, then the bombers. They began to arrive over the targets patrolled by Commander Dixon just before 11 A.M. Almost all the planes were *Yorktown* planes because the *Lexington* air group had a lot of bad luck. They missed the target, and most of them had to turn around and go home without attacking anything.

The *Yorktown* planes attacked, the torpedo bombers going in low and the dive-bombers coming down from on high.

As the American planes bombed and dropped their torpedoes, they thought they were creating great damage. One pilot went back to report that the *Yorktown* torpedo squadron had put a number of torpedoes into the carrier they attacked (the number varied from three to six). In truth, the *Yorktown* planes did some damage. When Admiral Hara came out of the gloom in the *Zuikaku,* he was shocked to see the *Shokaku* burning and listing. But the damage was slight enough to be contained; within an hour, the *Shokaku* was operating again. That fact was verified by the torpedo bombers from the *Lexington* who arrived over the target after the *Yorktown* crew had left. The *Lexington* bombers claimed five torpedo hits on a carrier.

When Admiral Hara counted noses, he discovered that the *Shokaku* was hard hit. She had lost more than a hundred of her crew, and she had big holes in her sides and on the deck. But she had no holes below the waterline, the fires were contained, and she could get back to Japanese waters. She left immediately because not even Truk could handle her damage. Therefore, she had to go back to a Japanese naval yard for extensive repairs.

While the Americans were attacking the Japanese, the fliers of Nippon were returning the favor. Capt. Frederick Sherman had warned his officers to expect an attack on the *Lexington* at about 11:00 A.M. Sure enough, it came. The Japanese had the great advantage of weather, sunny skies, and little wind, so that the attacking planes had a perfect view. They formed up, their commanders divided them to attack both carriers, and in they came.

The first great carrier battle of the Pacific War was in midstride. The Americans had made their attack. Now it was the turn of the Japanese.

The Japanese planes bored in on the American carriers. The American combat air patrol was low on fuel, thus more planes were launched. But there was a shortage of fighters, so dive-bombers were used to help the patrol. Not a very good idea considering the speed and maneuverability of the Zero fighters, which outclassed the American Grumman F4Fs, although the American fighters were superior in diving capacity and in armor protection—both important matters in this sort of action.

But the SBD, the dive-bomber, just was no match for the Zeros. Eight dive-bombers tried to knock down the Japanese over the American carriers. They were hit by Japanese Zero fighters, and four of the eight American bombers were shot down in short order. But the remaining four shot down four Japanese bombers, in turn. The effective tactic was a straight run and breakaway. The bombers could not turn with, nor outspeed, the Zeros in a climb.

Soon, the Japanese bombers were over the American ships. One plane put an eight-hundred-pound, armor-piercing bomb through the flight deck of the *Yorktown*, causing a good deal of damage below. Two boilers were knocked out, but the ship kept on moving.

The real damage to the Americans came to the *Lexington*. She was hit by two torpedoes and five bombs, she suffered many near misses as well. From a sailor's point of view, a near miss can be deadly. Half-a-dozen men were swept off the decks of the *Lexington* that day by near misses; so were men on other ships. But the torpedoes and the bombs that struck square made all the difference in the world. For a time, Admiral Fitch and Captain Sherman were optimistic. They thought they could control the damage. But at 12:47 P.M., just about an hour and three-quarters after the Japanese attack came and after the last Japanese planes had left the scene, an internal explosion rocked the *Lexington*. The force of it knocked out much of the fire-fighting mains, which created more problems. The *Lexington* began to fail. Her steering became almost impossible. The men of the *Lexington* tried hard, but by 5:00 P.M. it was apparent that the ship could not be saved. The fires below could not be put out, the steering had almost totally broken down, the boilers were giving out. So, Admiral Fitch ordered the *Lexington* abandoned. The men got off. The most important naval battle of the Pacific War to date was over.

The Japanese claimed a great victory on Radio Tokyo:

> In the great naval battle of the Coral Sea on 7th and 8th May the Japanese fleet succeeded in sinking the American *Saratoga* and *Yorktown* class and the capital ship of the *California* class, a British warship of the *Warspite* class, a cruiser of the *Canberra* class, was severely damaged, another was sunk. A twenty thousand-ton oil tanker was sunk and a destroyer sunk. Planes destroyed were ninety-eight. Japanese losses were negligible. One small aircraft carrier converted from a tanker and thirty-one planes.

That was not very accurate reporting. True, the *Lexington* was sunk, as were the oiler *Neosho* and the destroyer *Sims*. The carrier *Yorktown* was damaged, although not too severely. In exchange, the Japanese had lost the destroyer *Kikuzuki*, three minesweepers, and the light carrier *Shoho*. The fleet carrier *Shokaku* was also badly damaged and headed for home waters.

The battle really was a Japanese tactical victory but a strategic defeat. This because the Japanese had failed to attain their announced objective for the first time in this war. The invasion of Port Moresby had been called off while Admiral Inoue checked the losses and the condition of his one remaining carrier.

Japanese naval historians have faulted Admiral Hara for timidity in not pressing the attack on the *Yorktown*. Perhaps they are right, but Admiral Hara had lost a lot of planes that day; the condition of *Shokaku* was shocking to him. He did not know precisely what the Americans had left. The next day or two gave him plenty of pause. Admiral Inoue had decided to carry out the invasion of Nauru and Ocean islands, planned for May 10 after Port Moresby's fall. But the flagship of the Nauru fleet, the *Okinoshima,* was discovered by the American submarine *S-42* and sunk. Also there came a report that two more American carriers and all sorts of support ships were coming into the waters around Tulagi. Admiral Inoue did, indeed, get the wind up this time. He canceled the Nauru invasion and the Ocean Island invasion. So here was Japan, the great victorious Japan, having abandoned three island invasions in a row because of one battle and one ship sunk by a submarine. The tides of war did, indeed, seem to be slackening for Japan.

CHAPTER SIX

New Defenses

On the morning of May 8, the Japanese air force at Rabaul prepared for the day's operations. Twenty-four Zero fighters were made ready along with nine Betty bombers and six torpedo bombers to attack the American Fleet once again. But then the word came that Admiral Hara was retiring, and the land-based air operations against the American Fleet were called off. A few hours later, the whole MO Operation was suspended by Imperial General Headquarters (IGH), with the promise that it would be reinstituted in June.

The South Seas Detachment *(Nankai Shitai)* plus the naval landing force were put ashore again at Rabaul and told to wait. The Nauru and Ocean Island operations were also called off. The Japanese observation planes watched the American Fleet units from afar and saw that they were no more in the mood for another fight than themselves. Most of the light Japanese naval units of the covering force were moved into the Shortland Islands, where they would remain.

Because of the success at Pearl Harbor and in Alaska, of American naval intercepts of messages in the Japanese command's naval code, General MacArthur knew almost immediately that the Port Moresby operation had only been delayed by the Japanese, not scrapped. Any time after June 10, he was informed by Admiral Nimitz, he could expect a new Japanese attempt to take the islands. From Pearl Harbor, it appeared that it would be made by at least a division of Japanese troops and be supported both by carriers from Truk and by the Japanese land-based naval air force at Rabaul.

If information was ever a weapon, here it was. The result

of the intercepts was convincing to all concerned and a good pointer for the future.

The Australian reluctance to defend the continent at the approaches vanished. Australians and Americans were now of one mind about the manner in which the defense had to be conducted.

MacArthur's resources were slender, but at least he knew what he had to do with them.

On May 14, the 32nd U.S. Infantry Division arrived in Australia. So did the remainder of the 41st Division. Therefore, on May 15, the 14th Australian Infantry Brigade Group and attached antiaircraft troops, some four thousand strong, moved to Port Moresby, completely reversing the defense stance there.

The next important move was to begin construction of a new air base near the southeastern tip of New Guinea at Abau-Mullins Harbor. It was to be fifty-feet wide and fifteen-hundred-feet long, which meant it could handle fighters and bombers for attack against Japanese shipping and Japanese air bases to the northeast. It was not really suitable for heavy bombers, however. The code name for the new field was BOSTON.

Having sufficient assurances from Washington for some sort of assistance soon, MacArthur on May 20 announced plans to reinforce the whole area. Australia and New Guinea's air bases would be strengthened. The airfields in northeast Australia would be improved. Several new air bases would be built on the York Peninsula. The forward bomber line would move five hundred miles up toward the Japanese-held areas of New Guinea and New Britain islands.

But there's many a slip twixt cup and lip, as they say in Australia, and someone slipped here.

A survey party found Abau-Mullins Bay swampy and full of mosquitoes. Much better sites were discovered at Milne Bay, particularly a Lever Brothers' coconut plantation, which was already well developed with water, roads, viable port facilities, and a small landing field already in place. BOSTON was dumped and Milne Bay became the spot.

MacArthur also sent reinforcements to the Bulolo Valley. The Kanga Force was created. The hope was now that an attack could be launched soon against the Japanese at Lae and Salamaua to drive them off Papuan soil. It was to be a raid, in a sense. A limited force would attack the Japanese, drive them out if possible, and hold the area for two or three weeks. This ought to put a big crimp in the Japanese plans for Port Moresby and give MacArthur still more time. And so it was tried.

But just as the attack was about to be launched, the commander of the Kanga Force learned that the Japanese had exactly the same idea; they were planning an immediate attack on the Bulolo Valley. Thus, the Australians had to split their force, leaving half to defend the valley. When the attack came at the end of June, it went well enough in the initial phase, and the Australians killed some sixty Japanese in Salamaua. But the others held firmly, and soon up came Japanese reinforcements from Lae. The two units were too strong for the Australians, and they had to withdraw.

A week later, another raid had the same result. The Australians killed forty Japanese defenders, but reinforcements came from Salamaua and drove the Australians back up into their valley. It was going to take more force than MacArthur had in the Bulolo Valley to conduct any successful operations in the area.

One day a member of MacArthur's staff, looking over the map of New Guinea, noted that from Port Moresby there was a trail over the Kokoda Plateau in the foothills of the Owen Stanley Mountains. The trail led to a place on the northeast coast of Papua called Buna, which was otherwise undistinguished and unimportant. But if the Japanese could land a force at Buna, they could come across the trail to the Kokoda Plateau, and from there launch an assault across the six-thousand-foot mountain pass called the Gap. A telephone call to General Blamey's command indicated that no one there was particularly worried about the situation and nothing had been done to protect the trail. MacArthur then asked what was going to be done. Generally speaking, the answer, in soft tones, was: nothing. The situation was well in hand, said the Australians. They could depend on the district officer of the native administration plus the local Papuan Infantry. But when it came right down to it, the local Papuan Infantry was largely native and not very much infantry. It was true that these constabulary and district officers were moving about the area. But the fact was that the Japanese were moving about the area, too, and they were perfectly capable of reading maps. They were, in fact, several steps ahead and were already planning to move into Buna as soon as possible.

It took several days to shake the Australians up, but it was done. At General Blamey's headquarters, somebody realized that the old ways were not satisfactory in dealing with this new and extremely canny enemy, the Japanese army. Maj. Gen. Basil Morris, head of the New Guinea Force of the Australian army, ordered the Buna area reinforced and troops made available to be sure that the Australians controlled the pass at Kokoda. Thus came into being the Maroubra Force. It consisted of an Australian infantry battalion as well as the entire Papuan Infantry Battalion, which numbered 20 whites and 280 natives.

Then came June and the Japanese Combined Fleet's attack on Midway Island and the Aleutians. Admiral Yamamoto moved out in May. Already, as the fleet steamed eastward, the plans were being cut for the next operation, which would be the seizure of New Caledonia, Fiji, and Samoa by the Imperial 17th Army with the assistance of various naval units of the Combined Fleet. The Port Moresby operation was back on the calendar, too. All this would be done more or less simultaneously, Yamamoto was warned. So also was Lt. Gen. Haruyoshi Hyakutake, commander of the 17th Army. The purpose was just what Admiral King thought it was and what he had told the Joint Chiefs of Staff: to cut off communications between America and Australia and prevent General MacArthur from launching an offensive.

The Japanese now had three major infantry striking forces in the area. The South Seas Detachment at Rabaul had already landed at Lae. The Kawaguchi Detachment at Palau was ready, and so were the Yazawa and Aoba detachments at Davao in the Philippines. These small units, usually operating in battalion strengths, were much more powerful than they seemed to be and extremely well organized and efficient. Still, they were small units. The Japanese had been lulled by the ease with which they captured Singapore, Malaya, and the Dutch East Indies with forces that were numerically inferior to those of the Western armies. The Japanese had convinced themselves that a Japanese battalion was more than a match for a Western regiment. Except for the officers and men who had fought in the Philippines campaign, they knew nothing about the fighting qualities of the Americans except what their own propaganda told them. Unfortunately for General Hyakutake, the propagandists had gone wild with the succession of Japanese victories, and the truth was not in them.

The South Seas Detachment was assigned to take New Caledonia. The Kawaguchi Detachment was assigned to take Samoa with the help of part of the Yazawa Detachment. The Aoba Detachment was to land at Port Moresby. The Aoba Detachment had now been built up to be what the naval messages had informed the Americans it would be: all its units were reinforced and of infantry regiment size. The total operation would involve far more than a division of infantry.

In the interim, Admiral Yamamoto had to go to Midway. There he intended to capture the island as a naval base and then entice the American fleet out so that he could deal it the decisive blow that Admiral Nagumo had failed to do in December 1941.

Fortunately for the Americans, the breach of the Japanese naval codes again came to their assistance. They had advance warning of the coming of this enormous fleet, which included six carriers and most of the strength of the Japanese battleship line. Because of this and because of the enormous bravery of many young fliers who sacrificed themselves—one whole squadron of American torpedo bombers was wiped out over the Japanese carriers, a sacrifice that allowed the dive-bombers to come in and hit the carriers hard—the Japanese lost four of their major carriers, the *Kaga,* the *Akagi,* the *Soryu,* and the *Hiryu* as well as most of the pilots and aircrews of their planes. This loss was to be an important factor in Japanese naval aviation for the remainder of the war.

The Americans lost one carrier, the *Yorktown.* They had also lost many pilots, including all but one of the *Lexington*'s torpedo squadrons. But that loss to the Americans was not as important, figuratively speaking, as the loss in pilots to the Japanese because of the vast difference in naval pilot-training programs between the two countries. The Americans were just beginning a mass pilot-training program. The Japanese would not arrive at this stage for two more years.

The hard-won American victory was absolutely essential to the Americans and a stunning loss to the Japanese. They did not take Midway. They did land troops on the Aleutians. However, suddenly, instead of being an asset to further Japanese operations in the East Pacific, the Aleutians force overnight became an enormous liability.

Once the news of the defeat inflicted on the Japanese at Midway Island reached Brisbane and General MacArthur's headquarters, he and his staff were jubilant. At last, they could forge ahead with an offensive in the South Pacific. The plans were already made. Now they were sent to the Joint Chiefs of Staff. General MacArthur would launch a thrust through New Guinea and the Solomon Islands to retake Rabaul. MacArthur would be in charge.

But MacArthur did not reckon with Admiral King. King wanted no part of operations under MacArthur's command. The first task, he said, was the recapture of Tulagi to save it from becoming a Japanese seaplane base.

General Marshall was inclined to take MacArthur's side, but King would not budge. So, the Joint Chiefs of Staff compromised. They split the command: the Tulagi operation would be under the control of the navy. But the invasion of the Solomon Islands, particularly Guadalcanal—just across the sound from Tulagi—would be a MacArthur operation as would the following investment of Rabaul. It was not a very intelligent plan, dividing the authority the way it did, and it would put an enormous strain on the local commanders all through the Pacific War. But the army wanted MacArthur and the navy wanted to have control of the amphibious operations it was just learning to manage. So, the command was split. The commander of the Tulagi operation would be Rear Adm. Robert L. Ghormley, Nimitz's deputy in the South Pacific at New Zealand. In order to make it work the Washington wizards had to juggle a number of boundaries, but they managed. The navy had control of the lower Solomon Islands. The army had Australia, New Guinea, the Dutch East Indies, the Philippines, and, of course, Rabaul.

* * *

Since more attention was to be paid to Allied air defenses in the Southwest Pacific, a new air general was brought in, Maj. Gen. George C. Kenney. Headquarters of MacArthur's command was moved up to Brisbane from Melbourne. Everything was almost ready for some sort of offensive action.

The airfield construction was proceeding rapidly: seven fields at Port Moresby and three fields in Milne Bay. Buna also was to get a new airfield at Dobodura, MacArthur decided, and plans were made to send engineers and construction men up to do the job. But even as the Americans and Australians made their plans in the last days of July, the Japanese were moving. Word came from coast watchers that many small vessels had been seen moving out of the Rabaul area loaded with troops. Lt. Col. David Larr suggested to MacArthur's headquarters that the movement of troops to Buna ought to be speeded up lest the Japanese get there first. But General Sutherland, MacArthur's chief of staff, enumerated several reasons that made it impossible. Besides, he said, there was no indication that the Japanese were moving toward Buna.

They were very relaxed at MacArthur's headquarters, without much apparent reason except that they did not understand their enemy and his plans. The bomber crews, most of whom had served all through the Java campaign, were extremely tired. So General Brett, who was still in command of air activity pending the arrival of General Kenney, suspended all bombing operations on July 18. Next day he had to be chagrined: a B-17 spotted a flotilla of warships off New Britain Island and two merchant ships moving from Rabaul in their direction. Something was up. Probably, they now said at Brisbane headquarters, something that had to do with them.

Bad weather closed in on the area, and the airmen, try as they might, could not get a good look at the seas around New Guinea. On the morning of July 21, a plane did spot the invasion fleet—that is what it was now seen to be—about forty-five miles off Buna. A group of B-26 bombers attacked but without doing any damage. That evening the Japanese ships shelled Buna and the town of Gona to the north. Next morning, the convoy was found just off Gona by Allied planes. The troops were landing, but they had not yet all landed. Their main force was lucky. For some reason, there were no Japanese planes overhead, although the Japanese did, in fact, have control of the air anytime they wanted to take it. So, the Allied bombers came over. They dropped forty-eight tons of bombs on the landing operations, but they did not achieve very much. They set one transport afire. They sank a landing barge full of soldiers. They shot down a float-plane. But by 9:15 that morning of July 22, the invasion forces had left the area without further damage, and the Japanese were in control of Buna.

CHAPTER SEVEN

Overland Attack

In the early part of June, Imperial General Headquarters (IGH) in Tokyo made a basic change in the Japanese plan to conquer the South Pacific. The loss of four carriers at the battle of Midway had forced the navy to alter its entire Combined Fleet strategy. Earlier the carrier striking force had been prepared to support any and all army landings. But now, with the carrier force down to half-a-dozen ships, and not all of them first line, there was no further margin for losses. Therefore, the carrier force had to be kept intact for that day when it might meet the American Pacific Fleet with its several carriers. Since the Americans shuffled carriers from Atlantic to Pacific oceans, the Japanese were always a little bit off base, not knowing precisely how many carriers they might face.

In the first ten days of June, Operation MO was abandoned. The plans to take Samoa, New Caledonia, and Fiji were suspended indefinitely. A new plan for domination of Australia was offered by IGH. It called for the occupation of Guadalcanal Island in the Solomons and the building of an airfield there as well as the capture of Port Moresby by the army from land bases in Papua.

General Hyakutake was told to make a careful reconnaissance of the Buna–Port Moresby Trail. General Horii of the South Seas Detachment (*Nankai Shitai*) would be responsible for the reconnaissance. The IGH was giving him the 15th Independent Engineer Regiment, an extremely competent unit, to make the reconnaissance. On June 29, the engineers went down to Rabaul. Col. Yosuke Yokoyama was entrusted with the command of the mission. He was to land at Buna, then take his engineers across the Kokoda Trail, through the

Gap, and all the way down to Port Moresby. He was to report to General Horii as quickly as this was done. The Japanese were moving. On July 14, they reached Rabaul, and on July 18, they were preparing to embark for Papua. General Hyakutake made plans to capture Port Moresby and the island of Samarai, which is just off the southeast tip of New Guinea. There was a good harbor at the island, and the Japanese wanted it for a seaplane base from which they could attack Port Moresby.

Hearing that the Allies were building up their forces in New Guinea, the Yokoyama force left for Buna on July 20. Its mission had already changed. It was no longer just to make a reconnaissance, but to start the attack across the Kokoda Trail. Fear of Allied movement was why the Japanese had hurried that landing at Buna on July 22. The army was now to do the job with air support furnished by the navy from the naval air bases at Rabaul. On July 14, Japanese construction troops and a small garrison were landed on Guadalcanal to begin building there the air base from which the Japanese would cut the lines of communication between Australia and the United States. At the same time, the Japanese 8th Fleet was moved down to Rabaul.

In the last ten days of July, the Japanese prepared for a new assault on Port Moresby with the Buna landing.

The Japanese were on the northeast side of the Papua Peninsula and the Australians and Americans were on the other side. Between them was the luxuriant jungle rain forest, where the rainfall sometimes hits three hundred inches a year. The jungle covers most of the Owen Stanley Range, which rises as high as 13,000 feet. The only way to cross these sharp, crisp mountains was then by trail, and the best trail of all was the Kokoda Trail, which passed through the settlement of Kokoda, about fifty miles from Buna and a hundred miles from Port Moresby. Thirty miles southwest of Buna is Wairopi, which gets its name from the wire-rope bridge that then spanned the gorge of the Kumusi River. For the Japanese, the going would be easy from Buna to Wairopi, over rolling hills. But after Wairopi. . . .

The terrain suddenly changes into steep and rocky mountain country that runs all the way to Kokoda. And Kokoda is on a little upland plain at about twelve-hundred-feet altitude, between the foothills of the Ajura Kijal and the Owen Stanley Mountains. Here there was a single small airfield.

From Kokoda, the trail leads southwest along a gorge passing through several native villages, with several trail intersections. Then the trail climbs to Templeton's Crossing, at seven thousand feet.

Past Templeton's Crossing lies the Gap, the mountain pass that was the key to the capture of Port Moresby. The Gap is located twenty miles south of Kokoda: seventy-five-hundred-feet in height at its central point, about five-miles wide, with towering mountains on both sides. The trail runs six miles over the Gap, a ragged pitiful trail, where there is not room for more than two men to pass each other. The trail plunges down sharply from there, past many more villages, dropping to two thousand feet at Koitaki, which is about thirty miles from Port Moresby by road. Yes, there was a road there.

The Japanese quickly began to discover these facts, for on the very day of their landing, an advance force under Lt. Col. Hatsuo Tsukamoto was sent inland along the trail and told to keep moving. This force of nine hundred men marched swiftly. That first night it bivouacked outside Soputa, seven miles inland. The next afternoon it approached Wairopi. The only Allied troops in the Buna–Kokoda area were the three hundred men of the Papuan Infantry Battalion and Company B of the Australian 39th Infantry Battalion.

The Japanese and the Allies met for the first time on July 22 when a patrol from the Papua Infantry Battalion encountered the Japanese unit a few miles from the village of Awala. The next day, the Japanese attacked at Awala and the Australian force moved back to a position just short of the Wairopi Bridge. On July 24, the Australians crossed the bridge and cut the wires before the Japanese could make use of it.

There they were, the Japanese temporarily stymied in their attempt to cross the mountains, the Australians on the wrong side (the Port Moresby side instead of the Buna side). Thus, there was no immediate confrontation. On July 25, the Australian rifle company was ordered to march to Kokoda as quickly as possible.

The commander of the 39th Infantry Battalion, Lt. Col. William T. Owen, was ordered to make a stand at Kokoda.

When he arrived at Kokoda on July 24, he found that there was not much of a stand to be made with the troops at hand: they faced almost a thousand Japanese. Those Japanese were engineers; after the bridge was blown, it took them less than twenty-four hours to rig up a temporary suspension bridge across the gorge. They were now over in force and moving on Kokoda very rapidly. At Gorari, Capt. Samuel B. Templeton of the 39th made a desperate stand with about two hundred men. But the Japanese forced them back, using machine guns, mortars, and 37-mm field pieces. Templeton went back to a position only eight miles from Kokoda.

The trouble was that the Australians did not have the resources to do the job. On July 26, two flights were made into Kokoda airstrip by a light plane, bringing about thirty men. Half of them were kept at Kokoda. The other half were sent to Templeton. But that afternoon Captain Templeton was killed, and the Japanese surrounded the defenders at Oivi.

The Australians then had to evacuate Kokoda. They took up positions at Deniki, five miles southwest of Kokoda. Next day, they were joined by the men of the Oivi force who had succeeded in breaking through the Japanese circle. The rest were killed or captured.

At this stage, there was not much that could be done to help the Australians on the Kokoda Plateau. The Allied bombers came over on July 27, one B-17 and two B-26 bombers attacked. They wounded one Japanese soldier.

That day IGH ordered the 25th Naval Air Group to support the Kokoda operation. On July 29, Zero fighters from the Rabaul area staggered into Lae airfield.

That afternoon the Lae base was attacked by navy dive-bombers and Australian P-39 fighters, which struck the incoming supply transports from Rabaul.

On July 27, the Australians at Port Moresby sent up two small transport planes loaded with troops, and these helped Colonel Owen stage a counterattack and drive the Japanese out of Kokoda. At the end of the day, he was desperate for reinforcements.

That night, two more transport planes arrived from Australia, giving the Port Moresby defenders four transports to move troops up to the Kokoda Plateau. But events forestalled that. In the morning of July 29, the Japanese attacked at dawn. In the fierce fighting that followed, Colonel Owen was killed. A little later the Australians were again driven out of Kokoda. That also meant the airfield had fallen into Japanese hands.

But help was on the way, by foot over the trail. On July 31, a company of soldiers reached Deniki. By August 7, all five companies of the 39th Battalion were in action. The Australian force now numbered about 1,480 men, roughly half that of the Japanese.

On August 10, the Australians staged a counterattack in the Kokoda area and that afternoon recaptured the airfield. But the Australians had split their force, thinking that the Japanese they faced numbered only about four hundred. The Japanese attacked again from a different direction, and the Australians once more had to give up Kokoda and the airfield.

Meanwhile, more of Colonel Yokoyama's troops had come up, and he now had about fifteen hundred men in the Kokoda area. On the morning of August 13, he struck. The Australians were forced out of Deniki and Isurava, which was five miles away. The Japanese stopped and dug in here, in full possession of the high points of the plateau. They had a base for the attack on Port Moresby, just as planned. It was now up to General Horii to bring the South Seas Detachment of about five thousand men up to make the attack.

Back at Rabaul, General Hyakutake had orders from IGH to speed up the attack on Port Moresby. So, as of July 28, the Japanese planning was hurried along. Now came the delicate matter of securing the support of the Imperial Japanese Navy, which was really totally independent of the army. General Hyakutake met with Vice Adm. Nichizo Tsukahara, commander of the 11th Air Fleet, newly arrived at Rabaul and now to be the central air force of the region. He also met with Vice Adm. Gunichi Mikawa, commander of the 8th Fleet, also stationed at Rabaul. Admiral Mikawa was now responsible for naval operations in the Rabaul–New Guinea–Solomons area.

The army would take Port Moresby while the navy would move into Samarai. The latter operation would come first.

As soon as Samarai was taken, units of the 8th Fleet would move in and organize for the assault on Port Moresby.

Under cover of attacks against the nearest enemy by the Japanese army and navy troops at Lae and Salamaua, the Port Moresby assault force would be organized at Samarai. Then, the naval landing force and the naval escort units would move around to attack Port Moresby at the same time that Colonel Yokoyama attacked overland from Kokoda. All this would occur on X day, August 7, 1942. But, another landing was also planned for that day.

Under the agreement of the Joint Chiefs of Staff relative to military operations in the South Pacific, Admiral King was to have the first swipe at the Japanese in the Tulagi area. He had insisted that the Tulagi base must be destroyed, and the other chiefs had gone along with him, granting MacArthur control over the next two operations after that. For two months, the Navy had been preparing for an amphibious invasion of the area. The target in the plans was Tulagi. The island of Guadalcanal across the bay was not considered worth mention. There was nothing there of any note as far as the Allies could see. True, it had been the administrative headquarters for the southern Solomon Islands, but what did that mean? A handful of native villages scattered among the hills and rain forests.

But scarcely had Rear Adm. Richmond Kelly Turner been sent off to California to train troops for amphibious invasion, when an army intelligence officer in Australia looked at the island of Guadalcanal with a new eye. Photo planes making a routine run had filmed movement there. A few weeks later, photographs showed that the grass on the central upland plain had been burned off, leaving a spot very nicely gauged to become an airfield with a little work. Also, somebody was building a wharf at Lunga.

In June, Australian coast watchers got the whole story from natives. The Japanese were there. They were going to build an airfield and engage some native labor. They were only waiting for the arrival of the Japanese engineer units from Rabaul.

And then the radio intelligence people at Pearl Harbor supplied another part of the puzzle. The Japanese were sending the 11th and 13th Pioneer battalions (construction battalions) to Guadalcanal by ship. They would arrive on July 4 to begin work on the new airfield.

So, Admiral King got hold of Admiral Nimitz who got hold of Admiral Turner, and the whole amphibious landing program was stepped up. For some months, the Americans had been training the 1st Marine Division in the South Pacific. They were going to go into action now, probably before they were ready. But there was no time to wait.

King recognized precisely what the Japanese were up to. He would have been doing the same thing. Frustrated in one attempt to control the air and waters around Australia, they were going to go at it in a different way.

There were two plans for invasions on August 7, 1942, but only one of them came off. The Japanese fell into serious difficulties. At the end of July, their supply convoy heading for Buna—with engineers, bulldozers, and all the supplies necessary for the construction of an airfield—was caught by Allied bombers while at sea. One transport, the *Kotoko Maru*, was sunk, and five others were damaged, so that the whole fleet turned about and returned to Rabaul for repairs and reinforcements. At the same time, the Japanese engineers in Buna began to recognize that they had a very wet area on their hands and that the airfield was going to take some real building if it was to work at all. So, X day for the Japanese was advanced to August 16.

On August 3, the Japanese were in more trouble. A convoy of transports and cargo ships headed for Buna with many planes and plane parts for the new Buna airfield. Three ships were sunk by Allied bombers, and the whole enterprise was again a failure.

Then, on August 7, came the American landings on Guadalcanal Island and Tulagi. They came as a complete surprise to Rabaul, Truk, and Tokyo, the three headquarters directly involved.

At first, the Japanese were inclined to believe that the Guadalcanal landings were a raid or a feint. They had no immediate way of learning the strength of the forces because their garrisons were totally wiped out and the radio station went off the air before any real information could be passed. No one in Japanese high command was really much concerned. But they were ready. On the morning of August 9, the 8th Fleet sent its cruisers down between Florida Island and Guadalcanal in what was to be known to the Americans as the Battle of Savo Island. In short order, the Japanese sank four heavy cruisers, including the Australian forces' flagship, the cruiser *Canberra*. No one could fault the Japanese naval reaction. It had been swift and sure and enormously effective. The Americans immediately withdrew their fleet from these waters where the Japanese held naval and air superiority, and the U.S. Marines were then out on a limb.

But the Japanese made an enormous mistake at this point. The Americans had about 17,000 troops on Guadalcanal and Tulagi. The immediate dispatch of a Japanese division, landing under Japanese air control by Japanese ships that controlled the waters, could have been fatal to the American effort. But the Japanese army was so unaware of the nature of this invasion that one of its senior officers asked a naval officer just what an American Marine really was. He got the answer that *it* was something like the naval landing forces of the Japanese navy. Thus, he immediately concluded that the marines were—had to be—numerically a vastly inferior force. So badly had the Japanese military gulled themselves through their easy early victories in the Pacific War that this mistake could be made. Instead of dispatching one or two divisions to clean up the islands, the Japanese decided to commit the Kawaguchi Detachment—less one battalion, which meant about 7,000 troops. Operating on the principle that one Japanese soldier was worth two of the enemy, this seemed perfectly sound.

Beginning on the morning of August 8, the marines on Guadalcanal knew they had run into a buzz saw. The Japanese air force was out hour after hour: Zeros looking for anything that moved in the air and the Betty bombers unloading their explosives on the marines and all around them. The Japanese paid particular attention to Henderson Field (now so named by the Americans).

General Hyakutake was really in a quandary. He had so little experience with the Americans that he did not know quite how to react to their landings. Further, under the agreements set down by the directives of IGH, Hyakutake was bound to commit his entire mobile military resources to the Port Moresby, Buna, and Kokoda operations. What was left to meet this new threat? Only the Kawaguchi Detachment, unless he was to delay the whole plan for the assault on Port Moresby, which was already two weeks delayed, for the second time. The IGH would not like that.

So, General Hyakutake took the position that the Kawaguchi Detachment would be more than ample to wipe out the American threat on Guadalcanal and that the Port Moresby operation could remain relatively undisturbed.

He would not even give Col. Kawaguchi back that single battalion committed to the capture of Samarai and to be involved in the subsequent landing on Port Moresby. It was a moment at which a decisive Japanese action would have carried the day, without doubt, but the Japanese were so fuzzed by constant victory in the past that they did not see their danger.

Then came a new problem. The sinkings of half-a-dozen transports in these waters in the course of the Buna operation had created some real problems for the Japanese army's transport service. The army ran its own ships. To ask the navy for cargo vessels or transports was a matter unheard of in Japanese military protocol. General Hyakutake had a new problem. It was going to take him some time to get Colonel Kawaguchi's Detachment down from Palau, the staging center. In the interim, something had to be done.

Thus another unit was chosen to rush in and stem the tide of the Americans on Guadalcanal: the Ichiki Detachment. Actually, this arrangement was rigged up by the Japanese navy, whose Admiral Yamamoto seemed to recognize the American threat better than did General Hyakutake. Sitting at Guam and unemployed was the Ichiki Detachment. This unit was still (at least theoretically) under the control of the Combined Fleet because it had been scheduled to make the amphibious landings on Midway Island. When that was called off, there was so much confusion that no plan had been made for the reemployment of the detachment.

Admiral Yamamoto called that day for establishment of a Guadalcanal reinforcement force. By the way the Japanese army and the navy cooperated (almost not at all), it was again going to take some time. Therefore, the marines had some respite, some chance to dig in and learn the terrain and the climate in which they would be fighting. They would have just about a week.

But it would not be a peaceful week or anything like it. All day long every day, from before dawn until after dusk, the Japanese planes came over and plastered Guadalcanal with bombs. They strafed when they saw something moving. They retained control of the air, although the handful of marine and navy and Australian pilots—and later army pilots—who came in did their utmost to stop the attacks. But there were just too many Zeros and too many Betty bombers and not enough F4Fs and P-40s and P-39s.

Thus the Port Moresby invasion plan remained unchanged, and the Japanese set about plugging a huge hole in their defense perimeter with what was the equivalent of Kleenex. Adm. Raizo Tanaka, the man chosen to manage the delivery and resupply of the Japanese forces on Guadalcanal was indignant from the moment he learned what was being planned: less than a thousand riflemen and no heavy weapons. It was ridiculous and insane. But IGH had been told that there were fewer than two thousand Americans on Guadalcanal, therefore, nine hundred Japanese soldiers ought to be plenty.

Majestically, the Japanese counter to Guadalcanal got under way—with the navy bombarding and running up and down that bit of water between Guadalcanal and the other islands known as the slot and with the air force smashing the marines hour after hour. From the air and the sea, the Japanese preponderance looked so enormous to the army that no qualms were felt. General Hyakutake forgot one of the adages of warfare: no matter how powerful the striking force might be, there is no substitute for the capture and holding of territory.

And so the orders were given for the relief of Guadalcanal, but once again in a most gentlemanly and leisurely fashion. On the night of August 15, a thousand soldiers of the Ichiki Detachment and their colonel boarded six destroyer transports at Truk and headed for Guadalcanal. They did not expect much difficulty in either annihilating or driving the Americans off the island. On the night of August 18, they came down quietly past Savo Island and Lunga Roads, and sailed through Lengo Channel to land at Taivu Point. At the same time, Yamamoto sent a little insurance, the 5th Special Sasebo Landing Force of naval soldiers, who landed at Tassafaronga. Combined with the existing garrison, or what was left of it, the Japanese had perhaps fifteen hundred men on the island just then.

They would soon be in for a very rude shock and most of them would be dead.

But just then, in the middle part of August, General Hyakutake was serene and at Rabaul. He became just a little less serene when his air observers reported to him that the Allies had begun building an airfield at Milne Bay. That would make it duck soup for the Allies to attack the Japanese operations at Samarai, so that plan was hastily scrapped (showing how fast the Japanese could move when they had a mind to), and the island of Rabi was chosen instead. That stray battalion of the Kawaguchi Detachment would do the job here as it was to have done it at Samarai.

At Buna, the Japanese build up continued in spite of some fairly effective Allied bombing. One convoy, which had sortied from Rabaul on August 12, was attacked heavily several times from the air as it crossed the sea-lanes, but it arrived safely at Basabua on the afternoon of August 13. By dawn on the 14th, the ships were unloaded and on their way back to Rabaul.

Work then began on the Buna airstrip. The jungle was cleared for two miles. And another strip was also prepared— the second one, however, was a dummy that would be used to entice the enemy bombers while the Japanese carefully camouflaged their real strip and its revetments and aircraft.

With a slight allowance for the shock of the Guadalcanal landings, everything at Buna was going as planned. On August 17, the main body of the South Seas Detachment left Rabaul in three transports. General Horii's headquarters was aboard one. The entourage included infantry, signal companies, machine-gun companies, mountain artillery, field artillery, cavalry, antitank sections, a base hospital, several hundred New Britain natives for carrying, and a small part of the 5th Sasebo Special Naval Landing Force.

The Allies were asleep the day the Japanese reached Basabua without being detected. On the afternoon of August 18, they unloaded.

Almost immediately afterward, the Yazawa Detachment under Col. Kiyomi Yazawa set out for New Guinea. It sailed on August 18 with all the same sort of units that had gone with the South Seas Detachment. This convoy left Rabaul on August 19 and landed at Basabua on August 21. Once again, the Allied air force was caught napping, and the convoy soon unloaded without incident. At this point, almost all of the Japanese troops destined for the Port Moresby operation were on New Guinea. General Horii did not know it at the moment, but his chance of getting reinforcements was being whittled down every day by events on Guadalcanal.

So confident was Colonel Ichiki when he and his men went ashore on Guadalcanal that they had not bothered to reconnoiter and discover what they faced. One column of troops marched westward to find a bivouac area. So contemptuous of the enemy were the Japanese that they did not keep vigilant. Guadalcanal natives found the Japanese and led the marines along the way. The marines ambushed the Japanese and killed twenty-four of the thirty-one men in the column.

Then, the marines dug in along the west side of the Tenaru River and set traps on the east side. The Japanese did not bother to see what was going on. Led by officers waving samurai swords, they launched an attack on the evening of August 20. Their best technique against Westerners, they had discovered in earlier fighting in Malaya, was to attack in the dead of night, using flares and noise and screaming. At 1:30 in the morning, two hundred Japanese soldiers came storming over the bank of the river, hurling grenades and shouting. This technique had paralyzed the British in the earlier days of the war. But the marines were ready. They had their fields of fire. They turned their machine guns and M1 rifles on the enemy and let loose with everything they had. They cut the battalion of the Ichiki Detachment to ribbons.

By the time daylight arrived, all the Japanese who had forded the Tenaru River were dead, and the Ichiki Detachment was completely disorganized. Most of its officers had been killed. The fighting continued that day, August 21, and the marines launched a flanking movement. Colonel Ichiki had not been careful about his terrain, he found himself squeezed into a pocket in a coconut grove on the shore of the island. The Japanese could not escape across the river because of the marine machine guns. The Japanese launched a bayonet charge. The marines met it with one of their own.

The Japanese did not get through. Some Japanese soldiers took to the sea and swam to small islands, where they waited for rescue, or along the coast to get out of range of the marines. But nearly all the nine hundred men of the Ichiki Detachment were slaughtered that day. In the evening, Colonel Ichiki and several of his officers committed ritual suicide in expiation of the sin they had committed against the emperor and the army by losing the battle. Of the entire Ichiki Detachment, only fifteen men remained, prisoners of the marines.

The result of that disaster was to have its effects on the battle for Buna and Port Moresby. When General Hyakutake learned of the disaster, he ordered the battalion of the Kawaguchi Detachment scheduled for the Milne Bay operations to return to its parent group. It would now be sent to Guadalcanal. The Aoba force, which had been scheduled for reserve, was now detailed to the Milne Bay operations, leaving Hyakutake without a reserve.

By mid-August, the Japanese had about 12,000 troops in the Buna–Gona area.

The Allies did not believe the Japanese would really try a move overland to take Port Moresby. The idea was suggested several times, but each time General Willoughby, MacArthur's intelligence officer, indicated that it was impossible and should not even be considered. On August 21, General Horii went up to Kokoda to take personal charge of the attack through the Gap, the attack that Willoughby said was impossible. Still, Willoughby persisted in his claims that the Japanese could not possibly move that way.

The impossible, one might say, was just about to begin.

CHAPTER EIGHT

The Japanese Attack

Early in August, General MacArthur ordered the 7th Australian Infantry Division to split in two and move to New Guinea. The 18th Brigade went to Milne Bay and the 21st and 25th brigades went to Port Moresby. Finally, some real troop strength was being moved into New Guinea to oppose the Japanese.

In deference to the Australians (after all it was their country), MacArthur put command of the New Guinea Allied forces into the hands of Maj. Gen. Sydney F. Rowell. His task was to stop the Japanese penetration of Papua New Guinea and to retake Kokoda, Buna, and all the other places the Japanese had occupied.

But orders do not make victories. General Rowell had some work ahead of him. The Japanese at that moment were on the Kokoda Trail at Isurava, south of Kokoda. They were planning the landing at Samarai.

But the Japanese had committed one serious tactical error. They had failed to keep constant air watch on the New Guinea operations of the Allies. Therefore, they were not aware of the speed and efficiency with which MacArthur's engineers and construction men were building airfields and other facilities. Had they been aware, they might have bombed them so severely as to stop the work. Instead, the work progressed almost unmolested. In defense of the Japanese as well as the Allied air command, it must be said that the fliers had an enormous weather problem. Milne Bay was socked in most of the time. But the Japanese also had submarines and miniature submarines in the area, so that their reconnaissance facilities were far better than the Americans. They were not used very well. Once again, it was a matter of Japanese over-confidence.

Thus, by the third week of August 1942, the Allies had completed three airfields in the Cape York Peninsula, Australia. Three more were under construction, scheduled for completion by the first of October. All this in spite of a shortage of shipping, which MacArthur lamented, and a shortage of naval escort caused by the heavy losses of American naval units in the sea battles around Guadalcanal.

On August 19, the Australian 21st Brigade arrived at Port Moresby. Immediately, it was sent forward to Isurava, where the outnumbered Australian Maroubra Force was fending off the Japanese. That brought the forces in the Port Moresby area up to two thousand men, with another brigade yet to come. That would mean another six thousand men.

But all was anything but beer and skittles. The arriving men of the 21st Brigade were not used to marching in the Kokoda Track country of the Owen Stanley Mountains while carrying seventy-pound packs, and they began to show the pressure. The fact was that the Japanese were in much better physical condition, an element of the intense training—including "hot marches" and "cold marches"—that put a premium on endurance. And, a very successful Japanese air raid on Port Moresby had destroyed almost all the food and ammunition supplies immediately destined for the front line. Thus was an Allied counteroffensive stalled. The troops could not move until General MacArthur's air force could bring them in a thirty-days' supply of rations and ammunition. What now developed along the track at Myola was a series of skirmishes.

Down at Milne Bay on the tip of the peninsula, the defense force commanded by Maj. Gen. Cyril A. Clowes reached 950 men, Australians and Americans.

Once General Horii arrived in New Guinea, he began to press for swift action to strike simultaneously along the Kokoda Track and at Milne Bay. The information, just received, about the Allied build up caused the Japanese high command to move swiftly. The Aoba Detachment, which was supposed to take Milne Bay, was still sitting at Davao in the Philippines because of a Japanese army shipping problem. But Admiral Mikawa decided that the 8th Fleet's naval troops could manage the job without the Aoba Detachment and proceeded accordingly. Comdr. Shojiro Hayashi was in command of a very mixed naval force, including four different units. The troops would come in from Kavieng, and they would land at Rabi, three miles from the Gili Gili wharf area at the head of Milne Bay. Troops from Buna would meanwhile land at Taupota on the north coast and march to Gili Gili.

The operation began on August 24, the Kavieng detail leading in two transports. The Buna troops left that same morning in several large motorized landing barges. The latter were spotted by a coast watcher at Porlock Harbor that afternoon. He radioed in his report. The next morning a search plane found the barges as they came up to Goodenough Island. A dozen P-40s from Milne Bay took off as soon as the weather cleared early in the afternoon, and they found the barges beached on Goodenough Island while the Japanese prepared lunch. Up to this point, the Japanese attack had been a very relaxed operation. But . . . after the P-40s got through, all seven landing barges were wrecked on the beach and most of the Sasebo 5th Naval Special Landing Force's equipment was badly shot up. The troops were stranded on Goodenough Island, out of the battle.

The Japanese had been more careful with their main landing force, the Kure 5th Special Naval Landing Force. Its transports were escorted by destroyers and cruisers. The force was sighted on the morning of August 25 and the Allied air forces were ordered to attack, but the weather closed in. Royal Australian Air Force (RAAF) P-40s and Hudson bombers from Milne Bay as well as B-17s, B-25s, and B-26s were ready to go. But the weather had socked them in. Squalls, gusts, overcast, zero visibility—all made flying impossible. No attack was made that day.

The Japanese made their objective unharmed, and began the landing at 10:00 P.M. on August 25 on the north shore of Milne Bay five miles east of Rabi.

Almost simultaneously, as promised, the troops on the Kokoda Track launched an offensive against the Australian 21st Brigade.

The Japanese were quite methodical. They brought their

supplies ashore and set them up in dumps at Waga Waga and the Wanadala area. Their main bivouac was east of the K. B. Mission. Just before 2:00 A.M. on August 26, the Japanese met the Australians, and they started a firefight. It lasted until dawn. Somewhere during the fighting, the Australians saw tanks in motion. The enemy had really outclassed them. They ordered up antitank weapons, but there were none available.

Fortunately for the Allies, the Japanese had made another error in the darkness, once again because of insufficient preliminary reconnaissance. They had landed in the wrong place. Their proper landing spot was at the head of Milne Bay where the three airfields and the wharf were located. But they had landed several miles away from the cleared and dry plantation area on a jungle shelf flanked on one side by mountains and the other side by the sea. The bivouac area was sopping wet all the time.

So, a wet night was spent, with neither side quite sure of the strength or position of the other.

Before 8 o'clock on the morning of August 26, the P-40s and B-17s were taking off from their airfields and heading toward Milne Bay. The fighters strafed the Japanese supply dumps on the beaches and managed to destroy much of the food and ammunition. The B-17s went after a big transport unloading in the bay and damaged it.

Again, the Japanese were lucky. Their second echelon was coming in, and the Allied aircraft spotted it. But before they could attack, the weather closed in once more and the Japanese managed to come up and land in the cloud cover without mishap.

The Japanese attacked K. B. Mission that night of the 26th, and they forced the Australians back to the line of the Gama River, east of Rabi. As dawn came, the Japanese broke off the attack. During the day, a battalion of the 18th Brigade was sent up to the K. B. Mission to hold it. The Japanese attacked again that night using two light tanks with powerful searchlights. The Australians were pinned by the searchlights and raked by the Japanese machine guns. The Australian casualties were very high. The battalion was pushed into the jungle. Disorganized, it took several days to get back to the head of Milne Bay and Allied territory.

Having pushed the Australians off the road, the Japanese

then moved on toward Number 3 airstrip, with the intention of destroying it and the aircraft around the area. But here it was a different story: no jungle but a broad clear field of fire for the defending troops who would be shooting across a corridor with its southern end less than five hundred feet from the sea. The Japanese would have to run that cordon. Their tanks began to bog down in the soft ground.

Just before dawn, the Japanese came up to the strip. It was defended by Australians and Americans of the 709th U.S. Airborne Antiaircraft Battalion and two companies of U.S. engineers. The Japanese tanks bogged down in the mud and had to be abandoned.

On August 28, the Australians prepared to attack with new troops from the 18th Brigade. But then they learned of a new Japanese convoy on its way to Milne Bay.

And so it came, a convoy of transports escorted by a cruiser and nine destroyers with nearly eight hundred fresh troops to throw into the battle.

On August 30, the new contingent of Japanese, along with the old, attacked the 18th Australian Brigade in the battle for Airstrip Number 3. The Australians had worked out a field of fire that covered both ends of the line as well as the center. As the Japanese came up, they were slaughtered. Not a single Japanese soldier crossed that line of fire. On the 30th, the Australians were helped by P-40 fighter strafing attacks. The Japanese were in full retreat. Commander Yano told Admiral Mikawa that the assault on Milne Bay had failed. Mikawa offered him another twelve hundred troops of the Aoba Battalion and a smaller unit, but Yano said it was hopeless. His own men were worn out with disease and fatigue and unable to carry on. So, the Japanese evacuated all the men they could, and they went back to Rabaul, sick with dysentery, malaria, jungle rot, trench foot, and tropical ulcers. They had been devoured by leeches and ravaged by Australian fire. The Milne Bay operation had come a complete cropper, costing the Japanese some six hundred crack troops.

Meanwhile, the airstrips were being completed and soon the Australians and Americans were flying from them to attack the Japanese at Rabaul and other bases in the northern Solomons without having to cross the dangerous barrier of the Owen Stanley Range.

* * *

General Horii's Japanese army troops on the Kokoda Trail were now to come under the test of enemy action. General Horii had come up on August 22 to supervise one victory after another along the trail. On August 24, he had given orders for a general offensive. The Australians were pushed back steadily. Their supply problems were enormous, particularly after the sinking of almost all the supply convoy in the bay off Port Moresby. The Japanese were coming downhill and the Australians were fighting uphill in every sense of the word. By September 7, the day that organized resistance of the Japanese at Milne Bay ended, the troops on the Kokoda Trail had advanced past Isurava, Alola Eora Creek, and Templeton's Crossing. They held the Gap and half-a-dozen villages beyond. They were poised to take the last three villages that stood between them and Port Moresby.

Even without the pincers, it seemed quite possible that the Japanese would indeed capture Port Moresby, using the almost impossible trail overland to do so.

The Japanese were doing a remarkable job along that trail, improving it daily so that they might bring their artillery up. And more Japanese troops were coming in. The ships landed another fifteen hundred reinforcements on the night of September 2 at Basabua. They also landed three hundred packhorses for use on the trail.

General Horii now had five reinforced battalions on the Kokoda Trail, with a good strong supply base at Kokoda. The Australians had only three battalions up forward to oppose the enemy, and one of these was the 39th Battalion, which had been fighting for a solid month and whose men were nearly exhausted. Taking advantage of their superior position on top and their superior strength, the Japanese mounted a continuous flanking operation, and the Australians had to drop back before them. Two regimental combat teams of Japanese alternated in the attack. The Japanese attacked at Myola and seized the airdrop grounds, which had been used by the Australians as a major method of supply. Otherwise, supply had to be brought up by native carriers. Once the airdrop grounds were lost, it became ever more difficult for the Australians to secure supplies. The native carriers, sensing that the Japanese were advancing successfully, began to desert the Australians.

So, the Australians retreated, fighting stubbornly, but moving back. They retreated as far as Efogi Spur, and there they took a stand on September 6, 1942.

Until this time, General MacArthur had been under the mistaken impression that the Japanese strength on the Kokoda Trail was minimal. That being so, why were the Australians continually retreating?

The explanation came from General Rowell, the troop commander. He told MacArthur's headquarters that the general was badly misinformed: the Australians had been outnumbered for some time. Why MacArthur's staff should not have known this is a puzzle, showing how badly managed it really was in terms of liaison with the Australians who were doing the fighting.

General Rowell asked for more troops for the field. He pointed out that the Japanese seemed to have in the trail area the maximum number of troops they could manage and supply. What Rowell wanted was one of the two Australian brigades that had come in from Ceylon recently.

MacArthur ordered up the 16th Australian Infantry Brigade of the 6th Division, which he sent to Port Moresby. Then the 25th Brigade, which had been holding that position, was hurried up to the front.

By this time, some of the American troops who had been coming in from the United States were well enough trained that it was possible to commit them to battle. Lt. Gen. Robert L. Eichelberger, the commander of the American troops in the theatre, was given the order to make the assignments. He had decided that the 32nd Division was better trained than the 41st and, thus, should go into New Guinea. The best unit of the division was the 126th Infantry, so the 126th got the job of going in to assist the Australians.

America was very new to jungle warfare. The men of the 126th Infantry were wearing cotton uniforms and old-fashioned blue-denim fatigues. These were dyed a mottled color to decrease their visibility in the jungle of New Guinea. Soon, the riflemen would learn a lot of new tricks, including the use of condoms to protect the muzzles of their rifles from rust and filth. It was a brand new war for the Americans.

On September 11, MacArthur announced his plan. The Australians would continue to press the Japanese back along the Kokoda Trail. But the Americans would cut in at Wairopi in a movement that would put them behind the Japanese. They would march across the mountains from Port Moresby to Ropuana Falls and, ultimately, the Kumusi River. The air transports came, and the troops began to be airlifted to New Guinea.

Indeed, we were new at this war, and General MacArthur's staff was showing it. When the first echelon got to Port Moresby, wise old Australian hands informed Brig. Gen. Hanford McNider that the route chosen by MacArthur's staff was totally impractical. First, it would run into the Australians. Second, it would go over terrain so rough that the only way the troops could be supplied was by air-dropping. The real alternative was a trail that led from Jaure to Wairopi. This trail was not used by New Guinea natives because they believed it to be haunted. No white man had been there either, not since 1917. There was one small disadvantage. The trail had to cross a ninety-one-hundred-foot mountain. General Rowell said it was hopeless, and he recommended a trail from Abau to Jaure, where the altitude was never above five thousand feet.

But the Americans wanted to do it their way. General McNider sent survey parties out. The 126th Infantry and the 128th Regimental Combat Team arrived in New Guinea almost together at the end of September. It had been decided to send the extra troops. They would be needed. General Horii was still advancing apace along the Kokoda Trail.

The 128th Infantry was assigned by the Australians to the Port Moresby garrison. The 126th Infantry was assigned to the New Guinea Force for use at Wairopi.

General Horii was a real threat to Port Moresby just then. After the attack on Efogi Spur on September 8, the general had five reinforced battalions in action. Soon, there were five thousand Japanese troops ready to go. The Australians fell back again. They lost Nauro and Ioribaiwa. They drew back to the Imita Range.

At this point, the situation of the forces changed dramatically. The Australians fell back to a point where their supply situation was very favorable. The Japanese, on the other side of Ula Ule Creek, had a long supply chain that was becoming ever more tenuous as they moved. And General Kenney's 5th

Air Force was not helping the Japanese at all. They later admitted that Kenney's bombers and strafing fighters had completely disrupted their supply system. The major element was a new weapon, a modified A-20 attack bomber, which carried eight forward-firing machine guns as well as parachute fragmentation bombs. Every day that they could fly, the planes were out attacking the Japanese supply dumps, their landing barges, and the Buna airfield. Once every day or so the bombers and the Australian Hudsons would roar in and knock out the Wairopi bridge, too. The Japanese engineers must have repaired it fifty times.

Now the Japanese were in deep trouble and the real indication was that they were foraging for food—stripping native gardens and eating plants. The frontline ration was down from a pound of rice per day to less than a cup. On September 17, the Japanese troops who had just won another victory at Ioribaiwa did not have a single grain of rice to eat.

CHAPTER NINE

The Allied Offensive

Since the inception of the Port Moresby operation, the situation of the Imperial Japanese forces in the whole South Pacific area had changed enormously. Back in the spring, prospects had looked bright for an early capture of Port Moresby and the French and American islands nearby. The Battle of the Coral Sea had been a setback, followed by one far worse, the Battle of Midway, at which the Japanese naval superiority was brought down. Then came the invasion of Guadalcanal by the Americans and the concomitant increase in Allied naval activity in these southern waters. Allied aircraft were now fighting for superiority. They had not yet achieved it at Guadalcanal, but they had achieved it much more nearly in the New Guinea area.

On August 29, watching the deterioration of the Milne Bay operation, General Hyakutake at Rabaul ordered General Horii on the Kokoda Trail to stop, back up, and hold until the situation in the whole South Pacific region could be clarified. There was a great deal of difficulty in the reinforcement and resupply of Japanese troops at Guadalcanal. The Milne Bay operation had just failed. So General Horii was to move back to the Buna side of the Owen Stanley Mountains, stop, and hold.

General Horii did as he was ordered. He took his troops back through the Gap and looked for a suitable place on the other side to establish strong defensive positions. He chose Ioribaiwa as the place to make a stand. He told the troops that they would wait there for a month and after that would make the final push down the mountain to Port Moresby.

A few days after that decision was made, more negative changes came to the Japanese situation in the whole area. As far as the Japanese were concerned, the South Pacific and the Southwest Pacific were the same theater of operations. General Hyakutake was the army commander for operations in New Guinea and in the Solomons. Admiral Mikawa was the navy commander. Therefore, what happened in Guadalcanal was of direct and immediate significance to these commands.

On August 13, the Kawaguchi Detachment, once scheduled for New Guinea operations, was virtually destroyed in the Battle of Bloody Ridge near Henderson Field on Guadalcanal. The destruction of this second major military detachment brought home to the Japanese the tenacity of their enemy and the difficulty of their current position. The Japanese had waited too late and had put too few troops onto Guadalcanal in the period when the imperial forces had superiority in nearly everything. Now, the Allies were more and more successfully contesting the Japanese air superiority, and on the seas, the Americans now controlled by day, the Japanese controlled by night.

This worsening of the situation in the Solomons had its immediate results in New Guinea. There could be no major reinforcement of New Guinea just now. The South Seas Detachment *(Nankai Shitai)* would have to begin to think defensively and take on the defense of the Buna–Gona beachhead.

Two divisions of Japanese troops now were scheduled for Guadalcanal. After they had taken the island from the Americans, those troops would be sent to New Guinea to assist in the Port Moresby operations. Until then, the foot soldiers would have to hold.

These were all new shocking concepts to Japanese soldiers so long accustomed to unbroken successions of victories.

General Horii was told not to pay any attention to those messages of late August and early September, but to begin moving his troops down to the beach.

The troops at Ioribaiwa were to hold as long as possible and then retreat. The troops began coming down from the hills; as they came, they were enlisted in building bunkers and clearing fields of fire for defense. The Allied land forces were preparing to go on the offensive. On September 23, General Blamey arrived and took command. On September 26, the 25th Brigade began its attack on Ioribaiwa, which was captured on September 28 without much resistance because the Japanese—instead of following General Horii's instructions—had retreated. They moved so swiftly that the Australians could not follow them fast enough to fight. The real reason was not fear, but hunger.

As of October 1, then, the Allies in New Guinea were contemplating the offensive rather than the defensive (see map). The final objective was to drive the Japanese from the peninsula. But this was not going to be easy. The Japanese still controlled the sea-lanes in the South Pacific. What would happen in the New Guinea area was entirely dependent on what would happen in the Solomons area. General MacArthur was under no illusions that the battle had been won because the Japanese had failed to take Milne Bay or that their preoccupation with the Solomons had caused them to neglect the supply of their Kokoda units. He stated:

A local success attained at a time when the enemy is devoting attention to the Solomons, must not blind us to the fact that basic conditions which have heretofore limited our action in New Guinea are unchanged and that in the absence of secure lines of communication on the north coast of New Guinea we are still unable to maintain large forces there.

MacArthur, as the Australians put it, was "like a bloody barometer, always up and down." At one moment, he seemed near despair and was taxing Prime Minister Curtin because the Australians were not fighting hard enough. (His staff had never gotten it straight about the number of Japanese on the Kokoda Track.) At the next moment, he was talking of ultimate victory with the greatest élan. Then he was back down in the depths again as soon as another reverse came along.

On October 2, MacArthur flew into Port Moresby for one of those inspection trips of his that always had the look of a grandstand play. The correspondents and photographers were happy, they talked and snapped photos of the general and his staff. He was without doubt the greatest planner of media events of World War II. Later, the general went by jeep up the Kokoda Track as far as he could go. He made a few philosophical pronouncements for the press, which they could print, and said nothing about his battle plans, which they could not print. Censorship was very tight just then; the fact that some American troops had already been committed to the New Guinea battle was a deep secret. At the end of the line, MacArthur turned about and went back to Port Moresby. Next day he was back in Brisbane.

Part of MacArthur's plan was to send an American force up the Kapa Kapa Track, to the southwest of the Kokoda Trail, and intersect the Kokoda track at a point where the Americans could outflank the Japanese. At MacArthur headquarters on MacArthur maps, it made a whopper of a plan. But the MacArthur staff had again erred, and the Kapa Kapa Track turned out to be about twice as rough as the Kokoda Trail that had nearly licked the Australians. The track going was so desperate that it took the American party a week to cross sixteen miles of the Owen Stanley Range divide. By the time the Americans reached their objective, they had discarded most of their equipment and almost run out of food. They had come down with dysentery, so severe that many men cut away the seat of their trousers. They reached Jaure on October 28. What a mistake it had been! The 2nd Battalion of the 126th Infantry was very nearly destroyed by the trip, and the men were in no condition to fight even after a week of rest.

Also, there was another error by the MacArthur staff: just after the American troops had made this grueling march, it was discovered that it was all to no avail. There were plenty of places down on the coast, like Wanigela, where level fields of kunai grass would allow the landing of transport planes. The troops could all have been brought over by air.

The Japanese were still very powerful. Therefore, any offensive had to be carried out with the concern that the Japanese could stop it at any time and that the Allies had to be prepared to retreat on short notice to previously prepared defensive positions.

The 7th Australian Infantry Division was not doing what General Horii's troops had done before: but in reverse—attacking along the Kokoda Trail toward Buna. The Japanese had withdrawn through the Gap and by October 8 had reached Templeton's Crossing. They held there for a week. Then, under instructions from General Horii, they moved back to Eora Creek and made another stand there.

The Japanese were by this time more than half-starved and suffering from all the tropical diseases. As the Allies advanced against very strong opposition, they found evidences of cannibalism. Yet the morale of the Japanese troops, in terms of giving up, remained exceedingly high. There were virtually no surrenders. It was a slugging battle all the way for the Australians. But now they had fresh troops. On October 1, the 16th Brigade relieved the 25th Brigade, and the Australians pushed on.

Up from the beach came the Japanese 41st Infantry under Colonel Yazawa. At least, these men were not starved. They came up with all the food they could carry plus that carried by a whole line of Rabaul natives. Their defenses were laid at Oivi, where they planned to stay a while.

The Australians moved on into Kokoda, which they reached on November 2.

Following the Allied capture of Milne Bay, the Australian and American troops had begun to arrive there. They used boats and planes. The coastal shuttle became famous, even if it was never very efficient. They used every sort of craft. Trawlers (luggers) were the most available. They were bombed by their own air force and bitten by malarial mosquitoes. But somehow, they established supply dumps and got troops forward on the northeast coast of New Guinea. By November 2, the day the Australians marched into Kokoda and hoisted the flag, the U.S. 128th Infantry was at Pongani and Medaropu.

The task of these troops was to secure the coast between Milne Bay and Cape Nelson and to recapture Goodenough Island, which had been taken by the Japanese earlier. This job was given to the 128th Australian Brigade. In the last week of October, they set out and were landed by two destroyers on both sides of the island's southern tip. There were about three hundred Japanese on the island, most of them those troops who had been stranded when the Australian fighter planes and bombers had smashed up the landing barges of the Sasebo 5th Special Naval Landing Force during the preliminary Milne Bay operations in the summer.

Since that time, the troops had been resupplied and some

of them had been taken off the island by Japanese submarines. When the Australian forces landed on Goodenough, the Japanese resisted stoutly, but only for one day. That next night the rest of the Japanese were taken off by submarine to Fergusson Island where they were picked up by a Japanese cruiser and taken back to Rabaul. Only a handful of stragglers were left on Goodenough, men who had wandered away from the rest. They were soon mopped up by the Australians.

So many years after the war, it is difficult to recall the tensions that existed in 1942 during the battle for Guadalcanal. General MacArthur was extremely conscious of the battle over which he had no control. What if the Japanese recaptured the island? The next Japanese step would surely be to concentrate their resources against Port Moresby and Buna and to wipe the Allies out of New Guinea altogether. They would certainly be able to do it. For no matter what seemed to be happening along the Kokoda Trail, all that was unimportant if the full force of the Japanese Imperial Navy and the Imperial Naval Air Force could be turned against New Guinea. Thus, if MacArthur seemed almost totally preoccupied with the defensive aspects of this struggle, he was behaving as a sensible commander should, examining all the possibilities.

In this case, at the end of October and the beginning of November, sometimes the questions seemed more probabilities. The Japanese had been winning all the naval battles. Beginning on October 26 at the battle the Americans called the Battle of Santa Cruz, the carrier forces of Japan and the United States met again. The result was the sinking of a carrier, the U.S.S. *Hornet*, and the retreat of the American fleet in high gear. The Americans had already lost the carrier *Wasp* in these waters. The situation looked really desperate. The *Enterprise* had also been damaged in the battle of Santa Cruz, and the forced withdrawal of the American fleet from those waters meant the Japanese once more had undisputed sea control. They no longer had the same degree of air control, although their attacks on Guadalcanal in the last week of October were extremely fierce. But a handful of American and Australian pilots were flying mission after mission each day to keep down the damage.

From MacArthur's point of view, the situation was so iffy

that he told General Blamey—who wanted to prepare for a land attack against the Japanese—that until the Guadalcanal situation was resolved, it would be foolhardy to concentrate more than a single regiment in any staging area. That meant no broad attack. And, of course, MacArthur was right; if the Japanese could turn their naval air resources against the troops on the New Guinea coast, they could create disaster.

General Blamey then proposed that the American troops be concentrated on the Buna shore and that an early attack be made. They would come overland by trail and by airlift from Port Moresby. On November 2, MacArthur indicated his approval and the plan for an attack on November 15 was under way.

On the Kokoda Trail, the Japanese were fighting a rearguard action, and a very vigorous one, aided by well-placed artillery. On November 4, the Australians attacked at Oivi and at Gorari. The Japanese were caught, and Colonel Yazawa evacuated Oivi that night. With him was General Horii who had come up for an inspection trip and had been trapped by the Australian attack. The Japanese staff escaped into the jungle northeast of Oivi. Not a very comfortable situation for a general.

The troops of Yazawa's force stuck together, came out north of the Australians, and headed toward Gona. The Australians had kept on moving. The Japanese had fought them as hard as they could as long as they could, but their shortage of supplies and ammunition had grown desperate. On November 13, the Australians wiped out the Japanese rear guard at Wairopi, and that night, they built a temporary suspension bridge like so many that had been built there before. The troops began crossing the river.

The Americans were marching from Jaure toward the coast. They had a dreadful time. The 126th Infantry's 2nd Battalion pushed toward Gora and Bofu and reached Bofu on November 12. They had planned to receive supplies by airdrop, but all the way they had not found a single decent airdrop ground; therefore, most of the rations that came down for them were lost in the rain forest. By the time they got to Bofu they had been reduced to eating bananas and papayas.

Some of the troops were flown into the Pongani airfield and some to the field called Abel's Field. By November 14, most of the troops of the regiment were approaching their destination, and it would not be long before the attack would begin.

Over in the Solomons area, for a change, there was some good news. In the second week of November, Admiral Yamamoto organized a supply mission to relieve the starving Japanese troops on Guadalcanal Island, where more than two divisions had been landed after many errors. Once landed, those divisions had gotten virtually no resupply because of the interdiction of both the American air force and naval vessels. In the second week of November, Yamamoto had ordered an all-out effort to resupply the troops. A big convoy had headed south accompanied by the battleships *Hiei* and *Kirishima* and several other capital ships. The American naval forces had met it head on in Guadalcanal waters, and the battle had brought the sinking of several. One division had been landed but without supply because Admiral Halsey's naval forces wiped out seven of the eleven ships sent by Yamamoto to help out the Japanese on Guadalcanal. It was the worst disaster the Japanese had suffered. Many of the troops of the Japanese 38th Division were killed; the survivors found themselves ashore without food and without their equipment. The battle for Guadalcanal had entered a new phase. The Japanese were totally wound up in it, trying desperately now to supply the twenty thousand Japanese troops on the island. They had no extra resources at the moment to devote to the New Guinea campaign. So, the time for an Allied attack was precisely right.

CHAPTER TEN

The Japanese Stand

Buna. Beautiful, lush, green, stinking, deadly Buna—with its jungles and swamps; its tangles of scrub brush and clumps of knife-sharp kunai grass; its 125-foot coco palms; its rain, rain, rain; its leeches and snakes; and its chattering birds that could warn the enemy of a footfall. Many an Aussie and many a GI would wonder what the hell MacArthur or anyone else would want with this godforsaken coast, where the humidity averages eighty-five percent—averages, mind you—and the temperature averages ninety-six degrees Fahrenheit. It was a medic's nightmare: malaria, scrub typhus, two kinds of dysentery, dengue fever and another that was never even diagnosed except for the fever it brought at 4 o'clock in the afternoon, jungle rot, dhobie itch, ringworm, athlete's foot, conjunctivitis. You name it, Buna had it.

Already the Japanese had learned to suffer. There was no joke about it; more than half the Japanese casualties were from hunger and disease. Many a *Hei Watanabe* also was to wonder what General Hyakutake wanted with this Buddha-forsaken spot, but unlike the Diggers and the GIs, the Japanese soldier did not complain. He died silently praising the emperor in whose name he had been sent to this sticky death trap.

But the fact was the Japanese wanted it so they could control Australia, and that was enough reason for MacArthur to deny it to them. The process of denial was now to begin in the middle of November 1942.

The Allied attack plan was ready on November 14. The 7th Australian Division and the 32nd American Division would fight in the area bounded by the Kumusi River, Cape

Sudest, and Holnicote Bay. This was where the Japanese had begun and now, after all those weeks on the Kokoda Track, they were back at the beachhead with their backs to the sea.

The Allies would move on November 16: the Americans against Buna and the Australians against Gona and Sanananda.

It was not going to be easy. General Blamey had hoped for some Allied naval support by Rear Adm. Arthur S. Carpender, who had succeeded Admiral Leary. A bad choice as commander of MacArthur's navy, he refused to cooperate on the basis that these waters were too dangerous for his ships. So, the land forces would have to go it alone against the Japanese army and the Japanese 8th Fleet, whose Admiral Mikawa had no such reservations about putting his fighting ships at risk.

The attack began on schedule. The only real problem at the outset was the condition of the Allied troops. They had suffered—not as much as the Japanese but still a great deal—on the long march across the Owen Stanley Mountains. The Australian 16th and 25th brigades were tired, and many men were sick. The seven thousand Americans were not in tip-top shape either: some had marched across the Kapa Kapa Trail and some were just victims to the Buna Plain itself. The 32nd Division's men had been almost constantly in transit for a year; designated first for the European Theater of Operations (ETO), then moved about, and finally ending up here in the armpit of the earth. The division, by normal standards, was badly manned, badly officered, and badly trained. About jungle fighting they knew nothing at all. Maj. Gen. Robert C. Richardson, Jr., the commander of American troops in the Pacific, theoretically had supervised their training from his base at Hawaii. Actually, he had done nothing at all. When General Eichelberger had arrived in Brisbane, he was, to put it mildly, shocked at the state of the men's preparedness for combat.

Nor was their equipment what it ought to have been. The home-dyed uniforms were a mess. The dye clogged up the pores of the cloth and turned the uniforms into plastic sacks, which caused jungle ulcers. The radio equipment broke down in the humidity of the jungle. It was never planned for use in this sort of climate. The men had rifles, but no carbines, in a terrain where the carbine was an ideal weapon. The Americans had virtually no machetes, although the only way to get through the jungle was to chop your way. They had no waterproof pouches. Thus their cigarettes, candy, rations, and ammunition were often amalgamated into one sodden mass.

Cooking equipment was either too heavy or not available, and the cooks found themselves boiling coffee in gallon fruit cans. There was not enough fuel to build fires hot enough to boil the kitchen equipment, so that nearly all the troops had dysentery. Add leeches, malaria, jungle rot, and the Japanese, and the Americans had plenty of trouble.

What the Americans did not have was artillery. The generals quarreled among themselves over that explosive question. General Kenney, the air force commander, said, "In this theater, the artillery flies," but the infantry generals did not believe the concept. What was to be done about a barrage on the day that the air force could not fly?

The problem was that MacArthur did not have the shipping to bring the artillery to the Buna coast. Even most of the 81-mm mortars had been left behind in Australia—"to be shipped later."

Nor were the Allies prepared for the terrain with the sort of special troops they needed. The Japanese had come in and looked and then sent a force that was fifty percent engineers. That was the intelligent way. The Allies had not looked but had come with virtually no engineers. And the engineers who arrived had almost none of the tools of their trade: not one block and tackle, for example, and no axes, no picks, no shovels.

With all this wealth of problems, one would expect the Allied troops to be downhearted. But no, they were totally overconfident. The Japanese, they said, would now be pushovers.

The reason for this attitude was simple enough. The Americans did not see any Japanese. Ergo, there were no Japanese in the area. For a month the Allied Air Force had been reporting a dearth of Japanese at the beachhead. There was no indication that they were fortifying the area. "I think it is quite possible that the Japanese may have pulled out some of their Buna forces," said General Harding, the commander of the 32nd Division. On October 20, he suggested that it would all be over by November 1.

Down on the line, the overconfidence was far, far worse. Ultimately, the men who were going to do the fighting were told by their company officers that there were not more than two squads of Japanese troops in Buna village and that the other enemy positions were similarly weak.

In fact, the Japanese were preparing for a very tough battle. General Horii had been told by General Hyakutake to hold on the Buna coast until the 8th Fleet and the 17th Army could clean out the American invaders at Guadalcanal. There was no doubt in the minds of the men at Imperial General Headquarters (IGH) that this would be done. The ways of victory had been learned. The ways of defeat had not.

General Horii's troops had established a whole series of strong defensive positions along an eleven-mile front from Gona to Cape Endaiadere. The defense plot covered an area of about sixteen square miles. The three major positions were at Gona, on the Sanananda Track, and in the Buna area. Each was an independent position.

The major Japanese base was located at Giruwa. The reason the Allies did not see any Japanese in the open was that by the time the Allies became seriously interested in the area, the defenses were all built.

The defenses consisted of blockhouses, bunkers, trenches, and many many outposts—as the Allies would learn very shortly. The Japanese were masters at concealment. Every treetop was a Japanese position. In those treetops would be one or more Japanese, a sharpshooter, perhaps, or a pair of soldiers with a .25-caliber light machine gun. They would have some method of communicating with the "trees" around them and the positions on the ground. It might be a flashing mirror. It might be the waving of palm fronds. It might even be radio. But the communication was complete. And what looked like innocent jungle and sandy track was a fortified area. One heavily fortified position led to another. Everywhere fields of fire had been laid out, with distances carefully calibrated for the mortars and knee mortars (rifle grenade launchers). For example, one major Japanese position was located three miles south of Sanananda Point where the track to Cape Killerton joined the main trail from Soputa. The area was wooded but dry. The soil at the junction was sandy. And here were the bunkers. Two miles south, several forward outposts commanded views of everything around them. One-half mile to the rear of the junction another trail branched off from the track to Cape Killerton. Here, the Japanese had another heavily fortified position. Beyond that was a third fort. These positions were all on dry ground—the only dry ground in the area. The attackers would have to move through sago swamp as deep as four feet, and they would have to fight in this muck, muck that got into their eyes and noses and mouths—and worse, into the breechlocks of their machine guns, into their rifle muzzles, into their ammunition clips.

There were not many Japanese trenches. The water table was only three-feet deep. So, the Japanese had built hundreds of coconut-log bunkers, most of them mutually supporting.

In this area, the Japanese had nearly six thousand men, just about twice as many as General MacArthur's intelligence indicated. It was true that the Japanese were even sicker than the Allied troops because they had been exposed to the New Guinea ambience longer. But this was not true of all the Japanese troops. Every week more arrived in small groups; and these new men were well fed and well clothed and shod, for General Hyakutake had more than a year's supply for his army stowed away at Rabaul, stockpiled in the halcyon days when the capture of New Guinea seemed just a stone's throw away. The worst shortages of the Japanese on New Guinea now were in small arms, food, and medicines. Not all of the Japanese troops had weapons, so many had been lost on the Kododa Trail retreat. Colonel Yokoyama, commander of the 15th Independent Engineers, was in charge of the army forces in the continued absence of General Horii, who was lost out there somewhere in the jungle. Captain Yasuda, the senior naval officer present, was in command of the naval troops.

Colonel Yokoyama told the men who did not have weapons to tie bayonets to poles. If they had no bayonets, they were to sharpen stakes and use them as spears. They were to carry these weapons at all times; the hospital patients had them beside their cots.

Even before the battle, the Japanese situation was nearly desperate, at least by American standards. One Japanese soldier wrote in his diary as the battle was joined:

The patients in the hospital have become living statues. There is nothing to eat. Without food they have become horribly emaciated. Their appearance does not bear thinking upon.

And yet the Japanese morale was very high! First of all, they had plenty of ammunition and these very strong fortified positions. Second, they expected assistance from Rabaul at any moment. To them as well as to their officers, it was inconceivable that Imperial Japan could ever suffer a major setback. They had been well trained in the Imperial Way.

And so, the Americans and the Australians began their battle on November 16 against an enemy that was as confident as they were. On the eve of the battle, the Japanese had word that help was, indeed, coming. A new command, the 8th Area Army, had been established under Lt. Gen. Hitoshi Imamura by IGH. It would have under its command the 17th Army, under General Hyakutake, and the 18th Army, under Lt. Gen. Hatazo Adachi. The 17th Army would retrieve the situation at Guadalcanal. The 18th Army would win the battle of New Guinea.

The Japanese soldier in the line did not quite understand what all this was about. What it really meant was that IGH was moving the 18th Army down from the Dutch East Indies to the Rabaul area. No other change, except administrative. But it sounded very, very good at Buna.

On November 16, the Allied attack on the Buna coast began. The Americans were on the right and the Australians were on the left. Everyone advanced very quickly, everyone was sure of an early victory.

The Australian 25th Infantry Brigade coming down the track from Wairopi was the first to bog down. The enemy was not the Japanese but malaria and heat prostration. On November 17, men began dropping like flies. On the afternoon of November 18, one company moved forward from

Jumbora toward Gona to see if there really were any Japanese at all left in Gona.

They soon found out. There were, in fact, about a thousand Japanese there, in their fortified positions. The defense was centered on the Gona Mission at the head of the trail. Every approach was covered by weapons. The Australian company that had gone on ahead ran into these defenses. The first position they hit was about a thousand yards south of the mission buildings. The Japanese had cleared fields of fire, and they pinned the Australians down. Next morning, when the Australian battalion came up, it found sixty men pinned down under heavy Japanese fire. The 2nd Battalion of the 31st Regiment attacked but could not dislodge the enemy. By dark, the Australians had lost thirty-six men and had gotten nowhere. Yes, there were enemy troops at Gona.

If one had to characterize this whole Buna coast campaign from the viewpoint of both sides, it could be called the hunger war, for now not only were the Japanese suffering from lack of food, but so were the Australians. The men of the 33rd had outrun their supply; they were not only under counterattack by the Japanese, but under attack by hunger. For three days, the soldiers suffered without food. On November 21, supply planes got through and dropped food successfully.

The Australians were really very confident. Brigadier General Eather of the 33rd was reinforced at about this point and had around a thousand men. He did not realize that the Japanese defenders were almost equally matched in numbers. How could he? The Japanese were virtually invisible in their log blockhouses and connecting defense systems.

Early on the morning of November 22, the Australians attacked. Three battalions moved out. Moving through the swamp, the troops came as close as possible to the Japanese positions. The 2nd Battalion of the 31st Regiment then staged a bayonet charge. They just reached the Japanese frontline positions when they were hit by such waves of enfilading fire from right and left that the attack collapsed. They pulled back into the swamp and counted noses. They had lost sixty-five men killed and wounded.

The next day, the Australians tried again. This time they reversed positions, and the 2nd Battalion of the 25th Infantry

Brigade attacked from the east. But it was exactly the same. The Japanese waited, let the Australians come up almost to their position, and then from the sides came devastating fire. The Australians pulled back again. Once more they had lost more than sixty men.

In three days of fighting, the brigade had lost more than two hundred men killed and wounded, and for this they had nothing to show.

On November 24, the Australians called for an air strike in Gona, and it was carried out. They next day, they attacked again. Their attack was the best planned yet. They had twenty-five-pound artillery pieces in support and these fired 250 rounds before the infantry took off. This time the Australians got inside the Japanese main position, but once more the fire was so intense from the prepared positions that the attack had to be called off.

Piece of cake?

Hardly.

The Japanese were showing their true mettle and the excellent planning of their officers.

The Australian 25th Brigade was by this time used up. It had been involved in the long battle along the Kokoda Track. Its three battalions were now down to less than 750 men *in toto*. Most of these men were sick with malaria or dysentery. So, the wand was passed to the 21st Brigade, held in reserve, to do the job. Its strength at this point was eleven hundred men. It had been stationed in Port Moresby and had been out of the action.

But the 21st Brigade's attacks on Gona seemed no more successful than had the others. After two weeks of attack, the Japanese still held it, and the Australians did not really even know what sort of defenses they faced.

The story was very similar for the 16th Australian Infantry Brigade that was advancing on Popondetta, and then Soputa. The going was slow. The problem was the same, torrential rains, disease, and hunger compounded by a very tough Japanese enemy's presence. The first real resistance was encountered just outside Soputa on the evening of November 19. But the next morning when the Australians were ready to attack, the Japanese were gone from this place. On November 20, the brigade hit the enemy's southern outpost. Here Colonel Tsukamoto had left a rearguard, whose task was to delay the enemy until the main position at the junction of the Cape Killerton–Soputa Track could be made perfectly ready to receive them.

The going was very difficult. Three Australian companies began a wide frontal attack—center and two flankers. By noon, they were bogged down. Many men were killed. Capt. B. W. T. Catterns put together a force of ten officers and eighty-one men out of two companies. This unit made the best progress. Observing that the Japanese were very powerful in the kunai flat, he made a wide detour and infiltrated two miles behind the Japanese position. In the evening, the Australians crept forward, caught the Japanese at their evening meal, killed eighty of them, and established a perimeter just off the track. Next day, November 21, the Japanese attacked from three sides. The Australians fought them off all day long. On their right, the brigade then moved forward about a mile and a half and captured a rice dump just east of the track. The Japanese counterattacked, and the day's movement for the Australians was brought to a halt. But on the left, Captain Catterns attack had caused the Japanese to withdraw from their positions.

It was the first real victory for the Allies on the Buna coast. But was it expensive? Captain Catterns had lost sixty-seven of his ninety men. And the 121st Brigade was down from a force of nineteen hundred to just about one thousand officers and men. They had made a big dent in the Japanese line, but they were out of the fighting. The next attempt would be made by the American 126th Infantry Regiment.

The 126th had been scheduled to march on Buna, but when MacArthur learned of the difficulties in the Gona area, he diverted this regiment to the command of General Vasey on the Gona front. General Harding, who thought he was about to capture Buna, could not understand why half his troops were taken away from him, so he protested. It did him no good. The 126th continued to march.

On the evening of November 21, the Americans reached Soputa. The next day, they were to attack. The Australians of the 16th Brigade, who were worn out, could now watch. Some of the Americans had been doing a good deal of talking. The Aussies, they said, could now take a backseat and watch how real soldiers did it.

So the Australians watched.

The Americans proceeded to make a great bollix of the situation, largely because of the jealousies of the generals.

General Harding was still smarting from MacArthur's order that the 126th Infantry be taken from his force and given to the Australians. On the eve of the 126th attack, the 2nd Battalion was in reserve, and he demanded it to reinforce a position on his left flank. Early on November 22, the tired 2nd Battalion, which had just settled into a biovouac after a tough march across the Owen Stanley Range, was called on to move up to the river crossing half a mile away and help General Harding. But when they got to the river crossing, they found the river flooded. It took them until later in the day to put a cable across the swollen river and to move across in rafts. They then moved into action on the eastern side of the Girua River. West of the river was Colonel Tomlinson with the only troops on that side: Headquarters Company, the 126th Infantry Headquarters itself, the 3rd Battalion, and some special troops—about fourteen hundred men in all. His reserve had been taken away.

Colonel Tomlinson, the commander of the 126th, knew that the Japanese position was an inverted **V**. In order to take it, he would envelop it with a larger **V**. Thus, he said, he would squeeze the Japanese out.

Just before 7:00 A.M. on November 22, the Americans moved in to attack. They had two days' rations, all the ammunition they could carry, and hand grenades. The antitank company was still at Wairopi, so they had no artillery support except mortars, each with twenty rounds of ammunition.

They passed through the Australian lines and moved ahead. Major Bond's 3rd Battalion was the key force.

At 11:00 A.M., one company moved out into the no-man's-land on the Australian left and another company swung out wide around the first company's flank. They ran into Japanese patrols but dispersed them without much trouble. The terrain was rough—heavy brush and swamp. The Japanese tried to counterattack several times in ambushes. The Americans fought them off, but the going was slow. At the end of the day, they were only 350 yards ahead of the old Australian positions. The second company, moving up to the left of an old banana plantation, was stopped by Japanese fire after moving 200 yards. That night, the Japanese counterattacked, but they were fought off successfully.

The next day, November 23, was spent reorganizing and straightening out the front of the three companies so that a new attack could be launched. Meanwhile, the Allies were getting the advantage of some delayed supply shipment, which included rations and more 81-mm mortars. But the Japanese had some planes, too. They counterattacked on the night of November 24 and threw the American line into confusion. Once again, on November 26, the line had to be straightened out. November 26, was the day for the general assault.

At that point, the situation was not very encouraging. On the right, Company L of the 3rd Battalion had made no progress. It was just where it had been three days earlier: on the outskirts of the rice dump two hundred yards from its point of departure.

When the senior American and British commanders of the line companies were killed by Japanese mortar fire, Maj. Bert Zeeff, executive officer of the 3rd Battalion, took over command of the Americans. Together with the Australians, they established a defense perimeter in the Company L area. And on November 26, the three companies attacked. The fighting was very stiff, and although some progress was made, it was not nearly enough to claim any sort of victory. That night the Americans and Australians dug in for the night in foxholes. In an hour, the foxholes were full of water.

On November 27, the Sanananda Road area seemed to be in stalemate. Colonel Tomlinson, who had such hopes for an easy victory now commuted a hundred casualties. The cannon and antitank companies finally came down from Wairopi, arriving hungry and exhausted.

On November 27, Colonel Tsukamoto's Japanese attacked all day long on the flank of the track junction.

By this time, casualties among the Americans and Australians had been such that the units were thoroughly mixed up. Major Zeeff had about seventy men from two other companies under his command now. Company L still existed, but it was not according to the table of organization.

On November 29, Colonel Tomlinson tried to restore some order. He sent up Major Baetcke, his executive officer, to take command of the troops, which meant Companies I and K, elements of Company M, 3rd Battalion Headquarters, and the newly arrived cannon and antitank companies. Major Bond still had command of Company L and its allied units and the new force moved up to his group's rear. Early on the morning of November 30, the American 126th Infantry attacked the Japanese on the right, on the left, and in the center. The only real success came on the left.

Major Bond's force started off at 9:00 A.M. after a mortar and artillery barrage. But as they moved through a large patch of kunai grass about four hundred yards out, they were met by heavy Japanese fire. Major Bond was wounded and had to be taken out. Major Baetcke came up and rallied the troops. They drove the Japanese out of the kunai grass area. Captain Shirley took over for Major Bond.

The skill of the Japanese planners now came into play. The Americans had eliminated the resistance on the kunai flat, but a thousand yards farther on they ran into jungle and swamp. The Japanese had fire lanes commanding the swamp, which was knee-deep. They stopped Captain Shirley's advance with knee mortar and machine-gun fire. Finally, Shirley's troops got out of the swamp and dispersed the enemy beyond. A little farther on they came to a Japanese bivouac area. They stormed it, set up a perimeter, and settled down. That night the Japanese counterattacked and the soldiers spent the whole night fighting. But in the morning, they found that they had won a really fine victory. They had captured this bivouac area, an open oval-shaped space—about 250-yards long and 150 yards wide—lying across the track. Here, they could establish a roadblock.

Major Zeeff was not far away. He wanted to link up with the Shirley force to strengthen that roadblock. But the Japanese had other ideas. On the afternoon of November 30, Zeeff's force moved across the track and caught about thirty-five Japanese, whom they killed. Zeeff reported to Colonel Tomlinson that he had crossed the track. But the Japanese kept harrying them. Colonel Tomlinson ordered Zeeff to move back to the east side of the triad and push north to make the junction with Captain Shirley's men. Zeeff tried. The enemy kept up a steady fire as they withdrew. There were certain acts of heroism that day and the next.

One hero was Pvt. Hymie Y. Epstein, a medic. On November 22, to help wounded infantrymen he had crawled into an area swept by enemy machine-gun fire. On December 1, he did the same.

Major Zeeff recalled his heroism:

I was prone with a field musette bag in front of my face. Epstein was in a similar position about four feet on my left. Private Sullivan was shot through the neck and was lying about ten feet in front of me to my right. Epstein said, "I have to take care of him." I said, "I'm not ordering you to go, the fire is too heavy!"

Epstein then crawled on his stomach, treated and bandaged Sullivan, then crawled back. A few minutes later, Sergeant Burnett was shot in the head, lying a few feet from Sullivan. Epstein did the same for Burnett, and managed to crawl back without being hit.

The next morning, Pvt. Mike Russin was hit by a sniper. Epstein went over to him. But he was shot and killed. His luck had run out. They buried him there.

Major Zeeff had high hopes of linking up with Captain Shirley the next day, but he was to be disappointed. The troops were digging in that night a few yards east of the track and about five hundred yards south of the roadblock manned by Shirley's men. Sergeant McGee went out to look over the prospects. He came back to report to Major Zeeff that the Japanese had very strong positions about two hundred yards ahead of them. Just then it was growing dark, and as if to emphasize McGee's words, the Japanese surged up in a new attack. Zeeff's men fought them off, but five men were killed and six more wounded.

That night Colonel Tomlinson decided that Zeeff's position was impossible. He ordered Zeeff to move out. Zeeff would be subject to a mortar barrage the next day, he said. The situation was very serious and had to be rectified. Those Japanese had to be wiped out. Zeeff should bring back his wounded, said the colonel, but forget about the dead. There was no time for that. Zeeff was to get going.

First, Zeeff's men had to make stretchers for the six newly wounded. The stretchers were constructed in the darkness, and at 1:30 the job was done and the troops were moving. Eight soldiers were assigned to each stretcher. Four would carry it for fifty yards, then the other four would take over. Two stretchers broke down on the march. But somehow the stretcher bearers got the wounded to safety, walking south for nine hundred yards and then into the little stream that led to the banana plantation. Shortly after daybreak, the group reached the stream and safety. They had been in combat for eleven days. They had moved into and through the main Japanese defense position, with two thousand enemy soldiers around them. And they had come out again, bringing their wounded with them. It was one way to be blooded by fire. But if the whole operation had proved anything, it was that the Allies did not have enough troops on the Soputa–Sanananda Track to force the issue. The 16th Brigade was down to 909 effective riflemen, and most of them were sick with malaria. The effective strength of the Americans was 1,100 instead of 1,400 men. And of the 1,100 perhaps half were now sick with malaria or dengue or dysentery. So the word *effective* did not meet the textbook definition. The Americans still had 1,100 men on their feet, was what it meant.

As of December 12, the fact was that Colonel Tsukamoto's Japanese defenders outnumbered the Allied attackers.

CHAPTER ELEVEN

Buna

On the other side of the Girua River from Gona, the American 128th Infantry began its attack on Buna on November 16, as the Australian troops on the west attacked Gona.

This force had some artillery, not much, but some. General Waldron, the 32nd Division artillery officer, had found a Japanese barge at Milne Bay and had commandeered it for his artillery. He now had two 3.7-inch Australian mountain howitzers and two hundred rounds of ammunition to use against difficult enemy positions.

As with all the others involved in this bloody battle for New Guinea, the men of the 32nd Division soon discovered that nature was as much their enemy as the Japanese. The problem again was supply. Until an airfield could be established, the troops would be dependent on airdrops plus the efforts of six small trawlers that were carrying supplies back and forth. The six trawlers had already been spotted by the Japanese air force. On the day that the attack on Buna began, the Japanese descended on the trawlers.

Three of the trawlers, the *Alacrity,* the *Minnemura,* and the *Bonwin,* as well as the Japanese landing barge with its howitzers were on their way forward with supplies. One was full of soldiers, one was full of ammunition, and one had a mixed cargo that included a lot of 81-mm mortars. They were protected only by machine guns. Because the American navy would not come into these waters on the eastern side of New Guinea, there was no naval presence at all. Late in the afternoon as they steamed along, the trawlers were absolutely alone. They had no air cover because the Allied aircraft in the area had left long before sunset to be sure to make it back to base in the light.

The craft were rounding Cape Sudest when suddenly eighteen Japanese Zero fighters from Rabaul's 11th Air Fleet appeared without warning coming down from the northwest. The planes came in with guns blazing and did a very good job of strafing. The Allied troops fought back with their machine guns but did not have any effect on the attackers. Soon, the barge and all three trawlers were on fire. The ammunition began to explode. Everybody aboard the *Bonwin* had to take to the water. General Waldron swam ashore.

Soon, all three trawlers and the barge were a total loss. The personnel casualties were heavy, but worst was the loss of guns, ammunition, and radio equipment. The next morning, the Japanese air force was back again. This time they hit two of the remaining three trawlers. These, too, were destroyed. Thus, in less than twenty-four hours, the Allied "navy" at Buna was wiped out. One small trawler, the *Kelton,* was all that remained to supply the troops east of the Girua River.

The Japanese had caused a real catastrophe for the Allies. There were no replacements in sight for the trawlers. Nearly all the artillery pieces and many of the machine guns, mortars, and other essential supplies for the attack had just been lost. The entire system of supply for the Buna operation had been thrown out of kilter. Now, the Buna troops either had to be supplied by the air force or receive nothing. Fortunately, the air force indicated that it could handle the job. Unfortunately, for the troops in the line, the air force was unable to live up to its own expectations in the days ahead.

H hour for the Allied Buna attack was 7 o'clock on the morning of November 19, 1942. As it turned out, the Americans were committing a small force (less than a reinforced regiment) to do the job of a division. And then came the stunning news that General MacArthur had ordered the switch of the 126th Infantry (less one battalion) to the other side of the river. Now, General Harding had a battalion in reserve, and he had to commit that to the battle.

If there was ever a day in which an attack was going to be difficult, it was November 19. The day opened with a torrential rain that was followed by an entire succession of thunder showers. The troops were soaked to the skin and the aircraft were grounded. No air support would come this day. General Kenney might have been a little optimistic when he had announced that day from Brisbane that in the Southwest Pacific Theater of Operations the artillery "flies." What he should have said was that the artillery flew, weather permitting. At 7:00 A.M., the artillery—those two remaining mountain guns that had not been aboard the ships—fired a few rounds and the attack kicked off.

The 1st Battalion of the 128th Infantry moved toward Buna, so did the 3rd Battalion. Because of the efficacy of that Japanese air attack, the men had only one day's rations and just about one day's supply of ammunition.

Colonel McCoy's 1st Battalion moved toward Cape Endaiadere, two miles away. Here, Colonel Yamamoto had built his main line of resistance, which ran from a point about 750 yards south of the cape inland to the Duropa Plantation, past the plantation to the eastern end of the new airstrip, and past the airstrip to the bridge that was located between the two Japanese airstrips. It was marked by many cleared and overlapping fields of fire. The positions were concealed and manned by troops who had been well instructed in the techniques of defense in depth.

The 1st Battalion had gotten about half way to the plantation when it was met by heavy machine-gun fire from positions west of the track. The troops scattered and deployed, but their attack was much hampered by the heavy jungle growth. Mortars were not very much help in this jungle. Grenades did not help much either because the troops could not see the enemy and did not know where the fire was coming from—Japanese rifles and machine guns gave off no flashes. And now the Americans, who were totally untried in battle, began to learn about total defense.

Maj. David Parker, an engineering officer who was observing this maneuver, saw what was happening, he said:

Snipers were everywhere. They were so well camouflaged that it was nearly impossible to discern them. The enemy habitually allowed our troops to advance to very close range—sometimes four or five feet from a machine-gun post—before opening fire. Often, they allowed troops to bypass them completely, opening fire then on the rear echelons, and on our front elements from the rear.

Yes, this was a lesson, indeed.

The 1st Battalion moved forward very slowly. The Japanese resisted every foot of the way. At the end of this first day, the Americans had learned a great deal, but there were not so many of them any more. The handful of dead Japanese bodies they saw turned out to be well fed and with plenty of ammunition. The story was not at all what the intelligence officers had been feeding them these last few days.

The 3rd Battalion had a similar experience. Colonel Miller led them to the trail junction between the old and new airstrips. There the Simemi Trail broke down into a narrow causeway with swamps on both sides. The Americans tried to cross an open area three hundred yards from the junction. The Japanese opened fire. The fire was so intense that the Americans were stopped. It came from the western end of the new airstrip, from the bridge between the strips, and from other scattered machine guns.

The Americans learned something else. They had been fording swamps up to their waists and chests all day. The Australian grenades (Mills bombs) they were using got wet. After that, most of them failed to explode. One squad approached a Japanese position with grenades. They could see a dozen Japanese in the fortification, and they lobbed in seven grenades. Not one exploded. The Japanese were aroused and began firing off three mortars (rifle grenade launchers); these were very effective against the massed American troops. Their casualties were quite high: the Americans lost about thirty percent of their number.

At the end of the first day, Colonel Miller's troops were pinned down on the edge of the clearing south of the junction, and they were virtually out of ammunition. For some reason that Colonel Miller did not understand, Colonel Yamamoto did not counterattack that night or the next day. The reason was simple enough. Yamamoto was ordered to hold out for a long time. He did not want to waste strength or resources in counterattack. He was waiting for Rabaul to come to his rescue.

But even without counterattack, the Americans were stymied.

On November 20, Colonel McCoy's 1st Battalion was resupplied by air with ammunition and food and continued its assault. It attacked towards the cape. The men moved forward several hundred yards and captured several machine guns. But again, it was foot-by-foot fighting, and the casualties were heavy. Then, 1st Lt. John W. Crow led Company B in a very effective series of attacks against machine-gun nests. But while charging one of these, submachine gun in hand, Lieutenant Crow disappeared and was never seen again. Later, he was posthumously awarded the Distinguished Service Cross.

In the evening, there was another ration distribution to both the 1st and 3rd battalions. Also, reserves came up, Colonel Carrier's 2nd Battalion and Major Harcourt's Independent Company. They were already exhausted, having marched twenty-five miles from Pongani with full fieldpacks. The men were told that they would join Colonel McCoy's battalion in an assault on Cape Endaiadere the next morning.

The Americans had now pulled their resources together. The three battalions of the 128th Infantry and their supporting troops would attack the cape. The troops of the 126th Infantry would move on their left. The attack would start with a heavy air bombardment.

But when? That was the question. And the ground troops were not given the answer. Early in the morning, the A-20 attack bombers and the B-25 medium bombers came over and dropped their loads. They did knock out a few enemy machine guns. But they also bombed one of Colonel Miller's forward positions and caused six casualties.

General Harding called for an air attack at 12:45 P.M. The time came, but no air force. Another air attack was laid on for 4:00 P.M. It lasted six minutes and accomplished nothing. One flight bombed the sea; hard on the fish but not on the Japanese. One bomber unloaded its bombs in the midst of Companies B and C, killing six men, wounding twelve, and scaring seventy others half to death. Some of the men fled, and it took the officers a while to get them back into the line. General Kenney's flying artillery seemed to leave something

to be desired. It was 4:30 P.M. before the attack got started—
and then the Americans saw that although their lines had been
hit by the air attacks, they had done nothing to the enemy.

As the day came to an end, the officers realized that the
attack had been almost a total failure. The Australian Independent Company, operating at the eastern end of the airstrip, had made a little progress. The American battalions
had made virtually none. And casualties were very heavy.
Company C had lost sixty-three men in three days, including
four officers.

Colonel Miller's battalion had done no better. It had started
out with a bang and seemed to be getting up to the bridge,
but then the Japanese really opened up on them. The Americans found that they had been allowed to infiltrate behind
strong positions that now turned on them and produced a
withering fire. The battalion was pinned down. It lost forty-
two men and could not advance another yard. Just before
6:00 P.M., Colonel Miller called the troops back to a safer,
but retrograde, position.

That night it was clear that the 3rd Battalion was not going
to be able to take the bridge. So, a rear guard was left to
hold the position they had achieved, and the majority of the
battalion was moved around to operate on the right flank
against the cape.

There was one bright spot in the day. The air force began
operating at the Dobodura airstrip. And somewhere somebody had found five new trawlers to bring up supplies. One
of them was wrecked on a reef, but the other four joined the
Kelton, the last-remaining vessel of the first series. It looked
as though the Americans had a little navy at last.

General Harding saw that tanks would help in the assault
on the enemy bunkers. He asked for three to be sent up. They
were loaded aboard captured Japanese barges. That was a
mistake, but how were the Americans to know. They had no
specs on the barges and did not know how much weight they
would carry. The answer was not that much. The barges
promptly sank. No tanks.

The general was not very confident of his officers, so he
sent up Lt. Col. Alexander MacNab, executive officer of the
128th Infantry, to take over the attack. MacNab brought up

mortars and a handful of field guns; he connected them by field telephone and found an observation post in a tall coconut tree. Thus, the Americans for the first time had a bit of real artillery. On the morning of November 22, they began firing on the enemy positions. With that support, the infantry made a little progress that day.

On November 24 and November 25, nobody moved much. Colonel Miller's battalion replaced Colonel McCoy's in the line. Back in the rear, the staff was preparing for a new big attack on November 26, Thanksgiving Day.

By this time, the Americans and Australians had managed to scrounge up eight artillery pieces, a dozen 81-mm mortars, and the services of the thirty-five aircraft assigned to the area. This would enable them to stage a fairly powerful attack on the Japanese positions.

But what would happen was anybody's guess. Anyone could get hurt around this area. General McNider came up from his headquarters at Hariko to observe the attack and left on a stretcher. He was wounded by an enemy knee-mortar round that came in among the troops he was looking over. That sort of thing happened all day long, every day. The Japanese defenses were very tight indeed.

The next day's attack, it was decided, would begin with the best barrage yet devised. General Harding had high hopes for it and decided to come up himself to observe. He caught a ride on one of the trawlers, which was carrying up ammunition that evening. But seven miles out, the craft ran up on a sandbar and was stuck. So, General Harding finished his journey in a rowboat, getting into Colonel Hale's command post just before 5 o'clock in the morning. Ultimately, he made his way to Colonel Miller's command post.

This day the air force performed very well. The fliers delivered a screaming raid by Beaufighters, P-40s, by A-20s, and B-25s—and for once, the bombs were in the right place. The artillery fired its rounds, the mortars popped off, and the heavy machine guns banged away. Colonel Miller's battalion moved on the right. Colonel Carrier's troops moved on the left.

But once again, the Allies had failed to reckon with the completeness of the Japanese defenses. During the air raid, the Japanese troops retired within their bunkers. When it ended, they came out to their firing positions and when the Americans came along, the Japanese let them come, let them get past the forward firing positions, and then opened up. Colonel Miller's battalion suffered fifty casualties by noon. Company K was hit worst, and pinned down. Company L was caught by Japanese fighters from the 11th Air Fleet at Rabaul, which also destroyed that trawler hung up on the sandbar.

Colonel Carrier's battalion ran into a fiasco of its own. It got turned around and ended up in the rear of Colonel Miller's battalion after a long march through waist-deep swamp. Ultimately, the battalion got straightened out and lined up alongside Miller's battalion, but little progress was made that day.

Nor was it just the 126th or the Americans. Both the 128th and the Australians, on either side of the 128th positions, failed to make any gains that day. The Japanese were very, very tough, and they had been preparing these positions for months.

The Americans fought hard; some of them fought well. Pvt. Howard Eastwood of Company C was out scouting and discovered a ten-man Japanese patrol and attacked it single-handedly. He stood up in the tall kunai grass and opened up with his Thompson submachine gun. He killed several of the enemy, causing the others to flee. But a few minutes later, Eastwood was killed by an enemy sniper in a palm tree.

One thing was certain: the air forces had better start getting more accurate. On November 27, Allied aircraft that were supposed to be bombing the Japanese dropped a string of demolition bombs on an American company. Three men were wounded and the company pulled back into the jungle, sacrificing position in order to get out of the line of attack of the Allied planes.

That sort of bombing accuracy was not particularly conducive either to good relations with the air force or to good morale of the ground troops.

The going was just about the same on the other side, where Colonel Smith's 2nd Battalion of the 128th Infantry was advancing toward Buna. The unit was moving toward the Buna Mission. The men were coming up against the Yokosuka 5th and the Sasebo 5th Naval Landing units. That defense position was under the command of Captain Yasuda, and he had more than twice as many men to defend as Colonel Smith had to attack. Of course, the Japanese had made the best possible use of terrain, forcing the Americans to come up through swamp and jungle. The strong Japanese bunker positions lay astride the trails that led into Buna Village and Buna Mission, and both those areas were full of their fortified positions.

Up came the 2nd Battalion of the 128th Infantry, innocent of any knowledge about the enemy or the terrain. Sgt. Irving W. Hall of Company F caught the first glimpse of the Japanese. He saw an enemy machine gun about fifty yards off. He turned around slowly, as if he had not seen it, and motioned to his men to get off the track. Then he turned back and fired a burst from his submachine gun at the position. A firefight began. One American was wounded, but the Sergeant had saved his men from slaughter.

The Japanese machine guns seemed to be everywhere. Colonel Smith saw that he could get nowhere with a frontal assault and began flanking operations. He needed some reinforcements, he said.

And that is how General Harding asked for his 2nd Battalion of the 126th Infantry to come back and support his operations. Lt. Gen. E. F. Herring agreed and the battalion was again diverted from what it thought was its objective. The whole group then became known as the Urbana Force.

What a mess they were in! The terrain was composed of equal parts of mud and water, tidal swamp, and jungle, with Japanese machine guns everywhere.

The Urbana Force was attacking an area called the Triangle. The attack did not go very well. It was not helped much by the air force attempts to bomb and strafe. The P-40s missed the target entirely on one run, and they were just as likely to be strafing the Allied positions as the Japanese. And here the Americans learned another lesson about jungle warfare.

On November 25, the Urbana Force was trying to flank the Triangle. Company G started northwest through the sago swamp. About two hundred yards out, they came upon a group of Japanese working on an antiaircraft position. There were more Japanese than Americans, so that the firefight did not go very well. The company suffered several casualties and moved back into the swamp. Darkness found the troops pinned down on the edge of the airstrip.

The main body of Company G was held up outside the right-hand fork of the Triangle. The Japanese from the Government Garden position moved forward to fire on the kunai flat where the Americans were strung out. The Japanese attacked just as darkness was falling, killing one man, wounding five others, and causing great panic. After all, the Americans were not familiar with the terrain and the Japanese knew it by heart. Worse, the Americans had trouble with their weapons. They had not been careful in caring for them. Their officers had made no provision for weapons care, and they did not have any oil with them. Some weapons were wet. The mortars got wet and the propelling charges did not function properly. Machine guns jammed because the belts were wet and dirty, and the belts had shrunk. Thompson submachine guns and Browning automatic rifles (BARs) were full of dirt. The M1s only fired well for one clip, and then jammed because the other clips were wet and full of swamp muck. The men had been hip-deep and sometimes neck-deep in the swamp muck for more than twenty-four hours. The Americans pulled back from this position, leaving their machine guns and some of their mortars behind them.

The big attack on Buna Village was slated for the night of November 30. The Americans had learned a great deal in a short time. Colonel Mott, General Harding's chief of staff, had come forward to coordinate the attack and he had his command post in a palm tree that overlooked the front.

First, the Americans put up an artillery and mortar barrage before the troops jumped off.

Here is the recollection of Lt. Robert H. Odell:

As soon as it was dark, preparations began. When these were completed, we each grasped the shoulder of the man in front and slowly shuffled forward through the pitch black of the night. Our only guide was the telephone wire leading to the jump-off point, and the troops in the foxholes along the way who had been holding the ground recently captured. There was no trail and consequently several hours were required to travel as many hundreds of yards. We all had bayonets. Rifle fire was forbidden until after the attack was well under way. Japs encountered along the way were to be dealt with silently.

That turned out to be more of a joke than an order.

At 4:00 A.M., three companies of the 126th Infantry began their attack. It was dark. They did not know quite where they were. About one hundred yards from the starting point, they found out. They were right in front of a line of machine-gun posts.

Lieutenant Odell continued:

All hell broke loose. There was more lead flying through the air than it's possible to estimate. Machine-gun tracers lit up the entire area and our own rifle fire made a solid sheet of flame. Everywhere men cursed, shouted, or screamed. Order followed order. Brave men led and others followed. Cowards crouched in the grass . . . frightened out of their skins.

The attack gained momentum. The brave men forced their way through the machine-gun posts and gained their first objective, the eastern end of the airstrip. That element comprised Companies E and F. Company G, which was to have captured the track to Buna Village, overran a strong enemy blockhouse that let it go by. The company got lost and stuck in a swamp on the northern edge of the airstrip.

Company E was assigned to take the village. At 6:00 A.M., it started. Three hundred yards from the village the company ran into a strong enemy bunker line and was pinned down by cross fire.

Up came Captain Harold Hantlemann of Company H and some troops. They tried again to take the village, laying on a furious mortar barrage. But those Japanese bunkers were tough, and the barrage did not dislodge the troops. The attackers came again, and were repelled. They fought all day. At the end of the day they had made virtually no advance but had taken many casualties.

As for the 128th Infantry, Company F managed to secure its objective, but the rest of the companies of the 2nd Battalion did not do much. In mopping up, the troops found that they had captured a Japanese headquarters, with all sorts of papers and radio equipment. They saved the papers (for Allied Intelligence) and the radios and then burned the building to the ground.

General Harding was more or less stalled. He wanted armor and asked for tanks. There was no transport for the tanks, so they sent him Bren carriers (tracked vehicles that carried machine guns). Not quite the same thing. As for artillery, the Australians had a few guns, and the Americans had a single 105-mm howitzer. A flight of Australian Wirraway aircraft showed up. This was the heavy equipment.

Another attack was made on November 30. The Bren carriers had failed to arrive and the attack was made without them. The field guns and the bombers spoke out at 6:15 that morning, and there were three more bombing attacks during the day. But the job was the infantry's job. And on they went into the sputtering of Japanese machine-gun fire. They made very little progress. Company A of the 128th Infantry going along the coast advanced less than a hundred yards. Then it ran into a massive log barricade that the Japanese had erected across the track. Of course, there were plenty of Japanese guns behind that barricade and, as usual, all the enfilading positions that could be employed. The company was stopped cold. That night it was relieved by Company B.

No movement. That was the story all the way along the line. If the Americans and Australians wanted to take Buna and its many positions, they were going to have to do a lot more back in Australia than they had been doing to give the men in the front line something to work with.

So far, the U.S. 32nd Division had failed. Despite two weeks of attacks on the Japanese at Buna, there had not been one single penetration of the Japanese line. The regiment had sustained nearly five hundred casualties. The situation looked very grim, indeed.

CHAPTER TWELVE

The Buna Blues

The Australians had not taken Gona. The Americans had not taken Buna. At Brisbane, General MacArthur could not understand why, which shows how totally inadequate his intelligence operations had to be. No one on the Allied side had any real idea of the strength of the Japanese, the planning that had gone into their defense operations on the Buna coast, and the determination of the emperor's soldiers to hold the line to the death if necessary.

This was, after all, only November 1942 and the most serious fighting of the Pacific War was still ahead. To be sure, the Americans were winning the battle for Guadalcanal, but after Bloody Ridge, in which the marines held the line against repeated Japanese attacks and attempts to take Henderson field, the land war on Guadalcanal settled down to a war of attrition. The Japanese were the victims of hunger and disease more than of American military action on the ground. In the air and on the sea, the Guadalcanal battle raged unabated during November and December. The odds were changing as the might of American production released more than a dribble of supply for the South Pacific.

So, the New Guinea campaign continued, with no very clear understanding by General MacArthur and his staff of what they faced. The reaction at headquarters was to be a growing dissatisfaction with the leadership in the field, unmindful of the enormous difficulties the rear echelons presented to the line troops by their inability to supply them with any but the most simple infantry weapons.

Australians and Americans on both fronts were exhausted. They had begun this phase of the campaign exhausted, and the jungle, the heat, and the enemy had not helped a bit to ease the pain. The transfer of the 126th Infantry to the Australians had left General Harding with a feeling of resentment against higher headquarters and a physical problem: he had no reserves to help his tired troops. When he finally got back the 2nd Battalion of the 126th on November 23, that unit was half shot up. Still, there were no reserves because the 2nd Battalion had to be incorporated into what was now called the Urbana Force. This unit was created because heavy casualties had destroyed the effectiveness of two regiments.

The Americans, like the Japanese (except for the replacements that trickled in from Rabaul), were half-starved. They were living on about one-third of a C ration per day: one-third of their normal requirement. Their feet were in bad shape from jungle rot, athlete's foot, and every kind of fungus that could grow in hot, steamy shoes. They had virtually no protection from the torrential rains. It had been more or less standard operating procedure (SOP) to throw away one's shelter half, which the infantrymen were issued—almost as much of a nuisance, it seemed, as gas masks. Anyone who had no shelter half had nothing to protect him from the rain. The poncho was almost nonexistent. Most of the men had malaria. Later on, the medics would introduce the Atabrine tablet, that bitter, yellow substance that suppressed malaria as long as the soldier took his daily pill. But the tablets had not come yet; nor had quinine in sufficient quantity to help the men; nor had salt tablets to stabilize their systems, which were losing enormous quantities of fluid; nor had chlorination tablets to protect their water. The lack of fresh fruits and vegetables threatened the men with scurvy, and they did not have vitamin pills or lime juice to help them. Supplies and supply planning were woefully inadequate. The Americans frankly did not know what they were doing, and they were unwilling to take instruction from the Australians. Thus the mess continued at Brisbane and beyond. The victims were the men in the line.

Dysentery and malaria were the great weakeners and virtually everyone in the field had one or both. Even after a battle, when there was time for niceties, a medical officer tested the survivors and found that fifty-three percent of them had temperatures, ranging as high as 104 degrees Fahrenheit.

There was nothing to be done, given the failure of higher headquarters to provide reasonable rations or reasonable cooking facilities—even pots and pans. All the trawlers save one had now been destroyed. The provision problem was worse than ever. The only supply method at the end of November was by air. By the end of the month, less than sixty tons of freight had been brought in by air—the equivalent of the tonnage that two of those little trawlers could carry in one trip.

Weapons maintenance was virtually impossible because when gun oil did get up front, it came in fifty-gallon drums, and who was to use that? So the BARs and the M1s kept jamming at crucial moments, giving the enemy with his simple .25-caliber rifle a very big edge.

After two weeks of fighting, the Americans had begun to learn that the Japanese soldier was a very tough fellow. There was no longer any talk about walking into Buna. No one knew just what sort of enemy dispositions they faced because the Japanese had been so artful at concealment and camouflage.

What the soldiers needed were tanks, which could not be shipped across from Australia because of the failure of transport; flamethrowers, which were not available anywhere; and grenade launchers to match the Japanese knee mortars. They could also use some real artillery, some more mortars, and at least enough mortar shells to service the mortars they did have. All these items were in short supply. There was almost no way to approach a Japanese blockhouse. The one solution tried by many of the troops was almost suicidal. It was to crawl up to the blockhouse and lob in grenades. That was all right—as long as the men were not seen—except that the Japanese were very good at picking up the grenades and lobbing them back before they exploded. But the problem the Americans did not yet understand was that the Japanese system of defense was far more sophisticated even than it looked. It began with the central blockhouse. On all sides of that blockhouse were smaller positions, well dug in, that housed a machine gun or perhaps two. On the outside of these positions in a great circle were what the cavalry would call outriders—lookouts in the trees for the most part—who had either radio connection or a series of hand signals to tell their fellows when the Allied troops were approaching. Time after time, the snipers and scouts in the outer edges of the position would spot the enemy coming in, and they let them come. The Americans would move forward carefully, stopping and reconnoitering constantly. The Japanese would freeze. Once the Americans launched their attack, then from the rear and the sides and above the Japanese would open up on them in concert with the blasts of fire from the major position. The result had almost always been disastrous. And that was why the American casualties were so high. The Japanese light Nambu machine gun, especially, was ideal for work in the palm tree groves.

As far as air support was concerned, at the end of November it was a dreadful tangle. The medics were yelling for medicines and bandages. The engineers were yelling for shovels. The antiaircraft gunners were yelling for ammunition. And the men up front were yelling for food and bullets—and not getting them. Each element of the attack force conspired to get its own, and the result was almost total confusion and an enormous shortage of supply.

General Harding was the commander at the wrong end of the stick. He had asked for tanks, and he got a promise of Bren carriers, but no Bren carriers showed up. He had asked for artillery in November and was told that he might get half of what he requested—sometime in December. He had asked for reserves—the 127th Infantry was available at Port Moresby—and was told that he did not need them.

One problem, of course, was the diversity of command. General Harding was an American. General Herring, his immediate superior, was an Australian. On November 30, the two met. General Herring indicated his belief that if there were any spare troops around they should go to the Australians—on the other side of the river in the Gona area—who had been fighting longer and were more tired than the Americans. He was right, of course, but that did not make General Harding any happier. That was how it was going when they met at Dobodura. Then along came General Sutherland from MacArthur's headquarters to add to the confusion. Sutherland agreed with Herring that the 127th Infantry should not be brought up front. His reasoning would be alarming to any field commander. If they brought new fresh troops into the battle, they would have to supply them and supply was short. Therefore, until enough supply could be brought in to create a surplus, no fresh troops would be sent.

It was a very fine rear echelon view but quite impractical if anyone wanted to win the battle. Sutherland showed how little he knew about the situation up front when he indicated that the Americans were not fighting very hard. Obviously, they could not be or they would have won already, he believed. But the reason for that was that General Blamey, another Australian, had spoken disparagingly to MacArthur about the fighting qualities of the 32nd Division. And Blamey had done that because MacArthur had spoken disparagingly earlier to Prime Minister Curtin about the fighting qualities of the Australian brigades and the 7th Division.

Thus, all the little jealousies and misunderstandings ultimately had to be borne by the troops in the line who were "having a helluva time," according to the handful of newspaper correspondents who visited them.

The Blamey remarks to MacArthur were especially damaging because of MacArthur's dreadful ego and paranoia. It seemed to him as if the Australians were bent on giving him a personal insult. MacArthur began to develop anger against Harding because he had put MacArthur in the position of being criticized by others. MacArthur's ego was always a big problem. Now it was to cause heads to roll.

From the rear, came a stream of observers who went back to report to headquarters that the 32nd Division wasn't much. Of course, it wasn't much. Not much had been sent over to New Guinea from Australia. Even less had been sent over to Australia from the East Coast of the United States, where the 32nd thought it was in training to go to Europe—and its training had scarcely begun. All along the line, the rear echelon generals and their staffs were throwing the blame where it did not belong, on the men up front who were doing the dying because the rear echelon generals had not given them the training and the weapons and the support that they needed.

General Sutherland asked General Harding how Colonel Hale was doing. He did not like Colonel Hale, who had a brusque way about him and who had apparently ruffled Sutherland's feathers at some time. Sutherland now indicated that he did not think much of Hale's qualities as a commander. Sutherland did not think much of Colonel Mott either, "He has a notable talent for antagonizing his superiors." Apparently, that meant General Sutherland. General Harding was noncommittal. He knew what the problem was, and it was not his subordinate's behavior. But that was his last mistake. General Sutherland was furious when General Harding did not kowtow to his opinions. He was, after all, MacArthur's chief of staff and when he spoke, lesser generals should rush to do his bidding. So General Sutherland flew back to Port Moresby that day and recommended that General Harding be relieved at once because he insisted on keeping subordinates whose competence was "open to question." And so exit General Harding, said General Sutherland.

At this point, enter General Eichelberger, who was just then trying to whip the 41st Division into fighting trim. All of that division had now arrived in Australia and was training. At the moment, Eichelberger was giving them a course in jungle warfare. Now, he was going to practice what he had been preaching.

Eichelberger was hustled off to Port Moresby and before he had a chance to unpack his bag he was called into the presence of General MacArthur. General Kenney, the air commander, was there and so was an unsmiling General Sutherland.

MacArthur put on one of his great shows. Striding up and down the room, grim faced, with his corncob pipe for emphasis in hand or jaw—whichever was more effective—the general lamented the fact that American troops had dropped their weapons and fled from the Japanese in the jungles of New Guinea. He had never been so humiliated in his life, said MacArthur, and he would not stand for it. He said nothing about why the American troops dropped their weapons and fled. MacArthur was never a man to take responsibility on himself.

What was needed at Buna, said MacArthur, was aggressive leadership. He had to admit that the men had been badly trained. He had to admit that they were mostly sick. He had to admit that the supply situation was dreadful. But, said he, real leadership, real true leadership, would take these men on to capture Buna.*

And with a final flourish, he dismissed Eichelberger toward the front with these words, "You will relieve Harding—and his subordinates—or I will relieve them myself and you, too. Go out there Bob, and take Buna or don't come back alive."

He pointed to Gen. Clovis Byers, Eichelberger's chief of staff, and said, "And that goes for Clovis, too."

After this Spartan sendoff, General Eichelberger spent the rest of the afternoon and evening and night in briefings. Early in the morning, after a hasty breakfast, the Eichelberger party left for Buna.

The general was not very favorably impressed by MacArthur's orders to triumph or die. Before the day was out, the story was all over the command. But, of course, that was not the sort of story MacArthur allowed to get out through the pens of the correspondents. While the men in New Guinea cursed General MacArthur and his staff, to the outside world he was fast becoming the Great White Hope of the war—so carefully was his public relations campaign tailored.

Eichelberger was a sensible man. The first thing he did was make an inspection. That first night he wrote General Sutherland that things really were not as bad as Sutherland seemed to believe (Sutherland had not made any investigation for himself).

Meanwhile, on the Urbana Front, facing Buna village, American troops moved up to within three hundred yards of the village but did not pursue the action. No one seemed to know quite why. That night of December 1, General Harding rushed up eight new mortars. The next morning, they laid down a barrage and then the infantry hurried forward. But the American infantry ran right into those well-laid Japanese fields of fire and again were stopped—for the fifth time. The men were exhausted. Some of the officers were not sure they could continue to push them. A visiting medical officer from Milne Bay came up that day, looked over the troops, and

*This is the strength-through-character syndrome for which the Japanese were so roundly criticized during and after the war.

went back to tell General Eichelberger, "They looked like Christ off the Cross."

Colonel Mott wrote in the battalion diary, "The troops that we have left are weak and tired and need rest and reinforcement."

These were the "cowards" who were embarrassing General MacArthur and ruining his public relations image.

General Harding was still around. General Eichelberger had not relieved him. Harding had decided that the two attacks could no longer be pursued simultaneously because of the shortage of everything. He shifted the main attack to the new airstrip area. Colonel Hale was to come up and give Colonel Carrier a hand.

First would come the air strafing and bombing of Buna village, the new airstrip, and the bridge between. In fifteen minutes of bombing, beginning at 8:00 A.M. on December 2, 1942, the bombers did their job and did it well except for one little thing: the last flight was to drop flares to indicate that the bombing was over. The infantry could then take over. But the air force forgot. Consequently, the infantrymen waited, while they waited, Colonel Yamamoto's troops pulled themselves together, got out of their blockhouses, and manned their prepared positions. When the Americans started forward the Japanese were more than ready for them.

It was another typical Buna day: men dropping from bullets, men dropping from heat exhaustion, men dropping from fever. Ultimately, the American military force was stopped cold again, with virtually no gain and with many casualties. Wherever the cowardice factor was that day, it was not on the Buna front.

But when General Eichelberger went forward to inspect, he was not pleased—and with very good reason, he believed.

What he saw was that there was a modicum of truth in the claims of General Sutherland. He questioned soldiers who looked to be in pretty good shape and was told that they had been sent back for rest. He went further forward and checked. From the Buna front had come a report to headquarters that a strong Japanese counterattack had been repelled. But up front, Eichelberger thought he found that the attack had been very weak, not strong. All that looked very bad. What the general did not understand was that the Japanese had little need to counterattack just now. They let the Americans attack and mowed them down.

Further, Eichelberger was furious to discover that the hungry men up front had not been allowed to build fires and cook captured Japanese rice. What he did not know was that all the wood in the jungle was wet and gave off huge columns of smoke when burned. To build those fires the American troops would have exposed themselves to merciless mortaring and machine-gunning, and some officer had the good sense to prevent them from committing suicide. General Eichelberger did not understand.

The general did not know a lot of things. He went up front and questioned three soldiers. They told him there was a machine gun up the line and that every time they went up, the machine gun fired at them. He asked if any of them had been up in the past hour. No they had not. Would one of them go for a medal? "Shit. A Goddamn medal. Hell, no," came the response.

The general was aghast. Medals were his business. He forgot that he was dealing with National Guardsmen, civilian soldiers. But to General Eichelberger it was inconceivable that a man would not stick his neck out for a medal.

He sent his aide up. The aide was no dummy. He used a different route, went to a different place, crawled on his belly to the edge of Buna village, and returned without being fired on.

See, said the general. A piece of cake. There had not been any machine gun there at all.

So, General Eichelberger erupted at Colonel Mott's command post. He accused the troops of not fighting at all.

Colonel Mott tried to defend his men. They had been having a very tough time, he said. General Eichelberger did not want to listen to that. "You're licked," he shouted at Colonel Mott. And then he stamped out of the command post muttering about all the cowards.

Over on the Warren front, the scene was much the same. Two members of General Eichelberger's staff had gone over there to observe. There had been heavy fighting earlier, but by the time they got there it was all over. They did not even hear any firing because the Japanese, having knocked down the Americans again, had retired to their blockhouses for a nap.

The staff officers observed grimly how the Americans did not seem eager to go wave flags in the face of the enemy. They were flopped out, resting, or bringing up supplies for the next day's slaughter. And so the inspectors concluded that there had not been any fighting at all and that all this talk of the Harding units was just sham.

The inspectors were particularly infuriated by the terrible condition of the troops.

All this was the fault of General Harding, obviously, and not of General MacArthur and the men back there who were supposed to be running the war and supplying the troops.

The staff officers from the rear had many bright ideas for the men up front. Why, if those men had any gumption they would be salvaging half destroyed equipment and cleaning up their litter. The inspectors did not ask what would happen to the war while the troops stopped to begin policing the area.

And so all the inspectors went back to camp; in short order, General Harding was, indeed, relieved. It was a long, long time before General Eichelberger would realize that he, and General Sutherland, and General MacArthur, and all the stooges had been dead wrong. Of course, General MacArthur never would allow such an admission even to cross his mind.

CHAPTER THIRTEEN

Buna Shock

General Eichelberger had convinced himself that General Harding was the root of all the evil that had so embarrassed poor General MacArthur. General Harding would have to go. Eichelberger had so decided on his own hook. If he had decided otherwise, he could have made it stick perhaps, although MacArthur's wrath was not easy to overcome. But Eichelberger also had friends in Washington and the relief of a corps commander does not go unnoticed. Therefore, it was really on his own responsibility that General Eichelberger had decided to relieve General Harding.

That evening of December 2, General Eichelberger held a meeting of his staff. He told them what he thought. Like good staff members, they all advised him that he had only one choice, to follow MacArthur's instructions and relieve General Harding.

Yes, said General Eichelberger, that is what he thought.

When General Harding came into General Eichelberger's tent that night with a new plan for the capture of Buna, Eichelberger seemed bored by the whole proceeding. He stopped listening; when General Harding saw that, he stopped talking.

Eichelberger tried the firing on for size. He spoke of the terrible conditions he had discovered along the line, with men not fighting. General Harding interposed some objections. But it quickly became clear to him that he was being fired.

"You were probably sent here to get heads," he said. "Maybe mine is one of them. If so, it is on the block."

"You are right," said General Eichelberger, and he told General Harding that he was putting General Waldron, the artillery commander, in command of the division.

General Harding left the tent to go and find transportation back to Port Moresby, where he would then be consigned to whatever bin MacArthur would send him.

Immediately, in came Col. Clarence Martin and Colonel Rodgers from their foray up into the Warren line where they had not seen any fighting either.

"Clarence, my boy," said General Eichelberger to his operations officer, Colonel Martin, "you have always said you wanted to command a regiment. I am going to give you one. You will take command of the 128th Infantry and the Warren front."

General Sutherland had his way. Colonel Hale was fired. Colonel Mott was fired. Colonel Martin took over the 128th Infantry and Colonel McCreary, the former executive officer of the division artillery, took over as commander of the 126th Infantry.

The heads had been rolled. The vision of the officers back at headquarters had been honored and their authority propitiated.

The war could go on.

And it did.

At Buna and Gona, the Japanese colonels waited for General Horii to come down out of the jungle where he had been caught. The Horii party, including Colonel Yazawa and the nine-hundred-man force cut off on the Kokoda Trail, made its way northward along the Kumusi River. Near the end of November, they reached the mouth of the river, at Pinga, about twelve miles northwest of Gona. There, they tried to cross the swollen Kumusi River on rafts. General Horii's raft upset and he and his chief of staff were drowned. Now Colonel Yazawa was stuck. But Colonel Yokoyama sent all his landing craft up the coast to the mouth of the Kumusi. The landing craft picked up about three-quarters of the force and brought them back.

On the way back to Gona, they were attacked by Allied aircraft and several landing craft were sunk, but Colonel Yazawa and about five hundred men reached Giruwa on November 29 and joined the beachhead garrison.

Nor were these the only Japanese reinforcements. On the night of November 28, nearly a thousand men left Rabaul.

They were the members of the 21st Independent Mixed Brigade, a force from Indochina. Their commander was Maj. Gen. Tsuyuo Yamagata. They came in four destroyers. But the Japanese could make mistakes, too, and they did this night. The destroyers were not covered by fighter planes. The next morning they were spotted by Allied aircraft and bombed and strafed. The destroyers were damaged enough so that they turned around and went back to Rabaul. There, they encountered the second echelon of the brigade, which had boarded four other destroyers.

General Yamagata joined this group, leaving the others to find new transport, and they set out again on November 30. This time the 11th Air Fleet provided air cover by Zero fighters. Allied B-17s attacked, but the B-17s were intercepted by about twenty Zeros. There was another air attack, but the ships reached Basabua on the early morning of December 2. The troops were landed at the mouth of the Kumusi. About five hundred more reinforcements were then ashore with more supplies. But their problem was that they were, with about another four hundred men of the Horii force, on the wrong side of the defense area. Between them and the beachhead was the Australian army force.

The Australians had been having heavy going at Gona, just like the Americans at Buna. The Japanese were very tough and very well organized. For example, a patrol investigated a small creek on the beach half a mile east of the Gona Mission and reported no Japanese in sight. The whole 2nd Battalion of the 14th Brigade set out for the position and ran into a nest of enemy that spouted fire. The Australians suffered thirty-two casualties before they could get away.

Every attack on Gona had cost the Australians dearly. The 14th Brigade had only been in battle four days and had already lost 140 men. The 27th Brigade lost 45 men on the afternoon of November 30 and gained virtually nothing in exchange. But the Australians did hold most of the beach between Basabua and Gona, even if Gona was very much Japanese.

But the trouble for the Japanese was supply and reinforcements. They were running out of everything, including fighting men. On December 1, they tried to reinforce Gona in the dark of night. They sent in three barges loaded with troops and they landed on the shore about sixty yards east of Gona. The Australians drove them off, and the reinforcements were not put ashore.

That morning the Australians attacked Gona once more. Again the Japanese resisted stoutly. Before the day was over, the Australians lost many men. One company lost fifty-eight that day. Once more, they had gained virtually nothing.

But the Australians were sending in fresh troops. The 30th Brigade, which had been in action on the Kokoda Track in the summer and had become exhausted, was now rehabilitated and it came down to fight. These troops took over from the 21st Brigade, which had lost 450 men in the past five days. These were more of the "cowards" about whom General MacArthur complained.

On December 6, the Australians attacked Gona once more. Again, the Japanese sent them reeling back. It was beginning to seem almost hopeless; in fact, the situation had changed enormously. The Japanese strength had been decimated in these attacks. The defenders were completely exhausted from fighting every day, and there were only a few hundred of them left.

On December 8, the Australians launched a mortar and artillery barrage; fifteen minutes later, a battalion attacked Gona from the southeast. This time they broke through and began clearing out the enemy troops. That night Colonel Yamamoto ordered the garrison to break out and make their way in small groups to Giruwa. A hundred men tried, but they were unlucky. They ran into the Australians in force, and the Australians cut them down with their Bren guns.

The battle for Gona ended. Australian patrols came into the mission area and mopped up. They found little but dead and wounded and sick. They took sixteen prisoners, ten of them stretcher cases, and they found almost no food or ammunition.

They found something else. Carnage. The Japanese had not had the time even to bury their dead in the past few weeks.

Rotting bodies sometimes weeks old, formed part of the fortifications. The living fired over the bodies of the dead, slept side by side with them. In one trench was a Japanese who had not been able to stand the strain. His rifle was still pointed at his head. His big toe was on the trigger and the top of his head was blown off. Everywhere, pervading everything, was the stench of putrescent flesh.

The Australians, who had lost 750 men killed, buried nearly 650 Japanese at Gona.

The Japanese were now in serious straits. General Adachi was doing all he could from Rabaul to help them. On December 7, the first anniversary of the Pacific War, Adachi sent a new landing force in six destroyers. It consisted of about eight hundred men. The ships were bombed the next morning by a single B-24, but the one destroyer that was hit was not seriously hurt and on they went to New Guinea. Now the B-17s came into the fight.

They attacked the Japanese force that afternoon. They set three destroyers ablaze and shot down seven Japanese fighters. Many of the troops were killed or wounded. The force commander turned around and headed back to Rabaul. Thus the air force had interdicted an important Japanese reinforcement attempt.

Up by the river mouth, General Yamagata was in serious trouble. His troops were being bombed every day by the Australians and the Americans. But at Rabaul, help was again on its way. General Kensaku Oda, the new commander of the South Seas Detachment (*Nankai Shitai*)—to replace the drowned General Horii—set out in five destroyers with eight hundred men on December 12 to reinforce the area. The weather turned sour—good for the sailors but bad for the airmen—and the ships moved in through the Vitiaz Straight, landing safely. This time, they touched at the mouth of the Mambare River, thirty miles north of the Kumusi River.

Early in the morning, the Allied planes attacked, but they were too late. The ships were already moving out. The supplies on the shore were hit, but only a few were destroyed. The Japanese reinforcement attempt had at least been successful.

But there is many a slip 'twixt cup and lip, as they say; in this case, the interfering factor was a coast watcher named Lyndon C. Noakes, an Australian army lieutenant. Noakes watched the whole unloading operation from a ridge above the beach, observed where the Japanese stashed their dumps, and informed the Allied air force by radio. Next morning, planes came over and blew up several of the well-hidden dumps.

The Japanese shifted the rest of the supplies, but Lieutenant Noakes was again watching. Next morning, again, more bombers came over and blew up more supplies. This continued every day for a week.

General Oda remained for several days at the mouth of the Mambare River. The Australians had blown up so many of his landing craft, courtesy of Lieutenant Noakes, that when he started for the Amboga River, he could take only a portion of the 1st Battalion of the 170th Infantry. Moving only by night and lying up during the day to avoid Allied air observation, the Japanese moved to the mouth of the Amboga on December 18. Not far away was General Yamagata; General Oda reported in.

The Australian troops of the 14th Brigade were up against Yamagata's men in this area, and they were knocking off so many of them that when Oda showed up, Yamagata immediately ordered all his troops into the line.

Captain Shirley's mixed unit of antitank gunners, machine gunners, communications men, and headquarters men was holding the roadblock at the junction of the Killerton and Supota–Sanananda tracks. The position was ideal—for the enemy. It was located in a comparatively open space, in the midst of jungle swamp. It was only a bit higher than the swamp around it and had no natural cover except some tall trees, some of them one-hundred-feet high. Ultimately, these were discovered to be full of Japanese. But that discovery would come later. The basic problem, still unknown to the Allies, was that the Japanese watched everything they did. On the morning of December 1 when a strong patrol set out to probe at the south end of the perimeter, the Japanese were waiting and ambushed them. Captain Keats and Lieutenant Daniels were killed. The men pulled back. In that area, the garrison repulsed five enemy attacks that day. Not fighting—said General Eichelberger. It was too bad he was back in the fleshpots of Port Moresby.

A supply column, carrying food and ammunition, fought its way to the roadblock that day. At 11:00 A.M., it arrived;

but the Japanese launched another counterattack on the main force and cut off fifty yards of the perimeter. Captain Shirley was killed just after noon. Captain Huggins took over.

For the next two days the Japanese attacked ferociously, trying to destroy the roadblock. The Americans held on. What was needed, as General Harding had seen saying, was more troops. But Harding could not get them; now when General Eichelberger asked for a troop transfer, General Herring turned the force of Colonel Tomlinson over to the other side of the river, just as Harding had wanted. Major Baetcke became chief of American troops on the eastern side of the river. This slender force along with that of Major Boerem was told to attack again and drive out the enemy from the roadblock area. They did, and lost ninety of the three hundred men they had between them. Higher headquarters did not seem to be willing to learn from experience.

Every day the "cowards" fought, sometimes three and four times a day. By December 6, they were down to one-day's rations and ammunition and no one could get through to them. They were sick with malaria. Captain Huggins was wounded, but there was no way to get him out or to get any other commander in, so he stayed in command.

On December 7, Major Baetcke and Major Zeeff came down with malaria, and Major Boerem took command of all the Americans on the Australian side of the river. There were about eight hundred of them left. That day the Australian 14th Brigade relieved the 16th Brigade and Boerem's Americans came under that command.

The Australians now tried to break through to the roadblock. At 9:45 A.M. on December 7, they launched an attack after a careful mortar and artillery preparation. It lost ninety-five men in about an hour and was stopped.

More attacks. By the end of the day, the Australians had lost 225 men. Colonel Tsukamoto was still there in strength.

At the roadblock, life was getting very difficult. On December 8, Lt. Dal Ponte managed to get through with a supply party. Captain Huggins came out with them. He described the roadblock as about two hundred yards square, with the command post in the center. Everyone had fever. Food and ammunition and medical supplies were low. The men lived in holes. Where did they defecate? In the holes. It was becoming a problem. There were 225 men left in the roadblock and only half of them were fit to fight, reported Captain Huggins.

But the "cowards" were still there.

On December 10, another small supply party got through and came back with a message from Lt. Dal Ponte confirming all that Huggins had said and announcing that matters had grown worse. The Japanese were all around them, so close that several times soldiers grabbed the ankles of passing Japanese and pulled them into their holes to kill them.

In the swamp off to the west were the men of Company K and the Cannon Company. They were just as badly off. Somebody brought up a load of canned heat. "The men haven't washed for a month or had any dry clothing, but we did get some canned heat and a hot cup of coffee. Sure helps a lot." So spoke the journal of Company K on December 10. Somebody should have sent a copy of the journal to General Eichelberger to forward to General MacArthur.

The Americans were falling by the wayside. On December 10, Major Boerem's force of 800 men was down to 635 fit for duty. Two days later it was 551. General MacArthur would have said they were malingering. It is not hard to malinger with a temperature of 105 degrees.

On December 12, Major Boerem asked Brigadier General Porter, an Australian, to relieve the roadblock and the garrison. Porter refused. The situation grew worse and worse, compounded by stupidities in the rear. Earlier, the Americans had radioed Port Moresby for supplies. They had asked for 81-mm mortar ammunition, .50-caliber machine guns, a 37-mm gun, and medical supplies. Major Baetcke, who sent the message needed some administrative help—even up here— to take care of the army's paperwork. "Send Todish," he had said, in closing his message; meaning send up Chief Warrant Officer (CWO) Frank O. Todish, a personnel man. But the decoding clerk at Port Moresby decided that the word *TODISH* was a garble and that what Baetcke meant was "send to *FISH,*" which was the code name for Pongani. The supplies were never delivered to the force east of the river.

Finally, disgusted with the lower echelons of command, Major Boerem went directly to General Vasey on December

14. After the meeting, the Americans—Company K and Cannon Company—east of the river were relieved by Australians and sent to the rear.

It was some time before the men at the roadblock got relief. It was December 22, in fact, and they had been fighting every day. That particular gang of "cowards" had been fighting steadily for twenty-two days, disgracing General MacArthur every day with their failures to take Buna. From Port Moresby, it was sad to contemplate the incompetence of the men at the front. It was also hard to assess the work of the "cowards" since the rear echelon stayed in the rear.

Every day the Allied troops up front learned more about the strength of the Japanese defenses and the news was not exhilarating. The Australians in the Sanananda area were unable to make any real progress. One reason was that the troops under Tsukamoto were not service troops but special attack-force troops, the toughest that the Japanese services could bring together. The Australians had broken through a portion of the Japanese line, but they could not capitalize on it. Every foot of the ground was contested.

Usually, the Japanese let the Allied troops come up against their defenses and mowed them down. But now that the Allies had broken through the line, the Japanese took to a more active defense.

On the night of December 28, forty Japanese soldiers armed with light machine guns that could be fired from the hip, rifles, and explosive charges infiltrated the Allied lines and blew up a field gun. Thirteen Japanese were killed and, wonder of wonders, one prisoner was taken. That was a rare occurrence. Not many Japanese asked for, or were offered, a chance to surrender.

The Japanese hit the Allied lines again on the night of December 30. A Japanese patrol infiltrated the lines of the Australian company immediately to the right of the Americans. The company commander and several soldiers were killed. The Japanese got off virtually without casualties.

The Sanananda front was a stalemate at the moment. Gona was captured, Buna was under siege, and Sanananda was up for grabs. It was going to take more than the Allies had here to do the job.

If General MacArthur or one of his staff had made a visit to the line here, they would have seen things that might have made them think. One day, Major Boerem counted 160 Australian and American dead before one position that had just been taken by the "cowards" after days of fighting. He did not even try to count the Japanese dead.

The food was dreadful, mostly C rations made in Australia, with Australian mutton substituted for American beef; hard-as-nails D ration bars of chocolate; and corned beef. And the American part of the line was falling apart. Major Boerem at Christmas time had only 400 men able to fight. A few days later, the number was 300. Of course, MacArthur would say they were all "cowards." The medics would say they were all about half-dead. Finally, on December 31, Major Boerem was relieved. His replacement, Major Irwin, arrived to find that the American fighting force consisted of one company of men. The Americans had suffered 979 casualties, and there were only 244 men who could fight.

But . . . Brigadier Porter, the Australian officer in command of this sector, had no troops with which to replace the Americans. Until troops could be brought in, they would have to stay where they were, fight, and die.

CHAPTER FOURTEEN

The Fall of Buna—I

West of the Girua at Sanananda, the Japanese continued to resist with every fiber. Three hundred reinforcements had come in on November 23. Theoretically, the defense positions were very strong. Actually, they were not so strong for the same reason that the Americans were not strong: disease, and exhaustion, and lack of food were using up the men. General Oda's troops not far away were on the verge of starvation. They were eating roots, grass, crabs, and snakes. The hospital at Giruwa was a charnel house. There was no medicine and no food. The drainage system had collapsed and no one had time to repair it. Most of the wards were under water.

On December 11, Colonel Yokoyama gave Rabaul a picture of conditions so bleak that the operations officer of General Adachi's staff did not believe it. It had to be exaggeration he told the general. But other news confirmed the dismal story. General Hyakutake promised relief. The Imperial Navy was going to devote many of its submarines to carrying supplies to New Guinea. They would be landed in Mambare Bay. They would be moved up to the places that needed them thereafter. But Lieutenant Noakes, the coast watcher, thwarted this well-laid plan, almost single-handedly. Every time a submarine landed supplies, he watched, and then he found out where they went and radioed Port Moresby. A few hours later, along came the bombers.

There was a new element: the American PT boats. A squadron was based at Tufi in December. On Christmas Eve, they sank the *I-18*, one of Japan's best fleet submarines, just off the mouth of the Mambare. This 344-foot deep sea I-boat was out of its element and paid the price. That same night, the squadron destroyed two big landing barges filled with Japanese reinforcements bound for General Yamagata's Force.

And the reinforcements continued to come in. About a thousand men got through safely in late December. General Yamagata arrived on December 29. It seemed that matters were taking a turn for the better for the Japanese.

But the situation of the American 32nd Division was also improving after the first of the year. Two new airfields were finished. A new fleet of trawlers replaced the sunken ones. A new track was finished across the mountains. All these changes helped the supply situation of the Americans and the Australians in eastern New Guinea.

When Colonel Martin, a favorite of General Eichelberger, went up to take command of the 128th Infantry Regiment, he discovered a few of the facts of life up front that he had overlooked as an inspector who was looking for the head of General Harding at MacArthur's request. For one thing, the troops had totally inadequate weapons and equipment. When Colonel Martin got up front, he discovered that his command post consisted of a single shelter half suspended like an awning five feet off the ground. The regimental telephone sat next to a stump on the ground beneath the shelter half. There were no files, no typewriters, no order blanks. He came up with some bad news for the exhausted troops: there would be no relief until Buna was captured, he said. He was not immediately the most popular officer in the command.

The Bren carriers had been offered by the Australians in lieu of tanks, which could not be shipped because of the shortage of oceangoing vessels. Everyone knew they were a poor substitute for tanks, with their light, almost nonexistent armor and their boxlike appearance.

Five Bren carriers finally arrived in December. They were employed in an attack on December 5. The Japanese attacked them with grenades, satchel charges, and one antitank gun. In a few minutes, the Bren carriers—all five of them—were out of action. The Allies got the guns and equipment out of three of the carriers. The Japanese got the remains of the other two. Thus it was established, when the men up front asked for tanks, Bren carriers would not do the job.

The first attack by the 128th and 126th after the new commanders took over was the same sort of failure that their predecessors had faced. Colonel Martin was quick to learn. After the attack failed, he called back to General Byers at Eichelberger's headquarters. "We have hit them and bounced off," he said.

So, General Eichelberger learned a little bit, too, about the reality of the war in New Guinea as opposed to General MacArthur's pipe dreams.

On December 5, General Eichelberger came up front to see what the troops would do now that he had solved all their problems by firing their commanders. An attack began that day, first with a B-25 air raid on the enemy positions, or what were thought to be their positions. The idea was to take Buna Village, which MacArthur wanted desperately to assuage his wounded ego. Eichelberger watched as the Americans attacked against Captain Yasuda's defenders. The troops reached the outskirts of the village, but that was all. One company was stopped about fifty yards from the edge of the village. The fact that they got this far was due principally to three men, Lt. Thomas E. Knode, 1st Sgt. Paul R. Lutjens, and Sgt. Harold E. Graber. Knode and Lutjens pressed their men forward and were both severely wounded. Graber leaped up and fired his light machine gun from the hip. He cleaned out a main Japanese strong point which had been holding up the advance, and he was shot dead.

Company G of the 128th Infantry, got to a point very close to the village. General Eichelberger was eager to have that village that day. He took personal command of the operation and ordered Company F to pass through Company E of the 2nd Battalion of the regiment. Colonel Grose, the battalion commander, protested the order, which he found to be fundamentally unsound. He wanted to save his reserve (Company F) and throw it in on the left when a good time came. He told Eichelberger there was nothing to be gained by hurrying the attack. General Eichelberger ignored him.

So on the general's orders, Company F came up. And here is what happened in the words of the company commander, Lieutenant Odell:

The Lieutenant General [Eichelberger] explained what he wanted, and after a brief delay I brought up the company and deployed accordingly. 1st Sgt. George Pravda was to take half the company up one side of the trail, and I the other half on the other side. We were given ten minutes to make our reconnaissance and to gather information from the most forward troops, which we were to pass. It was intended that we finish the job—actually take the village—and it was thought that we needed little more than our bayonets to do it.

Well, off we went, and within a few minutes, our rush forward had been definitely and completely halted. Of the forty men who started with me, four had been killed and eighteen were lying wounded. We were within a few yards of the village but with no chance of going a step farther. Pravda was among those wounded and the casualties were about as heavy on his side.

So, General Eichelberger, that great tactician, had sent a company up front against the advice of its battalion commander. The company had been mowed down (fifty percent casualties) in order to make General MacArthur happy, and Eichelberger had not even achieved that.

On the right, Company H under S. Sgt. Herman J. Botcher had given up the fruitless direct attack ordered by Eichelberger and had gone around the end, pushed north, reached the beach with eighteen men and a machine gun. They dug in and weathered several attacks from Japanese in the village and in the mission. The position became known as Botcher's Corner and was recognizable by the pile of Japanese corpses around it. This breakthrough isolated the village, and without unnecessary loss of life. From this point on, the Japanese could not reinforce Buna Village from Buna Mission. If the Japanese could not succeed in pushing out Botcher's men or killing them, the capture of the village could not be far off. It had nothing to do with General Eichelberger's way of doing things. It was Sergeant Botcher's way that counted.

During all the commotion about the capture of Buna Village that day, General Waldron was wounded, and General Byers, Eichelberger's chief of staff, succeeded to the command up front. General Eichelberger, having made enough mistakes in seizing direct command of operations of the day—in violation of military protocol—departed for Port Moresby at about 6:00 P.M., leaving the "cowards" behind him. Indeed, when he got back the next day, he wrote to General Sutherland that the troops seemed to be fighting and that MacArthur really did not have anything to worry about. The first statement was correct. The second was not.

General Eichelberger had finally discovered that the Japanese positions were too powerful to be breached by direct assault without artillery and superior force. He really did not know what force he faced, but that did not stop him from leaping to conclusions. He decided to wait for tanks and the fresh Australian troops who were coming up. In the meantime, the American troops would concentrate on softening up the enemy by taking a number of positions on the perimeter of the Japanese defenses. And this is what they set out to do.

But the Americans had no artillery with which to do the job. The 37-mm guns were too light. They had no effect on the bunkers. Neither did the Australian twenty-five-pounder guns. The only weapon they had that could be of much use was the single 105-mm howitzer, and it did not have any ammunition. It was the second week of December before the 105-mm howitzer began to be supplied with some shells.

On the morning of December 7, 1942, the Japanese decided to celebrate the anniversary of the Pearl Harbor attack by clearing out Botcher's Corner for good, and they sent out forces from the mission and the village. The hero of the moment was Corp. Harold Mitchell. He had seen the Japanese on the edge of the jungle just as they were preparing to attack. With a yell, he attacked alone, with bayonet. The Japanese were so surprised that he got away with it. They stopped for a moment. The other Americans then began firing, and the Japanese attack was confounded before it began. When they did attack, the machine gun at Botcher's Corner was waiting for them and they were cut down.

All that afternoon of December 7, the Americans and the Japanese fought for the village. At one point, they were so close together that a Japanese officer began talking to the Americans in English. That evening, Captain Yasuda sent boats toward the village from his headquarters in the mission, but Botcher, down on the beach, set the first boat afire, the others withdrew.

All day long on December 8, the Japanese and Americans fought around the village and the mission. The Americans received two very primitive flamethrowers that day and tried to use them against the Japanese bunker on the southern edge of the village. This bunker, located in the corner of a kunai grass flat and with dense jungle and swamp at the rear, could not be taken by frontal assault and could not be outflanked. The flamethrower seemed to be the answer. The first one was brought up. The operator, covered by the fire of twenty riflemen, moved up to a point about thirty feet from the bunker. He stood up and turned on his machine. A spurt of flame came out of the nozzle and set the grass in front of the operator afire, thus destroying his cover. Then it dribbled off. Not one spark hit the Japanese. The operator was immediately shot down. Two of the men covering him and the chemical officer who had supervised the whole mess were all killed.

That night, Captain Yasuda made another diversionary attack to help the Japanese troops in the village. One force of forty men counterattacked on the left. Captain Yasuda sent a hundred men against the right flank of the 2nd Battalion of the 126th Infantry. The Japanese came out in a *banzai* charge, screaming and yelling all the way. But the Americans turned their machine guns on them and quieted them down.

Next day, the Americans continued their succession of attacks on all sides of the village, but still the Japanese held fast.

The real difficulty was indicated in the tale of Lt. James G. Downer, now in command of Company E of the 126th. He led a patrol against the most important bunker, the one where the flamethrower had failed the day before. Covered by fire from his entire patrol, Downer moved up against the bunker. But he was killed by a sniper just before he got there with an explosive charge. What the Americans had not yet learned was the depth of the Japanese defense. All around their bunker areas, the trees were sentinel boxes, and in the trees were snipers. They might let a whole patrol go by and then pick the men off from the back, one by one. How did that happen? Because the Americans still had not learned to look up. Up in all those trees where the Japanese snipers were. They would wait for hours, sometimes for a day or two in the trees, and then when an enemy soldier really threatened the bunker, they would fire. It had happened so many times one would think that the Allied soldiers would be aware of the practice. But the jungle was thick, it was hard to spot movement, and the Japanese were more than adept at camouflage. Here, in New Guinea, the Allied troops would learn all these tricks. But they had not learned them yet, so Downer and others like him paid the heavy price.

The fight for the bunker went on all day. But sometime during that day there came a change. The preponderance of firepower was with the Americans. The Japanese were short of ammunition, and it showed. Finally, at the end of the day and after many American casualties, that particular bunker fell.

But there would be more.

That day the 2nd Battalion of the 16th Infantry made twelve attacks against Buna Village. All of them failed. By the end of the day, its companies were so depleted that they could scarcely hold their positions during the night. Company E had less than 50 effective men left. The same was true of Company F. The whole battalion totaled fewer than 250 men. These were the ''cowards'' whose relief was long overdue.

The joy of making the final attack on Buna Village, then, had to go to someone else. The unit was the 3rd Battalion of the 127th Infantry, which had just come up from Port Moresby on December 19.

Colonel Grose took over command of the 127th when they came in. That was good. For the first time a fresh American regiment came in to be greeted by an experienced commander who knew what he was doing—a man who could teach the newcomers something of the way of the enemy so that they would not have to learn by bitter and deadly experience—if only the high brass would leave them alone.

The new men began to make gains. At Botcher's Corner, they moved forward. The Japanese in Buna Village were now down to about a hundred men. On December 12 and 13, the village was subjected to constant artillery fire. Things had indeed changed. Field guns, mortars, and more mortars spoke up loudly all day long. The Japanese defenders figured out what was coming next, and that evening they slipped away to Giruwa, the center of Japanese resistance.

On December 14, the American barrage against the village began early. It continued for an hour. At 7:00 A.M., the advance began. It was conservative and steady. Three hours later, the troops overran the whole area. There was not a Japanese soldier in the place. The village had fallen finally without the firing of single shot. It could have been a lesson for General MacArthur and General Eichelberger.

What a mess Buna Village was. Its huts were blown to bits by the American bombs and artillery. The palms were splintered and broken. Shell and bomb craters dotted the whole place. But the bunkers stood, as sound as the day they were built: mute evidence of the power of man's ingenuity (palm logs and bits of tin) over high explosives in limited quantity. There was virtually nothing else in the place. A few broken guns. A little canned food. Some old *sake* bottles (empty). A few clothes that would do for souvenirs.

The next task would be the reduction of the area called Coconut Grove. It was captured after hard fighting on December 15. Here some real booty was found—two thousand pounds of rice and meal, many small arms, machine guns, and a hut full of ammunition.

General Eichelberger now had decided that his men were not cowards. It had taken him a long, long time. But now he said, "the boys are coming to life all along the line."

He was not quite right. Hundreds of those he had maligned were not coming to life. They were very dead, victims of the jungle, of the enemy, and of the ignorance and public relations demands of higher command.

By mid-December the word *coward* had been expunged even from General MacArthur's lexicon, it seemed. And it was true. The soldiers who were still alive were veterans now, experts in jungle fighting. Had they been given a little more training before the Japanese undertook to teach them the arts of war, there might have been several hundred more of them alive. The two task forces east of the Girua River had been in action for only twenty-one days and had lost 667 killed, wounded, and missing; 1,260 men were sick.

But things were looking up. The coming of the 127th Infantry helped. The pressure was off the 126th and 128th now. Supplies were beginning to come in in respectable amounts. A big freighter actually appeared in Oro Bay, and there were promises of more in spite of the U.S. Navy's reluctance to commit any forces here. The airlift was beginning to count its deliveries in tons instead of pounds. On December 14, the airlift brought in 1,178 tons of matériel to the eastern side of the Owen Stanley Range.

If the Americans would not supply naval forces, the Australians would. In came several corvettes escorting a convoy that included tanks. Yes, real tanks. The Australians sent fresh troops and four light tanks (General Stuarts) of American make but Australian manning.

A second group of tanks was brought in a day or so later. Now there were eight. A new attack was planned, this time with the Australians in the forefront. The Warren Force would move out to take Duropa Plantation and Cape Endaiadere, the New Strip, the Old Strip, and the bridgehead across the mouth of the Simemi Creek. Then the Urbana Force would attack. It would seize the Triangle, the track junction between Buna Mission and Giropa Point. Thus the Japanese would be separated into two camps, each facing total envelopment. Captain Yasuda and Colonel Yamamoto did not have a long time to go. The attack was scheduled to jump off on December 18.

CHAPTER FIFTEEN

Buna Mission

In the middle of December, the Allies began the construction of a road between Oro Bay and the Dobodura airfields. Such a road would make it possible to base bomber aircraft north of the Owen Stanley Mountains. But if the road was to be built and the area made safe for operations, first the battle of the Huon Peninsula must be won. The fall of Gona and the fall of Buna Village had been part of that procedure, but it would not be finished until the Buna Mission was taken and the Japanese positions at the Sanananda Track junction were reduced.

So, a new attack was to be made in the area of the Duropa Plantation and the new landing strips. The difference between this attack and all the others was as night to day, for the Allies would have tanks for the first time. The Japanese use of tanks in the battle for Milne Bay had been an instance of erroneous intelligence, the tanks were at the wrong place at the wrong time. The Australian tanks now brought in were suitable for the countryside and the terrain made it possible to use them without too much fear of bogging down.

The New Guinea Force was still woefully short of artillery, which is odd in a way, because artillery is the strong point of the American army. Just then, the American soldiers in New Guinea had to make do with a single 105-mm howitzer, a handful of twenty-five-pound Australian guns, and two 3.7-inch mountain guns.

At the same time, dozens of batteries of artillery were saving the day for the American soldiers fighting against Field Marshal Erwin Rommel in North Africa. Of course, that was the reason General MacArthur's troops did not have adequate artillery. The decision had been made months before: the Allied emphasis would be on defeat of the European Axis. Until this was accomplished, the Pacific War had to move in low gear.

The Duropa Plantation attack began on December 18 just after 6:00 A.M. The American troops drew back from their positions up against the Japanese defense line and the air force came in to bomb and strafe. For ten minutes all the artillery also fired. The Australians then passed through the American troops and took the lead, tanks in the front.

Two companies of the 2nd Battalion of the Australian 9th Brigade moved up the coast, led by five tanks. Company C with two tanks moved against the Japanese bunkers on the eastern end of the new airstrip. The Americans came along behind in support of the attack. But the enemy bunkers in this area were still very strong and the attack bogged down. On the coast at Cape Endaiadere, however, it was quite a different story. The tanks and the Australian infantry surprised Colonel Yamamoto's troops in the plantation area. Here is how Colonel McNab, the executive officer of the Warren Force, described the action, "The tanks really did their job. They apparently completely demoralized the Japs who fought like cornered rats."

Yes, the tanks made all the difference. As tanks they really weren't much. In the ETO, the Americans were learning that their Honey tanks with the 37-mm guns were almost useless, the 37-mm guns being like popguns compared with the German 88. But in the jungle against an enemy who had no tanks and not much tank destroying artillery, they were something else. The Australians and the Americans had gone for weeks trying to blast holes in those bunkers. The 37-mm guns did it. Within an hour, the Australians had reached Cape Endaiadere. They did lose two tanks, one to a Molotov cocktail and the second when its engine failed as it moved along the edge of a burning enemy ammunition dump.

Once the Australians reached the cape, they did not hesitate. They hurried on to the second objective, Strip Point. Some five hundred yards west of Cape Endaiadere they ran into a set of bunkers no one had seen before: so well camouflaged were they that they had escaped air attack. Here, the attack bogged down for the day. There were a lot of

Japanese left in the coastal area. More Australian tanks came up and finally reduced one set of positions near the new airstrip. When this area was captured after a whole day of fighting, it was found that it had consisted of twenty pillboxes, several of them built of concrete and steel in the first days of the Japanese occupation.

The Australians that day had 160 casualties and had lost two of their seven tanks, but the effort was worth it. It was one of the swiftest and most complete investitures made during the campaign.

General Eichelberger had finally been convinced that his troops faced serious difficulty. MacArthur, coached by his chief of staff, General Sutherland, still did not seem to understand. He did not see why the troops needed tanks to beat other troops. Eichelberger wrote a memo describing the steel construction of the bunkers and their interlocking passages, "It would have been almost impossible for infantry, unassisted, to get across," he said.

December 19 was a quiet day. Two new 4.5-pound howitzers were brought in. More troops came in, Australian and American. So did cargo, aboard some of the new trawlers.

Then the action began again.

On December 20, most of Strip Point was cleared by the Australians. The terrain changed to marsh. Two of the M3 tanks got mired. Simemi Creek presented a problem that took two days to solve. Finally, the Japanese were cleared from the area.

The new airstrip was secure. Next came the fight for the old airstrip.

Colonel Yamamoto was ready here. The area was filled with bunkers and trenches that extended from the swamp to Simemi Creek. The Japanese had plenty of good weapons here: two 75-mm guns, two 37-mm guns, several 25-mm pompoms, plus half-a-dozen 3-inch naval guns. The Japanese had not given up by far; on the night of December 23, the Allies had a reminder. That evening two Japanese PT boats came into the Hariko area and sank a trawler and shot up the shore defenses. The Americans fired back, but the Japanese got away clean.

That same evening, two more trawlers came in with two more tanks and four hundred tons of supplies. Times had, indeed, changed.

On December 24, the tanks led the Australian attack on the old airstrip. The Allies had believed those 3-inch guns were knocked out because they had been silent for so long. But when the tanks came, the guns opened up and wrecked two of them in short order. A third tank turned over in a big shell hole and then was destroyed by the Japanese guns.

Once the tanks were gone, the Japanese guns raked the airstrip and for two days no one could go near it. Forward observers located one of those 3-inch guns and the Allied artillery destroyed it. But no one could find the other guns; until they were found, the Australian commander decided not to commit any more tanks to the battle. The M3s had very thin skins. They were no match for 3-inch armor-piercing shells.

On Christmas morning, the Allies attacked. Colonel Martin of the 128th Infantry decided to send men around through the swamp to outflank the Japanese. But it meant going through swamp that seemed impenetrable. Lt. George J. Hess of Company A took the job with fifteen men. They moved into the waist-deep swamp and struggled through. By afternoon, they had established themselves on dry ground in the Japanese rear on the left. The Japanese discovered them and began sending mortar fire into the area. But the men held. The next day, December 26, more troops joined Hess, and that day they found two of the Japanese 3-inch guns.

No wonder they had not been found earlier. Each gun was surrounded by a four-and-a-half-foot revetment so overgrown with grass that it was impossible to tell it from the surrounding kunai grass except at a range of twenty feet or less. Bunkers and flanking trenches connected these guns with other bunkers. It was like a series of rabbit warrens.

The Japanese air force now took a hand again. On the morning of December 26, fifty-four planes raided Buna, but this time they were intercepted by Allied aircraft and the Japanese lost fourteen planes. The Allies lost one P-38. These P-38s made a lot of difference. They could not maneuver with the Zeros, but they were superb on a hit-and-run basis. Coming in fast, they could make a pass and zoom away, come back, and make another pass. Their concentrated firepower was enormous. A new element had been added to the air war.

On December 27, the fight for the airstrips was almost over. Colonel Yamamoto now withdrew to the area around the plantation at Giropa Point. At noon on December 28, organized resistance in the airstrip area was finished. It was now just a question of mopping up. But this was not easy. The Japanese took refuge wherever they could and fought to the death. Allied troops would throw grenades into a foxhole and the Japanese would throw them back. Three Japanese were shot out of a single tree. Five or six Japanese would come charging out of a hut swinging swords and lunging with bayonets. One by one, two by two, they were cut down. Some tried to escape by going into the swamp. They, too, were picked off one by one.

The Japanese were still not finished. On the evening of December 28, they began counterattacking against the Allied line at the plantation. They attacked at dusk and again at 11:00 P.M. The first attack was dispersed, or so the Americans thought. But about twenty Japanese had hidden in the area; at 11 o'clock, they came out again as the troops were settled down for the night. They attacked the command post of Company C of the 128th Infantry, shouting "Medic, Medic" as they came. They bayoneted a number of American soldiers in their sleep. They attacked others, most of whom had set their weapons aside. By the time the Japanese were driven out of the perimeter, they had killed fifteen men and wounded twelve, including Lieutenant Foss, the company commander. He was the fifth company commander for Company C in five weeks. Now there would be a sixth.

As the reduction of the Buna Mission continued meanwhile in the last ten days of December 1942, Colonel Tomlinson's Urbana Force was ordered to attack Musita Island behind Buna Mission and the Triangle. This would prevent the Japanese in the Giruwa area from reinforcing the Japanese east of the river.

The fighting was very vigorous. At the Triangle, for example, the 126th Infantry lost 40 men killed and wounded of the 107 who had launched the attack. That was only the first day. For the moment that was the end of Companies E and G of the 126th Infantry. There were practically no men left who had begun the battle for Buna all those weeks before.

The 127th Infantry took over the fight for the Triangle, failed, and failed again to dislodge the Japanese. But it continued to try. It exhausted the troops and Colonel Tomlinson, who finally was so sick he had to ask General Eichelberger to be relieved of command of the Urbana Force. Command then went to Colonel Grose, the leader of the 127th Infantry.

When a half-dozen attempts to dislodge the Japanese from the Triangle failed, the Americans decided they could bypass it and come back later to clean up. The Americans decided to try a ploy. What they really wanted was the track junction—stoutly defended by the Japanese in the area—that was in the Triangle. General Eichelberger wrote General Sutherland:

> General Herring is very anxious for me to take the track junction and I am most willing, but the enemy is strong there and is able to reinforce the position at will. I am going to pour in artillery on him and I am going to continue tomorrow morning. Then I am going to find a weak spot across Government Gardens.

On December 21, General Eichelberger ordered Company E of the 127th Infantry to block the Triangle from the north and Company F of the 126th Infantry to block it from the south. Then came the ruse.

Earlier the Americans had established a pattern of attack. First came a barrage of artillery and mortar fire. Five minutes of artillery. Then salvos of smoke from the mortars. Under cover of the smoke, the troops would dash across the bridge into the Triangle. In the past, they had always been thrown back here with heavy losses. Today, it was to be different.

The artillery began. It stopped and the mortars began firing smoke shells. The troops fixed bayonets and sent up a cheer. For two minutes they cheered as ordered. The Japanese pulled out of their bunkers as usual and prepared to meet the bayonet attack. But this time the mortars switched over and poured everything into the track junction area; under cover of the smoke, the troops stood fast. The barrage continued. But in the end, nothing happened. The Japanese were not dislodged.

And now came one of the prime stupidities of this little war, the result of a failure in communications.

General Eichelberger had decided that the Triangle could best be taken by an approach across Entrance Creek in the area north of the Coconut Grove and the Triangle.

The problem was where?

The best line seemed to be in a fringe of woods of the northwest end of Government Gardens. There was cover here and the fire was reported to be light. On the night of December 22, Eichelberger ordered the attack to force a bridgehead the next day.

Colonel Grose chose Companies I and K of the 127th Infantry to make the attack. By moving troops around, he put Company K across the creek from the bridgehead area, ready to cross.

Company I was on the west bank of the creek almost at the mouth.

The hard crossing would be that of Company K. The tidal creek was fifty-yards wide and very swift from the rains. It was also eight-feet deep.

When Colonel Grose looked over the sector, he was not pleased. He figured that if Company K could move into Company I's sector temporarily, it could cross and work its way up from this shallow and narrow area of the stream to the point demanded. He telephoned General Eichelberger and asked for more time to move the troops around. He was certain, he said, that under the overhanging bank on the other side of the stream would be a shallow ledge that the men could use to go safely to their own position from the downstream crossing point in Company I's area.

Eichelberger either was not listening or did not hear properly. He refused the time.

Captain Alfred Meyer, the commander of Company K, was ordered to make his crossing.

At 4:00 P.M. Meyer sent some men down to the creek to see how it would go. They were nearly blown off the bank by the Japanese fire. There was no ford, no safe place to cross. Captain Meyer said it would be suicidal to try. He went back to Colonel Grose and asked to be allowed to use the small footbridge that the engineers had put across the stream in the Company I area. They would cross that night, using ropes, pontoons, and whatever was available and would then move to their assigned position on the other side before Company I needed to use the bridge.

Colonel Grose had already been chewed out by Eichelberger. He had to tell Meyer the answer was no. If necessary, the men would have to swim across the stream.

Captain Meyer went back to his company. That day, as the light waned, he made several attempts to get men across. All failed. The enemy fire from the other side was too hot and too heavy. Men were sent out to find what aids they could. By nightfall, they had found a heavy rope. Lt. Edward M. Green, Jr., picked up one end of the rope and with several enlisted men began to swim for the other shore. He was killed by enemy fire before he had gone twenty feet. His body was swept away by the current. A few minutes later, one of the enlisted men lost his hold on the rope and was swept downstream. But finally the men in the water got the rope across.

The rest of the night was spent bringing the troops in full fieldpack across the stream. By 2 o'clock in the morning, about fifty men were across. By daylight, the number was seventy-five. The cost had been fifty-four casualties: men drowned, men shot.

Early on the morning of December 22, Company I crossed the footbridge. Sure enough, there on the other side, just as Colonel Grose had surmised, was a shallow ledge that led beneath the bank up to the positions of Company K.

All day long the bodies of the men drowned and shot in Eichelberger's crossing bobbed up and down in the stream, moved back and forth by the tides, mute evidence of the error of high command.

"When we put Company K across an unfordable stream in the dark against heavy fire the other night we did something that would be a Leavenworth nightmare," wrote General Eichelberger to General Sutherland on Christmas Eve. And it still should be. It was an unnecessary nightmare, created by the insensitivity of a corps commander to the needs of his men.

On December 22, the engineers repaired the south bridge between the island and the mainland. That afternoon a patrol of Company L crossed over, but as they approached the north bridge, between the island and Buna Mission, they began to receive heavy Japanese fire.

By midmorning on December 23, the island had fallen. All the Japanese were gone. The next step was to use the island as a base from which to attack the Buna Mission.

On the night of December 23, the bridgehead at the northwest end of Government Gardens was secure. The Americans and Australians laid down a barrage of fire all night long on the mission. The Japanese responded with constant harassing fire on the bridgehead.

At dawn on Christmas Eve Day, Company C of the 127th Infantry crossed the creek. After a barrage, the troops started an attack on a four-hundred-yard front. The drive across the gardens to the sea had about half-a-mile to go. The gardens had once been a spot of beauty but now were neglected and overgrown with kunai grass. The Japanese had taken advantage of every bit of cover as far as a swamp about one-hundred-yards wide. On the other side of the swamp was a coconut plantation about thirty-yards wide, and through this ran the coastal track between Buna Mission and Giropa Point. Captain Yasuda had prepared this area well for defense. The track through the gardens was full of bunkers and the hiding places in the kunai grass were many. Foxholes and trenches spotted and striped the whole area. One survivor of this fight observed:

There was very little cover on the eastward side of Entrance Creek. This forced troops to be heavily bunched up during the staging period of an attack. The gardens themselves were very flat, covered by a substantial growth of kunai grass, and accordingly provided excellent cover for the Japanese as well as a good field of fire. The surrounding swamp areas were infested with snipers in trees.

The two companies moved up. Company I took an enormous amount of punishment and was disorganized. It was sent to the rear to reorganize. Company G, the reserve, came up and took on the Japanese. In an hour, it had cleared a three-bunker strong point. But that was about as far as Company G got that day. Beyond were more bunkers, more fighting. The debris of the advance had to be cleared away and every Japanese fought until the last.

On the left, Company L was to have made the main penetration into the mission that day. It failed. Colonel Grose ordered a platoon of Company A to cross over and hold there. But that bridgehead did not last long. The Japanese spotted the men, killed eight of the twenty and forced the others back across the rickety bridge.

One platoon of Company L got out ahead of the rest. It was led by Lt. Fred W. Matz and Lt. Charles A. Middendorf. The platoon was not missed, got through the gardens unnoticed because the Japanese line had thinned out as Captain Yasuda sent men northwest to stop that drive over the little footbridge. Though threading a maze, the platoon remained remarkably unhurt. This single platoon moved on and on. Soon it was through the garden and on the outskirts of the Coconut Plantation. There, the troops ran into two enemy bunkers that stopped them temporarily. Sgt. Kenneth Gruennart set out to knock out the first one. Covered by his men, he crawled forward and threw grenades through the slits, killing the men inside. He was wounded but refused to go back. He crawled forward against the second bunker and forced the enemy out of it. But now he was shot down by a sniper in a tree, and his Medal of Honor was posthumously awarded. This was what it took in the jungles of New Guinea, Medal-of-Honor performances, to go ahead against the Japanese this day.

By the time that Gruennart died, the platoon was far out in front of its company and completely out of touch. The American and Australian artillery were firing in this area, and they killed Lieutenant Middendorf and wounded Lieutenant Matz, who was not badly hurt, but with him was a man who could not make it out. Matz stayed with him. While the rest of the troops withdrew back to the American lines, these two remained behind the Japanese line. Matz stayed until the area was taken eight days later.

Colonel Grose learned of the lost platoon and sent another to help. That platoon broke through the enemy line, which closed behind it, and then was trapped. The second platoon broke back through to its own lines without encountering the first one. What was left of that unit, seven men, marched through a hip-deep swamp in a great circle to get around the enemy line, and they made it back safely two days later.

Colonel Grose was stymied. He asked General Eichelberger for time to reorganize, but Eichelberger was under enormous pressure from General MacArthur, who needed some semblance of victories to assuage his ego. Eichelberger refused the request. Seeing the Christmas Eve Day attack fail "had been the all-time low" of his life, said General Eichelberger.

The Americans were ordered to attack on Christmas Day. Colonel Grose had eight companies of the 127th in the front line.

On Christmas morning, the Americans put down a big barrage on the mission, but then attacked across the gardens without preparation. The ruse worked this time, and the men of Company F moved forward swiftly into the Coconut Plantation. There, the Japanese rallied and surrounded the company. It began to take heavy losses in a position 200 yards west of the track, 250 yards from the sea, and 600 yards from the mission.

A detachment of Company A broke through to help the men of Company F. But the weapons platoon, coming just behind, was totally destroyed by the enemy. As night fell, the Americans of Company F and Company A were well out in front of the other Americans and in danger of annihilation. On the right, Company G and Company I attacked and were stopped. Capt. James Workman, the commander of Company C, tried to help, that help failed and Workman was killed while charging an enemy bunker. The end of the day found the enemy still in position, the Americans with heavy casualties, and not much progress except the elements out front, which were in danger of imminent destruction.

The fighting went on thus for three more days. On the morning of December 28, Capt. Yasuda was losing men, too, and he realized that when the Americans broke through the line in the Coconut Plantation, the Triangle would fall. That day he evacuated the Triangle. The Americans came up cautiously that evening and found fourteen empty bunkers and no Japanese. On that day, General Eichelberger's military education was again furthered. He toured the battlefront and discovered just how strong those Japanese bunkers and inter-locking positions had been, "It is a mass of bunkers and entrenchments surrounded by a swamp. It is easy to see how they held us off for so long."

The troops had done the job, although at enormous cost. Now the Buna Mission lay open to assault.

CHAPTER SIXTEEN

The Fall of Buna—II

The Japanese were now virtually surrounded at Buna Mission and Giropa Point, but this did not mean the campaign was over by any means. They continued to fight with enormous tenacity and vitality in spite of constantly worsening conditions.

On December 28, the Australians brought in fresh troops and began an assault on the area between Giropa Point and the mouth of Simemi Creek. They had four tanks. In the attack, the tanks got out ahead of the infantry and reached the first line of bunkers. The Japanese evacuated in a hurry and went back to the second line, unhampered by any Allied infantry. But when the tanks moved up to the second line, the Japanese infantry moved back to the first-line bunkers and there were ready for the Australian infantrymen when they came up. By this time, the tanks had expended all their ammunition, and the badly coordinated attack had to be called off.

This gave the Japanese time to regroup that night and the next day, all the original positions were even stronger than they had been before.

It took the Australians two days to regroup for a new attack on the mission. But fresh troops and supplies were now coming in apace. In fact, a sort of milestone was reached on December 31. Two trawlers came into Oro Bay bringing more supplies. The new set of trawlers had now brought in 4,000 tons of cargo in three weeks—1,550 tons more of supply than the 32nd Division had received in all the time the division was in combat. The trawlers were now augmented by real freighters. The supply problem of the Allies in New Guinea was on the way to resolution.

At 8:00 A.M. on New Year's Day, the attack against the Japanese began again in the Giropa Point and the mission area. Six tanks made their way through the plantation toward the coast, followed by infantry. The tanks reached the coast at 8:30. By evening, they had cleared the beach as far as the mouth of Simemi Creek. The Australians lost two hundred men in the day's fighting, but they put an end to the Japanese on the Warren front.

The Australians had invented a new field weapon, prompted by the necessities of the time. It was a shock bomb. It consisted of a Mills bomb screwed into a two-pound can of ammonal explosive. A tank would come up and knock the corner off a bunker, leaving an entry hole. An infantryman would rush up with a shock bomb, heave it inside, and then duck. The bomb would explode creating an enormous shock wave inside. The shock would paralyze the Japanese. Then other infantrymen would come up and toss cans of aviation gasoline inside. The machine gunners would fire tracer bullets into them. Pouf, the bunker would begin to burn and would go up fast in flames.

Thus the Japanese positions in this point area were reduced. Now, all that remained was the Buna Mission itself.

The brass came up for a visit on December 28 and visited Colonel Grose's Urbana Force. In the party, were General Eichelberger, General Sutherland, and a passel of colonels. Colonel Grose gave them a situation briefing. He had just taken the 3rd Battalion of the 127th Infantry out of the line for a badly needed rest. Eichelberger's ears pricked up at this. Without discussing the matter, without seeing the troops, Eichelberger ordered the battalion split into two elements in order to launch an immediate attack on Buna Mission. The battle was going very well. The Warren Force of Australians, now having taken their territory, were free to come up and help with the Buna Mission. But General MacArthur wanted this to be an American show and so did Eichelberger. Once again, the troops in the line were to be sacrificed to the ambitions of the generals. The fresh troops of the Warren Force were ordered to hold back, and the tired troops of the Urbana Force were ordered to take the mission.

One part of the 3rd Battalion was to advance on their mission from the island by way of the north bridge. The other element would start on the southern side of the island and embark in five Australian assault boats and then cross over.

Colonel Grose was so surprised by General Eichelberger's orders that he did not even react for a few minutes. Eichelberger did not know, or did not care, about the difficulties. The troops were very tired, having been fighting steadily for ten days. More important, the Japanese had a line of bunkers just off the northern end of the bridge. And the bridge was not a complete bridge. Maybe nobody had told General Eichelberger that a misplaced Allied artillery shell had hit the bridge a couple of days after it was captured by the Allies and had torn a great chunk out of the northern end.

Immediately, Colonel Grose had to devise a plan to meet Eichelberger's demand. The attack would open with fifteen minutes of artillery and mortar fire on the mission and the bunkers. Forty men of Company K would round the island in the assault boats. As soon as the fire lifted, they would land and establish a bridgehead. They would be backed up by troops of Company H on the island and Company E on the tip of the village "finger" with support fire. That should make the bridge and let the engineers repair it. As soon as the bridge was repaired, the rest of Company K would dash across followed by Company I and Company L. When they were all across, they would make a concentrated attack north in connection with another attack from the southeast.

Captain Hewitt, the S2 for the Urbana Force, went on reconnaissance and instructed the troops who would move around the island as to where they were to go.

Six volunteers came up to lay the timbers that would span the gap on the bridge, if it could be done. They moved into position in some brush on the south side of the island. The rest of the 3rd Battalion began to move forward to the bridge area. The men had been told they were to have a rest and there was a lot of griping. They moved slowly and did not get into place until the artillery barrage had actually begun. It was 5:20 P.M. The boats pushed off from their hiding place. But Captain Hewitt had misdirected the men. They were to land on the east side of Entrance Creek, but they landed instead on the mission "finger." The American troops there thought they were Japanese and fired on them. The Japanese knew they were American and fired on them. All the boats were sunk in the shallows, and the men were stuck.

On the bridge, the six volunteers moved forward. They put the timbers in place, although they were under heavy fire, and all but one man escaped to safety. Company K started to cross. Two men reached the northern end, then the newly laid planks fell into the stream because the pilings at the north end collapsed.

Thus, the attack also collapsed, proving once again that general officers who meddle in company tactics usually end up messing up a war. Fortunately for the men, General Eichelberger and his party retreated to their own headquarters and left the fighting to Colonel Grose.

On the morning of December 29, the 2nd Battalion of the 126th Infantry, now rested, came back into the line. They moved into the southeast end of Government Gardens. The 2nd Battalion of the 128th Infantry moved into the Triangle. Part of the 1st Battalion of the 127th Infantry moved to the sea and established a two-hundred-foot shoreline.

On December 31, the attack toward the Buna Mission was resumed. At 4:30 A.M., part of the 127th Infantry moved across toward the mission. The plan was to launch a surprise attack on the enemy positions opposite the bridge. The time would be daybreak. The men were ordered to keep quiet and not to fire their weapons until ordered. Just as the leading elements reached the spit of land on the mission side, someone in the rear threw a grenade into a landing barge on the beach. The whole area erupted. The Japanese shot up flares to light the beach, and the Americans were hit with grenades, rifle grenades, and fire from automatic weapons. The Japanese reaction was so strong that it put the American troops into a panic. Lieutenant Bragg, who was leading, was shot in the legs. Another lieutenant took over, but instead of running to the front, he turned around and ran to the rear. The men followed him.

Colonel Grose walked up to the trail, pulled out his pistol, and waited.

Soon the erring lieutenant and the following company of men came running up to him. He pointed his pistol at them and ordered them to stop. His own account of the incident states:

I told the lieutenant to return and he said he couldn't. I then asked him if he knew what that meant, and he said he did. The First Sergeant was wounded and I therefore let him proceed to the dressing station. I designated a sergeant nearby to take the men back and he did so. I then sent the lieutenant to the rear under arrest and under guard.

Soon Captain Cronk of Company F of the 128th took command of the disorganized Company E and put it back together. There was nothing wrong with the troops. Once again it had been a failure of leadership. After that, the company responded well and fought hard, although they did not get far that day. But the holdup was not through fear, but through staunch Japanese resistance.

In the annals of the Pacific War, Guadalcanal and the Solomon campaigns are given billing far above the New Guinea hostilities, but the fact is that nowhere in the Pacific was the fighting more fierce or the Japanese resistance more effective than at Buna. Captain Yasuda and Colonel Yamamoto were putting up a remarkable defense, contesting every foot of the land in the Buna area.

But now the end was in sight, Captain Cronk's old Company F was putting up a steady fire on one side; other American troops were on the other side. The Japanese in the Buna Mission now faced total destruction. They were being resupplied with food and ammunition by submarine, but there was no way out for them. General Eichelberger was about to give General MacArthur the plum for which he had paid so heavily in the lives of his subordinates. In December, the end was very near.

General Eichelberger wrote to his deputy chief of staff:

On the right, the Australians with their tanks have moved up to the mouth of the Simemi Creek and the entire area of the two strips is in our hands. The forces of the Urbana and Warren fronts are now only about six hundred yards apart. On the left, we have established a corridor between Giropa Point and Buna Mission and have moved enough men in there to make it hold. The famous Triangle which held us up for so long was finally taken, and our men also occupy the island south of Buna Village. Today we are moving on Buna Mission from both directions, and I sincerely hope we will be able to knock it off.

The crisis was apparent at Rabaul. General Adachi, commander of the 18th Area Army, ordered General Yamagata to move all his troops from the area north of Gona to Giruwa. He was to use them to rescue the Buna Mission garrison. If he failed, he was to move the troops to the defense of Giruwa and hold there until the last man died. Colonel Yazawa was ordered to take a special force to Buna Mission by way of the beach and attack the American left flank. He was to cut his way through to the troops in the mission, rescue them, and bring them back to Giruwa.

In the annals of the Pacific War, it sometimes seems that the Japanese commanders were so heartless as to recklessly sacrifice men who could have been saved. But this was not true. Only when a situation was totally hopeless were the men told that they must die for the emperor. If there was a ghost of a chance of getting a beleaguered garrison out, the Japanese admirals and generals took that chance. Indeed, in the New Guinea campaign, the Japanese navy put more ships at risk under more difficult conditions than the Americans ever did.

The Yamagata plan was perfectly sound. The American line on that beach flank was very slim and the Japanese had a good chance of breaking through there. Colonel Yazawa was the most competent and experienced line officer around. He had taken his troops up into the Owen Stanley Mountains, across the track, and back again.

But the move came too late, even though General Eichelberger did not get his victory that day.

On New Year's Day, the Americans launched their big assault. It began with a heavy barrage from the augmented supply of mortars brought in by the steamers.

Company B attacked east toward Giropa Point. The rest of the Urbana Force struck at the line around the Buna Mission. Captain Cronk attacked from the spit. Major Schroeder moved in from Entrance Creek. In the swamp, Company C moved forward. The rest of the companies, filling in the gaps and coming close from the rear, made progress. The Japanese could see the end approaching. That night some of them swam away from the mission, trying to escape through the enemy siege and make their way to Giruwa.

On the morning of January 2 just before dawn, a platoon of about twenty Japanese soldiers, with full packs, was led out of the mission by an officer. They were headed for the landing barges on the mission spit. The Americans saw them coming and turned on their .50-caliber machine guns. To a man, the Japanese were slaughtered. As day dawned, observers on the beach saw scores of Japanese in the water: swimming, clinging to rafts, trying to escape in small boats. Artillery, mortar, and machine-gun fire was turned on them, and from the air came attacks by B-25 bombers, P-39 fighters, and Wirraways.

In the mission, Captain Yasuda and Colonel Yamamoto came from the two ends to the center for a meeting. The end was very near. The two men greeted each other, and then parted again to commit ceremonial *seppuku*, with apologies to the emperor for failing to defend the sacred territory on which Japanese soldiers had trod.

It seemed that all the Japanese were gone. It seemed that way until the Allies tried to advance into the mission grounds. Then all hell broke loose. Major Schroeder, commander of the 1st Battalion of the 127th Infantry, was killed by a bullet. The battalion was taken over by Capt. Donal F. Runnoe. At 10:15 A.M., the troops started to advance after a brief but heavy artillery and mortar barrage. The attack went very well. Phosphorous shells set grass and trees aflame and exposed a whole line of enemy bunkers. Artillery was focused on them; when the Japanese began to emerge, they were met by machine-gun fire. But every bunker and every hole was likely to contain at least one Japanese soldier; each one had to be checked very carefully. The troops continued to advance toward one another, with the Japanese trapped in between. By 4:30 in the afternoon, the mission was overrun by the Allies. The remaining enemy soldiers were either flushed out and killed or buried inside the bunkers by explosives. By 5 o'clock, the fighting was over except for one pocket of Japanese down by the beach. They would hold out until the next day. It had taken the Allies six weeks, but they finally had captured Buna.

For several days, isolated pockets of Japanese claimed the

attention of the cleanup troops. That little thicket in the beach area was the last to fall. About twenty Japanese were holding out. They were finally routed from their bunkers and scurried down behind a wrecked barge on the beach. Finally, someone threw a satchel charge into the barge and blew it up along with the Japanese.

The only Japanese left in the area now were groups of two and three, half-starved and with nowhere to go, who prowled around inside the Allied lines, mostly looking for something to eat. For days, these stragglers would harry the lines, and sometimes a man would be shot. They slowly disappeared, one by one dealt with by the Allies or by nature.

One hundred ninety Japanese were buried at Buna Mission, thirty at Giropa Point. Fifty prisoners were taken, most of them terribly emaciated.

There was very little booty except for some hand weapons and flags. The Japanese had virtually no food left, so none was abandoned. They were virtually out of ammunition, so no ammunition was left behind. A handful of weapons were discovered, most of them broken. Several smashed aircraft were found at the airfield, including two Zero fighters, which created quite a stir, as most of the troops had never seen the famous planes unless they were being shot at by them.

One knew the battle was over and won because the generals began congratulating one another. General Marshall congratulated General MacArthur. MacArthur could not refrain from exhibiting his paraoia: "However unwarranted," he said, "the impression prevailed that this area's efforts were belittled and disparaged at home, and despite all my efforts to the contrary the effect was depressing."

Indeed, MacArthur had taken pains to have his efforts lauded at home. His promotional machine had been going full blast for months, so steadily and so heavily that Admiral Nimitz at Pearl Harbor was under pressure from Secretary of the Navy Frank Knox to mount a similar sales campaign. But Nimitz refused. He had nothing but contempt for the MacArthur press agentry.

MacArthur congratulated General Blamey, who congratulated General Eichelberger, who congratulated General Herring, who congratulated Brigadier General Wootten, who congratulated the colonels down the line.

Unfortunately, the congratulations stopped at the regimental level. The GIs whose necks were on the line all during those six weeks did not get any of them. One positive factor did emerge. General MacArthur stopped calling the men in the line cowards; apparently, he wanted to forget his fury when they had "humiliated" him personally by panicking in the first encounters.

The casualties of the campaign showed how difficult it had been. The Allies buried twenty-eight hundred Japanese. That represented almost all of the Japanese casualties; the Japanese themselves had not had time to dispose of their casualties. The Allied casualties were also about the same, but two thousand of these were wounded, not dead.

CHAPTER SEVENTEEN

End of the Papua Battle

Gona and Buna, the two major Japanese bases on the Papua Peninsula, had fallen to the Allies. But on January 3, General Herring reminded General Eichelberger that the job on the Buna coast was far from over. The Sanananda area was still alive with Japanese troops. For weeks, the Americans and the Australians had besieged the Japanese there, but without any real success. Sanananda and the Giruwa area, which the Japanese had fortified so long ago, were still going to be very difficult nuts to crack.

With the victories at Gona and Buna, the Allies had freed up the fighting troops used there, and the 127th Infantry and the Australian 18th Brigade with its tanks were now available to move to the Sanananda front.

The Allies had established roadblocks at Huggins and Kano, but the Japanese were still holding out in the area all around these spots. There were three fronts. One was south of the track junction. The second was in the roadblock area at Huggins. The third was in the Napapo–Amboga River area north of Gona.

Brigadier General Porter of the 30th Australian Brigade had two Australian battalions and what was left of the U.S. 126th Infantry, which had been decimated in the Buna fighting. It consisted of about two hundred men.

Fresh troops were coming. They would be the 14th Australian Brigade and the 163rd U.S. Regimental Combat Team. This consisted of the 163rd Infantry and five hundred attached troops. There was no artillery.

General MacArthur had stuck his foot in it again. On December 27, when the 163rd Infantry arrived at Port Moresby, he ordered it up to the Buna front without consulting anyone. General Blamey protested. There were plenty of troops on the Buna front, he said. The tired Australians of the 21st Brigade had to be relieved. They were in no shape to fight again. MacArthur, in the cocoon of his headquarters, did not know this and no one on his staff had bothered to find out. What annoyed Blamey, and he said it, was that MacArthur should choose to interfere without knowing anything about the consequence of his interference.

General MacArthur retrieved his blunder: the 163rd was sent to General Herring for use on the Sanananda front.

By January 1943, the Americans of the 163rd Infantry were highly trained and competent soldiers, something that could scarcely be said of the 32nd Division troops who had been thrown into the battle the previous year without any jungle training or any jungle equipment.

Headquarters and the 1st Battalion were flown into eastern New Guinea. Colonel Doe then took command of the Sanananda area's Huggins front. The movement began on January 2. For the next few days, field pieces and tanks moved up to the Sanananda front from the Buna area. On January 4, a high-level meeting was held between American and Australian commanders. When they sat down, they discovered they really knew no more about the disposition of the enemy troops on this part of Australian New Guinea than they had known about Buna and Gona. They did not, in fact, know whether there were a thousand or five thousand Japanese in the area, nor what weapons they had.

What they planned, however, was an envelopment of the Japanese, using the 18th Brigade, the 127th Infantry, and the 163rd Infantry. The first attack would be made on Tarakena by the 127th Infantry.

What a country! They had to fight Mother Nature as much as the Japanese. On January 5, headquarters of the 18th Brigade moved into Soputa with four tanks. But movement was abruptly halted. The reason: torrential rains washed out the roads. So, the rest of the tanks and the artillery had to remain on the eastern side of the river. General Vasey had expected to have all those tanks and all those guns from the Buna front, but he was not going to get them as his attack started.

The roads were so bad that not even four-wheel-drive vehicles could get through. That meant the supply line was closed off at least temporarily. The engineers had claimed that the airstrips at Dobodura and Popondetta were all weather ones. That was right, but the weather was Papua weather. The airstrips were completely mired in.

But so much had times changed that this problem was not insurmountable. Enough supply had been stockpiled in recent weeks—because of the arrival of the new batch of trawlers and the freighters—that the troops could get along.

On January 7, the fresh Australian troops of the 18th Brigade reached Soputa and were ready for action. On January 9, the 126th U.S. Infantry was relieved. The regiment had been decimated in recent weeks. These were the "cowards" who worried General MacArthur. Here is what Brigadier Porter, who had commanded their efforts in battle, had to say about them—and the men of the 127th and 128th Infantry regiments of the 32nd Division:

> By now it is realized that greater difficulties presented themselves here than were foreseen and the men of your division probably bore most of them. Your men are worthy comrades and stout hearts. I trust that they will have the opportunity to rebuild their depleted ranks in the very near future. With their present fund of experience they will rebuild into a formidable force.

The 126th had gone into action as a unit of 1,400 men. Only 65 men of regimental headquarters had transferred to Buna in December and no other transfers out had been made. On January 9, the 126th numbered 165 "cowards," most of them so sick they could hardly move. Three days later, they were down to 158 men and these marched to Buna, where they were received by a wet-eyed General Eichelberger, a man who perhaps, at last, had learned something about fighting the Japanese.

But if units were to be chewed to pieces in the Japanese meatgrinder, nonetheless the war had to go on. The Allied plan was to persuade the Japanese that the main attack would come against Tarakena and across Konombi Creek. Actually, the main drive was to be against Sanananda. The Japanese had pushed the Allied troops near Tarakena out of position and Colonel Grose had to order an attack to reestablish a beachhead on the far side of Siwori Creek. This was done by Company G of the 127th Infantry on January 5. In two days of stubborn fighting, the Japanese gave ground only bits at a time, but the Americans pressed forward until they captured Tarakena Village. But these attacks were costly. The 127th Infantry was losing men fast. The three companies that had attacked at Tarakena were in bad shape. Company F consisted of seventy-two men, Company A eighty-one, Company C eighty-nine.

The next step was to cross Konombi Creek, a body of water that denied the name *creek:* it was forty-feet across. Swimmers were sent out to fix guy wires, needed to keep the assault boats that would be used from drifting out to sea in the tide. This was a difficult process because the Japanese on the other side kept up a steady stream of fire on the crossing men. But by the evening of January 10, Company C and Company A were across the creek and fanned out along the shore. The men sought trails into the jungle but found none. Their position on the sandy beach was under water at high tide. They had to move forward into the edge of the tidal swamp then, and that was no place from which to launch an attack. So, their attack was delayed.

The coastal advance would have to wait until the 163rd Infantry and the 118th Brigade attacked Sanananda.

The Americans were learning every day. A new position was established on the old Huggins roadblock. It was now called Musket. It consisted of an inner and outer perimeter, with rifle and automatic weapons squads spotted around each perimeter. The war in New Guinea was becoming downright civilized, they even had field kitchens and hot food now. Within the inner perimeter were located the regimental and battalion headquarters, with switchboards, aid stations, and various dumps. Company headquarters were also located here, and the area was crisscrossed by trenches.

The Japanese were never far away, however—they were closest in the tall trees that surrounded the camp. Their snipers were active all day long, particularly at chow time. So Colonel Grose launched a campaign against snipers. Around the edges of the perimeter, he established observation posts. Their job was to find the enemy snipers in their trees. Then his teams would work on them. Americans would go into their own trees and from there fire on the Japanese snipers. Below them, American patrols of three men, covered by their tree-sniper buddies, would move up on suspicious-looking enemy trees and pick off the Japanese snipers from the ground. The Japanese were extremely hard to find. Their smokeless and flashless weapons helped them a great deal in maintaining security. But they had to come down sometime, usually at night. The Americans set booby traps. These consisted of two grenades tied to adjoining trees with their firing pins connected by a cord. If a Japanese soldier tripped the wire, he got two grenades. That was usually enough.

Old Huggins—new Musket—was becoming extremely refined. It had a water purification outfit. Dumps appeared all over. Orders were given about sticking to the slit trenches at night and no movement was permitted in the camp. In other words, the chicken shit had begun.

The 1st Battalion was waiting for the rest of the 163rd Infantry to come up. While they waited, they probed the Japanese line and discovered two strong areas between Musket and Kano about two hundred yards to the north. These could not be seen at all except close up. Something would have to be done about them in a hurry.

On January 8, Company B and Company C were to attack Kano. They did, covered by artillery fire. But the artillery was in trouble: it had only delayed-fuse shells, and these nosed into the muck and either never exploded or simply sent up mud geysers that did not do anyone any harm. So, the attacks failed.

There were more attacks up and down the line. More American troops came in. On January 12, Americans and Australians attacked in a combined operation against the road junction at Sanananda. The attack included tanks and field pieces, something the Allies now had in some strength; something the Japanese did not have. Or so the Allies thought. But Colonel Tsukamoto, who was in charge of this section, had been hoarding antitank shells and had mined the roads. As the first tank came up the road, its hull was pierced by a

3-inch antitank shell that destroyed its radio. The troop commander in that tank managed to get the tank off the road, but without a radio, he could not warn the following tanks. There were two of them, and within half-an-hour, all three had been knocked out of the battle by antitank gunfire and land mines.

The Japanese fought fiercely. That day the 189th Brigade lost 142 men. The Japanese maintained their line.

What to do?

General Eichelberger came up to see. He now had a much better idea of the realities of jungle fighting than he had nursed even two weeks earlier. He saw that frontal attacks were going to be enormously costly and decided to begin a siege. The Allies would surround the area and would cut off all supply and starve the Japanese out.

Once again, General Eichelberger had misread the situation. The Japanese had seen the handwriting on the wall. Surrounded, with the Allies having more tanks to throw into the battle and more fresh troops—who completely outnumbered their own—the Japanese had already decided to evacuate the Sanananda position.

Back at Rabaul, the eastern New Guinea fight was now regarded as a disaster—and with good reason. On the beach at Giruwa, General Yamagata had five thousand men. Most of them were half-starved. Supply was becoming more difficult every day, although they were using submarines for that purpose. In the first week in January, the supply of rice gave out completely. There was no food for the troops. The hospital wards were under water and the doctors had no medicines. The troops who were still in fighting trim were short of ammunition and some of them did not have weapons.

"We are now in the final stages," said General Yamagata. Imperial General Headquarters (IGH) agreed. Col. Masanobu Tsuji, one of the rising young stars of the Japanese Army* had just returned to Tokyo to tell IGH that the Buna campaign had been a tremendous blunder and should be abandoned. A whole new Japanese policy for the South Pacific area was ordained. Guadalcanal would be evacuated. On

---

*Col. Tsuji's report on the fall of Bataan and Corregidor and the "soft treatment" of the enemy by General Homma had brought about Homma's forced early retirement from the service.

New Guinea, the Japanese would retreat to Lae and Salamaua and start their offensive operations over from that point.

The initial orders were issued on January 4; thereafter, Admiral Yamamoto supervised one of the most brilliant troop withdrawal campaigns in the history of modern warfare. Seventeen thousand Japanese soldiers were taken off Guadalcanal without the Americans even being aware that they were going, until they were all gone. Meanwhile, the headquarters of the army and the navy air forces at Rabaul were doing everything they could to rescue a lost situation. The 11th Air Fleet was throwing as much power as it could into the battle for the skies, pilots flying mission after mission until they were exhausted. This was particularly true of the fighter pilots. The air battle for Guadalcanal had already turned around and the Japanese were now the underdogs. It took them five or six hours to get to the Guadalcanal operational area; when there, they had a very short time to operate if they hoped to get home and land. As the Americans and Australians brought in more air power, the Japanese were at a distinct disadvantage, and the American P-38 and late-type F4F fighter planes were a much better match for the Zeros than the P-40s and other fighters had been.

On January 5, the Japanese 102nd Infantry Regiment, reinforced, left Rabaul for Lae and arrived safely on January 7.

On the Buna coast, the Japanese were in desperate straits, and General Oda so indicated in a message to Rabaul on January 12 in which he urged reinforcement of his position:

> Most of the men are stricken with dysentery. Those not in bed with illness are without food and too weak for hand-to-hand fighting. Starvation is taking many lives and is weakening our already extended lines. We are doomed. In several days we are bound to meet the same fate that overtook the Basabua and Buna garrisons.

When that message reached General Adachi, commander of the 18th Area Army, he immediately ordered Yamagata to evacuate Sanananda and Giruwa. The troops would assemble at the mouths of the Kumusi and Mambare rivers and from there would march to Lae and Salamaua. But not all of them could march. These would be taken by motor launch to the Japanese bases. The troops who could march would be expected to make their way overland by slipping through the Allied lines to Lae. The launches would work under the cover of night, safe from the Allied air forces. The evacuation would begin on January 25 when the moon was down and would continue until January 29.

It was a desperate plan and not a very practical one. How were the Japanese to hold Sanananda and Giruwa if all the troops were to be evacuated. Somewhere, sometime, the Allies would learn of the movement and would descend on these places like the wolves of Albion.

That is precisely what happened.

Even as General Eichelberger lamented the inability of the Allies to defeat the Japanese in their bunkers, starvation was doing the job for him. After the failure of the attack of January 12, the Allied troops mounted a series of patrols to try to establish the true strength of the Japanese in the area. Two days later, a patrol of the 163rd Infantry came upon a sick Japanese soldier lying in some bushes south of the Musket position. He was taken back to camp for interrogation, and he said that the Japanese in the area were moving out. All the able-bodied soldiers, he said, had been told to move through the Allied lines and make their escape. He had followed these orders, but had collapsed on the trail.

General Vasey gave orders for an immediate offensive. So, the 118th Brigade and the 163rd Infantry started new attacks against all sides of the enemy perimeter. For the most part, they found the enemy positions evacuated. They did find about a hundred sick and wounded soldiers who tried without much success to fight, and these were killed. They captured a few arms and some ammunition but not much because the majority of the enemy had escaped and left behind the unfit to die. By default then, the Allies had won the victory of the Battle of Sanananda. What was left was scarcely more than mopping up.

On January 14 and 15, the Allies launched several probing attacks into the Japanese line in the Cape Killerton and Wye Point areas. The Japanese here were holding so that those in the area could escape through the line. On January 16, just a few Japanese defenders were left in the Killerton Village area.

Past Wye Point the Japanese were also holding so that their fellows could escape. By January 17, most of the Japanese around Sanananda Village had left and all that separated the Australians from the place was a wicked stretch of swamp.

The Allies also advanced on Giruwa Village, which had been the headquarters of Japanese resistance. The Japanese there were still full of fight, but there were very few left in this rear guard. The fighting was hard, but the Allies advanced almost steadily against a diminishing number of enemy troops. The Japanese were trying now only to slow down the Allied advance to give their fellows as much time as possible at the assembly points to get away. By January 19, the Japanese in the Sanananda area were reduced to possession of three pockets, entirely surrounded by the Allies, who had new supplies of 81-mm mortars and .50-caliber machine guns.

General Yamagata saw that his troops could not wait until January 25 if they were to escape the encircling and now-superior enemy forces. Thus, he ordered the withdrawal to begin on January 20. They would assemble at Bakumbari seven miles south of Gona; there, they would be taken by boat to the Japanese lines around Lae. General Yamagata left on January 19 with his staff. They went off in two launches and made it to safety.

General Oda and Colonel Yazawa were holding the last lines of resistance. Their orders told them to start moving out. That night of January 19, they did begin moving and tried to escape through the swamp. Both Oda and Yazawa ran into Australian outposts. Oda, at least, seeing the inevitability ahead, committed suicide with his pistol.

The Japanese were dispersed. They had put eighteen thousand men ashore on the Buna coast in the months since spring, and they had lost more than eight thousand men.

And so, organized Japanese resistance in the Sanananda area and in Giruwa came to an end. For several days isolated pockets and individual Japanese soldiers were hunted down and for the most part killed—some because they would not surrender, some because the Allied troops did not ask them to surrender. Some prisoners were taken, including sixty-nine at the Giruwa hospital. Many of these were unconscious and the others were too weak to resist. On January 21, 1943, the main Japanese center of resistance, the headquarters at Giruwa, was captured. There were virtually no Japanese left there. Only a handful of Japanese troops were left at the beachhead, the point at which they were once supposed to assemble for their evacuation. About five hundred Japanese troops were assembled here, and they were surrounded with no way out. On January 21, 1943, the Japanese finally lost Buna. It had been their most disastrous campaign, worse even than Gaudalcanal. In the long campaign on the Buna coast, the Allies had lost eighty-five hundred troops.

Many of those men need not have been lost had not the ego of General MacArthur been so great, his ignorance of local conditions so abysmal, his misunderstanding of the Australians so complete. The battle of the Buna coast would go down in American military history as a great victory. However, the fact is that the Allies had not won the battle, the Japanese had lost it. A fact well known in Tokyo where the entire enterprise was finally regarded as the greatest blunder of the war.

CHAPTER EIGHTEEN

Against Rabaul

As the campaign for the Papua Peninsula on the eastern New Guinea coast came to an end, the Allies thought they had won a great victory. To the contrary, the Japanese had suffered a great loss, and the major reason for it was not the efforts of General MacArthur, who took the credit for the victory, nor even the valiant efforts of the Australian and American troops who fought the battles. The real cause of the Japanese defeat was the Allied victory at Guadalcanal, which had prevented Admiral Yamamoto and Generals Imamura and Adachi from reinforcing the Japanese troops on the Buna coast.

General MacArthur, in fact, knew very little of what had occurred in New Guinea. His staff work was really incompetent. His intelligence was inept. He had insulted the American and Australian troops who fought under his command, and he had shown absolutely no understanding of the conditions under which they fought or the enemy they faced.

The Japanese troops who occupied Buna, Gona, and Sanananda were among the best in the Japanese army. The Australians, for the most part, were half-trained militia, the equivalent of the American National Guard, and by any normal standards, the men of the American 32nd Infantry Division went into battle with virtually no training at all. They knew nothing about jungle warfare. They knew nothing of the Japanese enemy. Their equipment was better suited to war in North Africa, where they had expected to go, than war in the Southwest Pacific. Even their camouflage uniforms were so ineptly made that they caused itch, infection, and rot.

The unsung hero of the war in the Southwest Pacific at this point was Lt. Gen. E. F. Herring, the Australian commander of the New Guinea force, under whom the Americans actually fought. He showed more consideration and understanding of the American troops by far than the MacArthur headquarters ever did or than General Eichelberger, the American senior troop commander, for that matter. And as MacArthur's strategic decisions were inept, so were Eichelberger's tactical decisions. He was constantly interfering and ordering attacks, and almost every attack he ordered failed. When he interfered in operations up front, men died, but very little was gained.

No, the Japanese in the Buna coast area were not so much defeated by the Allies as by nature and the inability of their rear echelons to supply them. When Colonel Tsuji returned to Tokyo after his survey of the operations on Guadalcanal and in New Guinea, he reported that the Guadalcanal campaign was lost through the superior performance of the Americans but that the New Guinea campaign was a dreadful bollix from the beginning and should never have been launched after the failure of Operation MO against Port Moresby from the sea.

Imperial General Headquarters (IGH) listened to this colonel. He was the man who had gotten General Homma cashiered in the Philippines for being "too soft" on the enemy.

The casualties of the New Guinea campaign told the story. Both Japanese and Allied sides suffered casualties of about eighty-five hundred men. The difference was that so many more Japanese died either of their wounds or of sickness because medicines ran out. But this was not a triumph for the Allies; it was a failure of the Japanese high command. That failure also existed in the Guadalcanal campaign but in a different way. There, the Japanese army totally underestimated the strength and fighting ability of the U.S. Marines, and the Japanese intelligence estimates as to the American order of battle were completely wrong. They started out by sending a reinforced battalion to fight a whole reinforced American marine division. When that unit was wiped out in short order, they might have sent a division, but they sent another reinforced battalion, and it was not until that one got into trouble that they realized a division was needed. Ultimately, they put two divisions into Guadalcanal, and nearly half the men died of starvation and disease. The Japanese navy tried valiantly to resupply the troops on Guadalcanal and sacrificed a dozen ships to that end. The American navy and the Allied air force prevented that resupply, leaving the Japanese with no margin for aiding the Japanese forces on New Guinea. The Battle of the Bismarck Sea, in which the Allied air forces destroyed a well-protected Japanese convoy, marked the end of the efforts to resupply Buna from the sea.

The Battle of Guadalcanal was fought by the Americans and Australians, largely on the sea and in the air. Ultimately, after suffering frightful losses, the Americans and Australians triumphed. They defeated the Japanese. In the end, the Japanese launched one of the most spectacular rescues of World War II: the bringing out of some 11,000 survivors of the Guadalcanal campaign by destroyer transport under the noses of the Americans, who never learned of the feat until it was finished.

Not so on New Guinea.

Most of the Japanese on the Papua Peninsula escaped to fight again at Lae and Salamaua, but they did so in small groups, many of them making their way through the jungles. There was no massive rescue as there had been at Guadalcanal.

Lae and Salamaua. Those places would be the next area of reduction.

General MacArthur had big plans. He still dreamed of his triumphal return to the Philippines, and it was to him the most important aspect of the war. The Japanese had touched him in his most sensitive spot: his ego. He, MacArthur, had been humiliated and all the resources of the United States must be made available to rectify his situation and punish the Japanese.

Fortunately for the Allied war effort, the Joint Chiefs of Staff had other matters on their minds and did not seem to recognize the enormous importance of MacArthur's ego.

They had laid out two more tasks for the Allies in the South and Southwest Pacific, given the limited resources they could then devote to the Pacific arena. The first of these was the capture of the northern Solomons and the capture of the rest of New Guinea. The second was the reduction of Rabaul, the major Japanese base in the area. Until Rabaul was cut down, the danger to Australia would always remain.

By February 1943, the plans were laid. Since all the fighting in this area was within the region designated as the Southwest Pacific Command, and thus under MacArthur's suzerainty, the general would be in charge at the highest level. But Admiral Halsey, the commander of the forces in the South Pacific was going to do it his own way. The confrontation between commands was avoided by the Joint Chiefs of Staff, who announced that the South Pacific forces would be commanded by Halsey, the Southwest Pacific forces by MacArthur. Each commander would go his own way except that all was "under the general directives" of General MacArthur. This was a sop to MacArthur's ego, and that was well understood at Pearl Harbor. Those lines were broad enough that even the navy, which had very little use for General MacArthur, found that it could live with the situation. Admiral Halsey paid a call on MacArthur and said all the right things, then went back to run his own show from Nouméa.

On March 28, 1943, the Southwest Pacific Command was ordered to seek new objectives for 1943. Airfields were to be established on Woodlark and Kiriwina islands. The Lae–Salamaua–Finschhafen area of New Guinea was to be taken, and western New Britain Island was to be seized. Admiral Halsey would take the Solomons.

With the increase in supply and personnel from the United States, MacArthur now pushed the Australians out of the forefront of the Southwest Pacific operations. MacArthur's headquarters was an American army headquarters. It had Australian officers and American navy officers, but they served in junior position. General Blamey, the Australian, was still theoretically in command of the land forces. But MacArthur and his staff pulled what the Australians always considered a fast one by establishing a new land forces' headquarters called Alamo Force. This was headed by General Krueger, who was also commander of the U.S. 6th Army. As commander of the 6th Army, Krueger was under control of General Blamey, but as commander of Alamo Force he was not. Therefore, MacArthur had direct control of Krueger and his army and the Australians were pushed into a backseat.

American Vice Admiral Carpender was in command of the naval forces, now called the U.S. 7th Fleet, or MacArthur's navy. And Rear Adm. Daniel Barbey was in command of the VII Amphibious Force, which was to be MacArthur's striking force. The only problem with MacArthur's navy was that it did not have any ships except a handful of submarines and the Australian naval forces. MacArthur demanded carriers, battleships, and cruisers, but Admiral Nimitz said the Pacific Fleet had nothing to spare. Ships would be lent to MacArthur for specific naval operations, after which they had to be returned to Nimitz's command.

The air power was under the command of Lt. General Kenney. It included the U.S. 5th Air Force and the Royal Australian Air Force (RAAF).

On April 26, General MacArthur put out his ELKTON plan. This envisaged the movement against the Japanese in New Guinea with the objective being the reduction or capture of Rabaul. The plan called for thirteen different invasions in the next eight months.

The first act by the Southwest Pacific Command would be the capture of Woodlark and Kiriwina islands, which would be used for air bases. Neither was held by the Japanese. Kiriwina is 270 miles from Rabaul and 30 miles from Bougainville. The new air bases could make it very tough for the Japanese.

As for the Japanese, their commands were basically unchanged. General Imamura was in charge of all army forces in the Solomons, New Guinea, and the Bismarck Archipelago. Vice Adm. Junichi Kusaka, as commander of the Southeast Area Fleet, was now in command of all naval forces. He was responsible directly to Admiral Yamamoto, the chief of the Combined Fleet, who by this time had moved his headquarters down from the Kagoshima naval base in Japan to Truk.

In the winter of 1943, IGH looked over its defense lines. The islands of the Solomons—the Russells, Santa Isabel, New Georgia, Munda, Kolombangara, the Shortlands, and Bougainville being the most important—were well garrisoned and seemed to occasion little worry on the part of Tokyo just then. With the aid of the navy's 11th Air Fleet and the 8th Fleet from Rabaul, as well as with assists from the Combined Fleet where necessary, the defense of the northern Solomons seemed a relatively simple proposition. So IGH turned its major attention to New Guinea. There the plan was to strengthen Lae and Salamaua, with an eye to returning to Buna and retaking Port Moresby at a later date.

Therefore, General Imamura gave orders to General Adachi, the commander of the 18th Field Army, to reinforce the Japanese garrisons at Lae, Salamaua, Wewak, and Madang. Thus the Japanese could dominate Dampier and Vitiaz straits and block any attempt to advance along New Guinea to the Philippines, as they knew MacArthur desperately wanted to do. In fact, he wanted to do it so badly that he had already launched his propaganda campaign in the United States. Thus General Imamura was well aware of the Allied plan. Oddly enough, this was all prophetic; at the moment, the U.S. Navy was in the saddle and their plan for movement through the Central Pacific was in ascendance. But MacArthur was counting on political factors that would help in the future to direct the war the way he wanted it to go.

All those Japanese survivors of the Buna coast were ordered to Salamaua. The Japanese 20th Division began moving to Wewak. The 41st Division went to Madang. Part of the 51st Division was sent to Lae and Salamaua. General Imamura's command boundary was the border of Dutch New Guinea. Above that line Field Marshal Count Hisaichi Terauchi's southern army was in control—that meant the north coast of New Guinea from the Vogelkop Peninsula to Hollandia.

The Japanese IGH was a little vague about the line in the Solomons that their army should hold. The army wanted to draw the line at Bougainville, saying it was too hard to supply the troops further south because they were within the air cover of the Allies. Admiral Yamamoto disagreed. He said that New Georgia and Santa Isabel islands were outposts for Bougainville and must constitute the line of defense. But if the navy wanted to defend these places, said the army, it would have to defend them itself. So, the army drew the line at

Bougainville and the navy took over the shore defense as well as air and sea defense of New Georgia and the central Solomons. Lt. Gen. Haruyoshi Hyakutake and the 17th army took the responsibility for Bougainville. The 6th Division was stationed there. But the army finally did send some troops down to New Georgia and Santa Isabel on the urgent request of the navy—some, but as it would turn out, not enough.

In the spring of 1943, then, the Japanese were preparing for an offensive in New Guinea and a holding action in the Solomons.

The first Japanese move was against Wau, southeast of the Huon Peninsula of New Guinea. It is 145 miles southwest of Port Moresby and 25 miles from Salamaua. The plan was to seize Wau, whose major valuable attribute was an old airfield, and then use the island as a stepping-stone for a new drive against Port Moresby. That move would outflank the Allied positions on the Buna coast and make all that victory worthless.

So that spring, as General MacArthur made his grand plans for the return to the Philippines and left to others almost everything in between, the Japanese 18th Army was strengthening Lae and Salamaua with serious intent.

And now into the Southwest Pacific picture came a new factor: air power.

Until this point, the air power in the area had been more or less divided. The Japanese 11th Air Fleet at Rabaul could put forth major efforts when it wanted, both in bombers and in fighters. It had been weakened by the attenuated battle for Guadalcanal, but once Guadalcanal was lost, that meant an end to those round-trip flights of a thousand miles and more for the fighters. Similarly, the Allies air forces, strengthened by the new fields on the Papua coast, found it much easier to hit Rabaul and the Japanese positions at Lae and Salamaua. An indication of things to come was the trial of the 102nd Japanese Infantry. That unit was ordered to go by convoy from Rabaul to Lae during the first week of January 1943. But General Kenney's air force was on watch; when the Japanese convoy came up toward Lae, the Allied planes interdicted it and sank two transports. Three-quarters of the 102nd

Regiment arrived at Lae, but half the supplies intended for the regiment were lost in two sunken transports.

Once at Lae, the 102nd had new orders. It was to move up the mountains and seize Wau in the Bololo Valley. Maj. Gen. Toru Okabe, the Japanese commander at Lae, decided that he would begin the attack from Salamaua by using old native trails that led from the coast into the mountains. He sent his troops there; by January 16 they were ready to move.

But General Herring learned of the Japanese plans and decided to reinforce Wau. Elements of the 17th Australian Brigade were flown up to the airfield from Milne Bay.

The Japanese began to move through the trail country. By January 28, they had reached the outskirts of Wau and there launched a dusk attack.

The Japanese attacking Wau were stopped at the edge of the airfield. The Australians held that position during that first night and through the next day. General Herring managed to send supplies and reinforcement to them by air, which landed virtually under the Japanese noses. In three days, Allied transports flew in 194 planeloads of supply. They brought arms, field pieces, machine guns, and plenty of ammunition. The airlift made the difference; it was the new factor in the New Guinea jungle war. It changed the odds considerably. The Japanese were not notably successful with the airlift concept. For one reason, they did not have any plane as suitable for this task as the Douglas DC-3 aircraft, christened by the army the C-47. This workhorse of the air changed the odds in many places.

The Japanese attacked valiantly for three days. But all their ammunition and supplies had to come up over the Bololo Valley trails. They could not keep up the pace with the Australians. At the end of the third day, they had to admit that the attack could not succeed as it was, and they began their withdrawal.

The Australians brought in more troops, and began pressing the Japanese back toward Salamaua. It was a long, difficult jungle battle once again, but this time the Japanese were forced back steadily, if slowly.

At this time, over in the Solomons, Admiral Halsey recognized that the Allied forces had established air superiority in the southern Solomons. He was preparing his next attack, the invasion of the Russell Islands, just north of Guadalcanal. He wanted these islands primarily as a base for motor torpedo boats that could then move up the Solomon chain. At that moment, the question of overall command of the southern Pacific operations was still being discussed in Washington, but the navy still balked at letting MacArthur really run the show. They thought he was a wild man. President Roosevelt did nothing to force this issue. He knew what the problem was: MacArthur's hope to take the war up through the Philippines; the navy's intention was to move through the Central Pacific to strike the penultimate blow at Formosa or the China coast. Roosevelt's preoccupation that February and March was with events in Europe. The North African campaign was not going all that well at the moment. Field Marshal Rommel had wiped up the Kasserine Pass with the Americans, and the British were speaking of Americans as "our Italians" in the same sarcastic manner that the Germans spoke of their gallant allies. The sea war was still raging in the Atlantic. The plans had to be made for further invasions of Europe. Stalin was protesting that the Allies did not seem to have any intention of establishing a second front.

So, as long as the Allies in the South and Southwest Pacific were proceeding with some gains and not demanding too much support, Roosevelt was content to let the generals and the admirals fight it out among themselves.

As for the navy, things were stirring. At about this time, Admiral King succeeded in creating a new unit, the 5th Fleet, under Vice Adm. Raymond Spruance. This organization would immediately set to work, planning the first Central Pacific invasion: the taking of the Gilbert Islands in the fall of 1943. Already, the new carriers and battleships and hundreds of destroyers, service ships and transports, were coming off the ways of the American shipyards. At about this time, also, Admiral King decided that he needed a fighter with a little greater punch than that shown by Admiral Carpender in the Southwest Pacific. Carpender was moved out and Vice Adm. Thomas C. Kinkaid, who had made a reputation for himself in the Aleutians Islands, was moved down to Australia to become the chief of MacArthur's navy. The

7th Fleet, from this time on, would have far more importance than in the past.

In January, Admiral Nimitz had brought Secretary of the Navy Frank Knox out for a look at Guadalcanal, and had laid plans with Admiral Halsey for the move up the southern Solomons, almost without reference to General MacArthur's planning. On February 7, the day that the Japanese so stealthily and so successfully completed their evacuation of thousands of troops from Guadalcanal, Admiral Halsey ordered his invasion of the Russell Islands. At that time, Vice Adm. Richmond Kelly Turner, the senior naval officer on Guadalcanal, was going to begin a campaign of amphibious landings that would take him to the forefront of the Pacific War. His command was located at Koli Point on Guadalcanal. It was called the 3rd Fleet Amphibious Command. Two days after the invasion of the Russells was ordered, Admiral Turner learned that the Japanese had just evacuated the islands. That was tough luck for a man trying to set a sort of training program in motion. But they would go through with the details anyhow, just for that training, even if the Japanese could not be expected to put up much, if any, resistance. On February 20, the Russells were invaded. It was a walk-in—no Japanese resistance at all. Only at sea and in the air was there any fighting here.

In the air in the South Pacific there was also another change. Vice Adm. Aubrey W. Fitch, who had commanded the carrier *Lexington*'s task force at the battle of the Coral Sea—actually he ran the whole operation—was now Halsey's director of land-based air forces. And land-based air forces were going to play a large part in the campaigns for the Solomons and New Guinea in the months to come.

In New Guinea, the Japanese failure to take Wau brought an intensification of the interest on the part of Rabaul. On February 19, a convoy of supplies landed safely on New Guinea. The ships had come from Rabaul. Three ships had run the gauntlet of Allied air power and made it safely. So, the Japanese continued their plans quite unaware of another build up that was going to change their war completely.

At home in America, the factories were working at double time and producing thousands of aircraft, enough to meet the needs of the European theater and leave quite a bit for the

Pacific. Thus General Kenney's 5th Air Force was expanding. That meant more P-38 fighter planes, more B-25 medium bombers and A-20 attack bombers, as well as heavy B-17s and B-24s. The Allied air forces on the Papua side of New Guinea now numbered 200 bombers and 130 fighters.

In the beginning, the American bombers had not performed with great skill. The B-17 technique, developed for bombing German industrial targets, was not effective against fast-moving ship convoys, the principal target in these parts.

The B-25 medium bomber had some difficulties of its own. In the B-25 H model, common in the South Pacific, the bombardier sat in a plastic nose bubble in the front of the aircraft; from there he was supposed to be able to operate his Norden bombsight with great precision. But once again, the aircraft did not meet the need. The need was for planes that could get in fast, attack hard, and get out at mast level just as fast. That was the way in which convoys and enemy warships could be hit hard. The level-bombing technique just did not do the job.

So, General Kenney took the bombardiers out of the B-25s and put in eight .50-caliber machine guns instead of the Norden bombsight. The pilots also learned the skip-bombing technique. This technique had all the aspects of a kid on a riverbank hurling flat stones across the surface and watching them skip. In this technique, the pilots came in fast, unloaded their bombs on the water just before they came up to the ship, and let them skip against the ship's sides. For a while, there were incidents of bombs skipping clear over the ship, but sometimes those bombs then hit the ship beyond the target. By the end of February 1943, the pilots of the B-25s and the A-20 attack planes had become quite adept at skip bombing. Soon enough, they would have a chance to try their new technique on a big scale.

CHAPTER NINETEEN

The Battle of the Bismarck Sea

The failure of General Okabe's efforts to seize Wau as a base for overland operations against Port Moresby created some serious difficulties at Rabaul. General Imamura and General Adachi conferred. They needed to reinforce Lae and Salamaua if Okabe was to have the troops he needed to try one more time to capture Wau. They conferred with Admiral Kusaka, who was not only commander of the 11th Air Fleet at Rabaul, but who had been given command of all Japanese naval units in the area. He conferred with Admiral Yamamoto and all agreed that under the Imperial General Headquarters' (IGH's) new plan, first attention must be given to New Guinea, and this meant a major effort to reinforce Lae and Salamaua. The troops ready at the moment were the remainder of the 51st Division.

The problem was logistical. The generals and admirals at Rabaul were aware of new air power that gave the Allies air control of the waters around southeastern New Guinea. To reinforce Lae and Salamaua the ships would have to sail into waters now under observation by planes from the Papua airfields. And from those airfields, the Allies could launch attacks on shipping.

Work was proceeding in February on the Allied Papua fields. Dobodura, the field nearest Buna, had 207 medium bombers and 129 fighters. As February came to an end, General Kenney concluded that the Japanese would make a major effort to reinforce Lae and Salamaua. Thus, the Allied air searches of the Bismarck Sea became broader and more careful. The Allies were waiting for a chance to pounce with their new air power.

Eight transports were brought into Rabaul and loaded with supplies for Lae and Salamaua, including many drums of aviation gasoline. Eight destroyers were sent down from Truk to escort this important convoy along the coast of New Britain Island, then through Dampier Strait, and finally to the coast of New Guinea. Rear Adm. Masatomi Kimura was in command of the escort and the convoy. The sixteen ships sailed at 11 o'clock on the night of February 28. It was an ideal night from a convoy commander's point of view, stormy and overcast. The ships moved along the Bismarck Sea at seven knots. The main concern of the lookouts was submarines.

Morning dawned on March 1, still heavily overcast with occasional squalls. The weather could not be better. And no submarines appeared.

But shortly after noon, the storm dissipated and headed off west into the Solomon Sea; the sun came out above the ships sailing westward. Out of the clouds appeared a B-24 heavy bomber. It was not on a bombing mission but on an aerial reconnaissance. In a few minutes, the word reached General Kenney's headquarters that a large Japanese convoy had been sighted, and the message gave position, course, and speed. The convoy had to be heading for New Guinea.

The facts were a little wrong, the sighting was only six destroyers, but it was accurate enough for the purpose. The Allied air forces were called to the alert.

All afternoon the B-24 stuck with the convoy, shadowing.

At Rabaul, on receipt of Admiral Kimura's message that an Allied plane had found the convoy, the 11th Air Fleet was asked to provide air cover for the ships. Before dark, two flights of Zeros were over the convoy, all seemed serene. All air activity ended with darkness, the B-24 went back to its Australian base and the Zeros returned to their bases in Wewak and Madang.

To reach their destination the ships of the convoy would have to run through two narrow bodies of water, Vitiaz Strait and Dampier Strait. It would be like running two gauntlets, with the ships bunched up when passing through. If the Allies could master the air, then the convoy was going to be in big trouble.

At Rabaul, Admiral Kusaka knew this, and the 11th Air Fleet was giving every cooperation. On the morning of March 2, the air cover over the convoy was renewed. The ships steamed on.

That same morning, Allied bombers began taking off from fields on Papua. Twelve B-17s and seventeen B-24s were escorted by sixteen P-38s of the 39th Fighter Squadron located at Port Moresby. It was Japanese weather—so bad that the Allied P-38s had trouble keeping track of their bombers. They bucketed and surged through the air, avoiding thunderheads and trying to stay out of squalls. The weather over northern New Guinea was really terrible, everybody agreed. The P-38s looked for enemy fighters and found three. These were Oscars, Japanese army planes. They had nothing to do with this convoy, for the army planes were engaged only in supporting army operations. These Oscars were flying harassment missions against the Allied troops in Papua. The P-38s shot down one of the Oscars and sent the others scurrying for the clouds. The P-38s went on.

As the convoy steamed toward New Guinea, out of the clouds appeared seven B-17 heavy bombers. Something new had been added. The usual B-17 technique was to come in at ten-thousand feet and depend on the bombsight to give them accuracy. Three of these bombers did just that. They bombed and they missed. The ship's captains had expected that. The inaccuracy of the American heavy bombers against ships was a joke among the skippers of the South Seas. But the other four B-17s did not bomb at ten-thousand feet. They dropped down to six-thousand feet and then let go their bombs. As the Japanese antiaircraft gunners banged away at them, the bombers flew steadily on, and the convoy was in trouble.

The transport *Kyokusei Maru* took a direct hit on the Number 1 hatch, and began to burn. Another bomber hit the Number 3 hatch.

The fires grew worse. They got into the aviation gasoline drums and these began to explode, spreading gasoline all over the ship. The 115th Infantry Regiment was aboard this vessel. Twenty minutes after the bombing, the troops began deserting the ship. Fifty minutes later she sank.

The B-17s did a good job. They put near misses up against the transport *Saiyo Maru* and the *Kenbu Maru*. Both ships were badly damaged. That meant they were slowed down, among other things. Up came the destroyer *Asagumo* to rescue more than eight hundred men of the 115th Infantry as they struggled in the water. The staff of the 51st Division, riding in the *Saiyo Maru*, was taken off for safekeeping by the destroyer *Yukikaze*. The two destroyers then parted company with the convoy and put on full power to get to Lae after dark and land their passengers.

The B-17s went away, and the afternoon sky was serene. The battered but intact convoy steamed onward. But Admiral Kimura had the sense of being followed, and he was. The Americans were not notable in these waters for patient shadowing. But back there was a B-24 doing just that, moving in and out of the clouds, making it hard for the Japanese fighter cover to undertake two tasks—to shoot down the intruder or to cover their charges. Naturally, the fighters chose to cover the convoy and the shadowing plane hung on, radioing messages about the convoy's position, course, and speed.

In midafternoon, another flight of B-17s appeared. This group was not as deadly as the first, but the bombers did manage to put fragmentation bombs into two more transports, killing a number of men.

The convoy moved on in the lengthening shadows; behind it, but not far behind, was the shadowing aircraft of the Allies.

Urgent messages to Rabaul brought doubling of the air cover. Four more Allied bombers came over that afternoon, but they were driven off by the threat of that massed fighter attack.

As evening came, the convoy was nearing Uinbari Island. This was now dangerous narrow water, and Admiral Kimura was a worried man. Allied planes came over and dropped flares to keep the convoy in sight. But there was no attack. That much he could be thankful for. And that night the submarines did not come either, as he had half expected.

The convoy traveled at nine knots, heading for Dampier Strait, the most dangerous part of the voyage. Once they passed Dampier Strait, it was an easy shot across to Lae, and they would be safe. The convoy reached Uinpoi Island, which was just on the edge of the territory occupied by the Japanese.

Before dawn, the lookouts reported air activity around the convoy. But at dawn came forty-two Japanese fighters, most of them navy Zeros. They remained at high altitude waiting for the B-17 bombers to show up.

The Allied planes began taking off. The B-17s were escorted by thirty-two P-38 fighter planes. When they all reached a point thirty miles from the convoy, the B-17 pilots saw the Japanese fighters up there and disengaged. They moved down to medium altitude while the American fighters went after the Japanese fighters. Then something new was added. The Japanese at Guadalcanal had learned that to counter an attack by a torpedo plane they should turn into the enemy or away from him, thus presenting the narrowest possible target. And that is what Admiral Kimura's skippers did this day.

It was about 10 o'clock, Dampier Strait time when the first attacking medium bombers arrived. They came in at mast height, something the Japanese had not before encountered. The first to come were forty A-20 attack bombers. In the air also were several dozen B-25 bombers with the modified nose, machine guns instead of bombardier filling the bubble.

The escorting Zero fighters were getting low on gas, and they turned away toward Rabaul when they saw their replacements coming in. Just then, the attack arrived at the position of the convoy.

The Japanese fighter pilots were looking high, at and for the B-17s. Then in came the A-20 bombers, so low over the water that their slipstreams churned up waves. True to form, the Japanese ships turned into the attackers. But these attackers, the A-20 bombers and the B-25s with eight machine guns in their noses, wanted a nice long target. They came in, guns spitting, and strafed the ships from end to end. The ship gunners were at an enormous disadvantage. Only the bow and stern guns could be brought to bear on the attacking planes. The explosive bullets from the attacking planes cleared furrows in the decks of the ships. Men fell. Fires started. Ammunition began to blow up.

Then the bombers turned and came back athwart the ships. This time they dropped their bombs, but they dropped them at mast level and well before the target. The bombs hit the water, traveling with great momentum, skipped and slammed into the sides of the vessels. Some of them exploded at the waterline, giving a torpedo effect.

Thirty minutes later the attack ended. It had been enormously effective. The Allies lost one B-17 and three fighters. The Japanese lost five Zeros in attacking the B-17s. The B-25s, A20s, and Australian Beaufighters got off scot-free. Of the thirteen ships in the convoy, all had suffered damage, some of it quite serious. The destroyer *Shirayuki* sank. She was the admiral's flagship, thus he had to move. The destroyer *Tokitsukaze* began to sink. She was carrying members of the staff of the 18th Army on their way to observe the success of the reinforcement operation. The destroyer *Arashio* went dead in the water from fires that put out her boilers. Her sister ship, the *Asashio*, came up to help.

The convoy was spread all over Huon Gulf.

One transport had sunk and several were burning. The *Oigawa Maru* was barely afloat. The convoy was a total wreck. There was no way the orderly landing of troops could be accomplished. But what could be done was move the troops from the transports into landing barges and get them ashore as quickly as possible. Land was not far away.

While the plans were being made, the naval officers tried to bring the convoy back together. But it was not an easy task.

The destroyer *Tokitsukaze* sank. Just about then the second wave of Allied fighters and bombers reached the scene. They attacked everything that they could see. The *Asashio*, trying to help her sister destroyers, was badly damaged. The *Oigawa Maru* was finished off in a few minutes, and she went down. She carried many troops and so many bodies and bits of flotsam came to the surface that the water was filled with debris. A group of twenty bodies, not tied together, came up and floated around in the water, sticking together as if by glue.

The surviving destroyers moved around in Dampier Strait and tried to help rescue survivors.

Now there was no question of an orderly landing. What could be saved?

The army commander was landed from the *Yukikaze* at Finschhafen.

That was about all that could be done immediately. At Rabaul, where the army and navy commands were listening to the distress messages, no effective help could immediately be sent. The naval command at Rabaul did radio Truk and two submarines: the *I-26* and the *I-17*, were ordered to the scene. But Truk was a long way off for men struggling in the water at Dampier Strait. The *I-26* was off Goshu Island but that was at least a day's steaming from the scene. Search planes reported to Rabaul that a large force of enemy planes was heading for Dampier Strait. Rabaul reported to the convoy and the convoy's remaining destroyers—*Uranami*, *Shikinami* and *Asagumo*—all suspended activity and moved away from the scene to save themselves. Two squadrons of Japanese fighter planes appeared over the scene and tried to cover the men in the water. But the American force swept in and the planes began strafing, sinking ships' boats, floating rafts, flotsam, bodies, struggling swimmers, anything that moved. "The horror of the scene overwhelmed the eye," wrote one Japanese observer.

More Japanese fighters appeared and engaged the enemy. But now the Japanese faced the same problem that the Americans had faced in earlier times. They were too far from the base to have much time over the target. Thus they came and hit and ran and then had to go home. The Americans had four or five times as much time.

It was now about 1 o'clock in the afternoon. A whole new group of American planes appeared. The Japanese were learning how fast the Americans could produce and reinforce an area once they decided to do so. They had never seen so many American aircraft before. Along came the P-40s. They were too old and too slow for the original battle, but now that the job was strafing men in the water, they were admirable for the task. One P-40 attacked a Japanese barge loaded with troops that was heading for the Lae shore. Seven Japanese fighters got on the tail of this Australian plane. Six American fighters joined in and a general dogfight ensued. Two of the Japanese planes were destroyed.

At 4:30 P.M., the Americans began to run out of gas. The fourth wave of Japanese fighters was still trying to protect the men in the water. The destroyers *Shikinami* and *Uranami* went back to Rabaul, having picked twenty-seven hundred survivors out of the sea. They left behind the destroyers *Yukikaze* and *Asagumo* to deal with the remainder. But as night approached so did the American PT boats from New Guinea. They came out of their base at Tufi and another newer base at Kona Kope. Two of the boats hit debris left over from the day's battle and turned back to base. But the other boats went on, eight of them, and soon they were among the wreckage and the survivors. They found the transport *Oigawa Maru*, abandoned by her crew and the soldiers, and they put two more torpedoes into her. She sank immediately. By this time, the only ships still afloat in Huon Gulf were the sinking destroyers *Asashio* and *Arashio*.

The American PT boats then began looking for lesser game. They went out with their forty 20-mm and 37-mm guns to search for boats and barges. Hundreds, thousands of Japanese soldiers died that night as they were attacked again and again.

On March 4, the Japanese again sent an air umbrella over the gulf, but the Americans were back once more, hammering at the hulks of the two sinking destroyers. They sank both ships that day.

That afternoon the Japanese fighters above reported to Rabaul that they had spotted a large group of survivors in the water fifty-five miles southeast of Buin. But there was nothing to be done by the navy for them. The navy was too far away at Rabaul and Truk. An air umbrella was of limited usefulness. But the planes could drop lifesaving equipment, and they did in heroic numbers. On the morning of March 5, the two submarines arrived at the scene and began to pick up survivors. The *I-17* picked up 150 survivors and took them back to Truk. The *I-26* searched among the wreckage and found 54 survivors. She was still looking when along came two American PT boats. They fired torpedoes, but the *I-26* submerged and was saved. She hung around for a while. The PT boats moved in and out of the flotsam, dropping depth charges and firing at anything that moved. Finally, when the *I-26* came up again and looked around the surface of the sea, there was nothing at all to see. She headed out on the patrol she was starting on when the rescue operations were ordered.

* * *

For the Japanese the battle of the Bismarck Sea had been total disaster. Seven thousand men had been aboard that convoy, and no one would ever know how many of them survived. Twenty-seven hundred were rescued by the destroyers and landed back at Rabaul. A few hundred more were sent back to Rabaul, rescued by the other destroyers. A few hundred had been rescued by the submarines and some men had swum to shore. A handful of survivors even turned up eventually on Guadalcanal to be captured. But perhaps three thousand of the men were lost to the sea and the planes and PT boats. Further, not one of the transports survived, which was an enormous blow to the Japanese army transport system. Army and navy each had their own cargo and troop ships and up to this point, at least, they had not shared facilities. The Battle of the Bismarck Sea brought about a change in high policy, hereafter army and navy were ordered by IGH to cooperate in the field. The orders never did produce a major change in Japanese policy, the separation of powers was too deeply ingrained in the armed forces for that. But it would in future produce some local cooperation that, until this point, had been almost totally lacking.

The battle of the Bismarck Sea was a disaster of such magnitude for the Japanese that even in Tokyo it was realized that the war in the *Nanto Homen* (southeast area) had taken on an entirely new coloration. It was a disaster of such magnitude that it stunned both Rabaul and Truk.

Never again would a convoy of ships try to negotiate Kula Gulf during these operations in New Guinea. The Allied victory presaged the greater coming Japanese disaster.

CHAPTER TWENTY

Spring Offensive 1943

The disaster in the Bismarck Sea caused the Japanese to change their tactics in the Southwest Pacific, but not their basic strategy. Imperial General Headquarters (IGH) in Tokyo was determined that the original program should stand. New Guinea would be conquered; then the army and the fleet would turn their attention once more to the Solomons.

What this meant, of course, was that the implications of the defeat at Guadalcanal had not really sunk in yet in Tokyo. Admiral Yamamoto, the most farseeing of all the Japanese leaders in his estimates of American policy and power, grew steadily more morose about the possibilities of any sort of victory for Japan. But that feeling was not shared by most of the Japanese leaders. They regarded their setbacks in the South and Southwest Pacific as mere temporary reverses that could, in turn, be reversed in time. No one in Tokyo was paying any attention to the vast reservoir of logistic power that the Americans now had as compared to their position only six months earlier.

Since the Japanese had decided not to send any more convoys into the Lae area because of the Allied air control there, they had to find an alternative method of supplying their troops in Lae and Salamaua if they were to start up their offensive again. Their answer was a road that was to be built from Wewak through Madang to Lae. That way, the supplies could be landed at Hansa Bay and Wewak—well within the Japanese air umbrella—and shipped overland to Lae.

Construction of the road had begun in January. The Japanese 20th Division was given the job. But the road did not go well because combat troops are not labor troops. The fighting men resented the assignment and did not press forward. The engineers had made some mistakes, too, and part of the route led through impossible swamps. Most important, the Japanese did not have the proper equipment to build roads in this area. Their trucks broke down. They used horses, but the horses did not prosper on the swamp grasses, and they sickened and died. In the jungle areas, the trees protected the builders from aerial observation, but in the open spaces of the Finisterre Range the workers were subject to frequent Allied air attacks, which knocked out bridges and whole sections of road.

Thus, by June the road had been pushed only through the Finisterre Range.

After the Battle of the Bismarck Sea, IGH in Tokyo ordered a major air offensive to be staged by Admiral Yamamoto's naval air forces. The purpose was to knock out Allied air power, particularly in the New Guinea area. It was called Operation I.

Yamamoto stripped his Third Fleet carriers at Truk of their fighting planes and sent them down to Rabaul to join the 11th Air Fleet for the offensive operation. He had moved his flagship down to Truk from Japan during the Guadalcanal operation and there at Truk it remained. But Yamamoto himself moved down to Rabaul to direct Operation I. For the next few weeks, the aircraft would operate alternatively against targets in the Solomons and in New Guinea. The object was to crush the Allied air forces in both areas. *Crush, annihilate,* these were the usual sort of terms used by the Japanese military in referring to operations. They were a hangover from the days of the *samurai,* and they quite properly described the expectations of a military nation that had never been defeated in a war. The mind-set of the Japanese in the Southern Pacific waters in the spring of 1943 precluded any possibility of defeat and laid the groundwork for what was to happen in Operation I.

In the New Guinea area, General MacArthur was preparing for the invasion of Woodlark and Kiriwina islands, which would become Allied air bases. There were not any Japanese on the islands, it was reported, but still the invasion would be an amphibious operation. Over in Admiral Halsey's 3rd

Fleet area, the Americans were getting ready to invade New Georgia Island as a stepping-stone on the way to the envelopment of Rabaul.

On April 7, Admiral Yamamoto sent a large force of bombers and fighters down to Guadalcanal. The Americans that day were planning a naval bombardment of Vila and Munda islands, but the ships turned back and the Americans concentrated on getting air protection up around Guadalcanal. The Japanese swooped in. In the area around Guadalcanal, they sank the New Zealand corvette *Moa*, the American tanker *Kanawha* and the U.S. destroyer *Aaron Ward*. In the furious air battle, the Allies lost seven fighters. The Japanese lost thirty. But the Japanese pilots came home with glowing tales of victory. The air pilot's usual exaggerated sense of accomplishment in battle was exacerbated in this case by the official demands for victory. The generals and admirals at Rabaul believed that their air forces had, indeed, found an American task force and had sunk most of it. They believed because they wanted to believe, and there was no serious debriefing of the pilots that would have unraveled some of the stories. The pilots had gone into this battle in a sort of organized hysteria. Many of them wore the *hachimaki* (headbands with mystical patriotic writings on them) and expected to come home victorious. They reported an achieved victory, although they had not really accomplished much. The loss of the thirty aircraft was not as important as the psychological misrepresentation that made the Japanese believe they were winning. Thus they believed that what had been at best a standoff was a major Japanese naval air victory.

The Guadalcanal raid had been only a softener as far as Admiral Yamamoto was concerned. The real target was New Guinea. On April 11, the Japanese sent a hundred planes against Oro Bay. They sank a merchant ship and damaged another, so that it ran up on the beach. They damaged an Australian minesweeper. That raid was, indeed, a success, but limited once again because there was not much Allied shipping to bomb and strafe. Allied air power was not strong.

On April 12, the Japanese again struck New Guinea, this

time with 175 planes that bombed Port Moresby. Once again, the Japanese had calculated properly and the Americans had miscalculated. General Kennedy had been expecting a raid soon on Milne Bay, and that is where his fighter planes had gone. The Japanese raid did not do much damage because, once again, there was not much to hit except the shore installations.

On April 14, the Japanese air force attacked Milne Bay in strength. The Japanese planes were successful. A Dutch merchant ship was bombed and sank. Another Dutch ship was damaged. The pilots came back to Rabaul claiming an enormous victory and talking about the warships they had destroyed. For the entire Operation I, they claimed a cruiser, a destroyer, 25 merchant ships, and 134 aircraft destroyed. They had lost 42 planes.

The facts were that they had sunk a destroyer, a tanker, a corvette, 2 merchant ships and downed 25 Allied planes while losing 42. For an attacking force, that was not a bad ratio; in that sense, Operation I was a success. Admiral Yamamoto looked at the results, concluded that the Allied air and sea power had indeed been annihilated and sent his carrier planes back to their carriers at Truk. Operation I was declared to be a total victory and was called off. Thus, at the time that the Allies were building up their forces in New Guinea and the Solomon Islands, the Japanese high command in Tokyo had the erroneous belief that those forces had been whittled down. They were not looking in the right place. Allied power in New Guinea was very slight because it did not need to be strong. The Southwest Pacific forces were being massed elsewhere for an amphibious invasion, and so were those that would operate in the Solomon Islands.

Basically speaking, the Japanese estimates of the damage they had done (with the exception of overcalling the sizes and natures of the ships sunk) were ultimately more or less correct. The conclusions the high command drew were not.

Just after the end of Operation I, the Allies scored what they thought was a great coup. Through naval radio intelligence monitors at Pearl Harbor and in Alaska, the Americans learned of a coming visit by Admiral Yamamoto to various frontline air organizations in the southern islands. The Americans had broken the Japanese naval code months before. The decision was made (at the presidential level) to try to shoot Yamamoto down, and it was done on April 18 when his party was attacked on schedule near Buin by P-38 fighters. Yamamoto was killed and his chief of staff was injured. Only then did the American high command realize what it had done: possibly destroyed the future value of the naval intercepts. There was near panic at Pearl Harbor when an Australian newsman revealed the facts. Fortunately—particularly for the submarine force, which relied on the intercepts as a primary intelligence source—the foolish move was not caught out by the Japanese. Yamamoto's staff insisted that the code must have been betrayed, but the arrogance of IGH was so great that the military leaders would not believe this truth; thus the codes were left the same. It was a very narrow squeak for the Allies who were saved from the consequences of a dreadful blunder.

By June, the excellent Japanese air intelligence system revealed the extent of the Allied build up at Guadalcanal. On June 7, they began a series of air raids to cut down that power. Three raids were staged in rapid succession. The result was not very satisfying to Rabaul: a large number of aircraft were lost and only three Allied ships were hit. Allied air power had built up to the extent that the losses of the attackers were very high.

Even after this series of raids, the Japanese assumed that they could restore their air superiority in a short time through combined navy–army operations in the air. But the fact was that the Japanese would never again gain control of the skies in either the South Pacific or Southwest Pacific areas.

In May, engineering reconnaissance of Woodlark and Kiriwina islands indicated that there were no Japanese troops on either one. Thus, the engineers landed and began their work before the amphibious landings took place. The amphibious landings were really just a practice operation.

Units of the 112th Cavalry, the 134th Field Artillery, and the 12th Marine Defense Battalion landed on Woodlark Island on June 30. Even without the enemy, the landings were confused. Coxswains got lost and landed men on the wrong beaches.

But if the Woodlark landings were rough, they were smooth as silk compared to the Kiriwina landings. No Japanese were found here either, but that did not stop the landing force from nearly failing. On June 30, a dozen LCI (Landing Craft Infantry) sailed from Milne Bay escorted by six destroyers. When they reached Kiriwina, the LCIs grounded about three hundred yards out from shore. Then along came seven LCM, and a dozen LCTs. Most of the vessels grounded in shallow water and the men and the gear had to be hand-carried ashore. Several vehicles drowned in the process. Nearly everybody got wet, and a good deal of equipment was lost or damaged by salt water. The enemy would have added an element that might have caused the whole operation to fail.

But without the enemy, no one could do too much wrong. By the next month, the construction of the airfields was in progress and C-47s could land at Woodlark. By July 21, the 67th Fighter Squadron made its appearance there. Troubles continued at Kiriwina, occasioning a change of command, and it was not until August 18 that the RAAF's 79th Squadron set up operations there.

Meanwhile, the Australians and the Americans invaded Nassau Bay to give themselves another air base for attacking Lae. There were about a hundred and fifty Japanese sailors and soldiers here. A battalion of the 162nd U.S. Infantry was assembled and reinforced. It was now called the MacKechnie Force, after its commander, Col. Archibald MacKechnie.

Its job was to take Nassau Bay from the sea. The Australians would create a diversion in the Markham Valley.

On June 29, the force assembled at Morobe. PT boats, LCVPs and LCMs took the troops to the shore. They landed at night in heavy rain. The PT boats got lost, but the landings began after midnight on June 30. The troops got mixed up on the beach. The storm developed a high surf and seventeen of the landing craft were wrecked on the beach. The LCMs were swamped. But again, the Americans were lucky. There were no Japanese in sight, so their mistakes were not fatal. The Japanese, having seen the Americans coming, thought that the first bulldozer that landed was a tank and fled into the jungle.

So nearly eight hundred men were ashore safely, in two waves. The third wave didn't land at all; it sailed around for two days before coming back and landing. Meanwhile, the troops ashore had fought an engagement with the Japanese.

Back at the New Guinea force headquarters nobody knew quite what was going on because all of Colonel Mac-Kechnie's radios had gotten wet in the landings and none of them worked. It was nearly a week before communication was established. Slowly, the troops began moving, fighting engagements with the handful of Japanese in the area. At Rabaul, the Japanese decided against reinforcing this area, preferring to see how the Allied advance proceeded. On July 2, the Nassau beachhead was declared secure. The Americans had linked up with the Australian 17th Brigade and the drive north against the Japanese at Salamaua was ready to begin.

The most important landings at this period were those on New Georgia Island, carried out by Adm. William F. Halsey's South Pacific Command. Since the commands were divided more in fact than in theory, the progress of the war in the Solomons is not really a part of this book.*

The Marines landed first to create a diversion and hold Segi Point. The main landings came at Rendova. They were executed with considerably greater skill than the Southwest Pacific landings just described, but that is quite normal. In the first place, Vice Adm. Richmond Kelly Turner, the commander of the Allied landing forces in the Solomons, had considerably more experience than anyone else, having supervised the Guadalcanal landings and resupply from the early days. In the second place, he had at his disposal all the support he could ask for, whereas over in New Guinea Mac-Arthur's navy was making do with very little. The fighting on New Georgia was brisk; the Japanese were at their best; and the drive went slowly. By July 11, Enogai was secured and Bariroko was under attack. Munda was the real target, and it took the Allies a month to do the job. They had their troubles. The 43rd Division suffered an unusually high number of war-neurosis casualties, largely caused by poor leadership.

On August 5, General Sasaki, the commander of the Jap-

*The author has dealt with the New Georgia landings in another volume, *The Glory of the Solomons* (Military Book Club, 1983).

anese on New Georgia, decided that he must evacuate, and he moved his troops to Kolombangara.

The Japanese expected the Allies to try to march up the Solomons chain, and Kolombangara then was the next point of attack. But the Allies proved brighter. They decided to bypass Kolombangara.

Who made that decision? It is not quite clear. General MacArthur's staff took the credit for him. But the facts indicate that the decision was made at Admiral Halsey's headquarters and was probably proposed by some bright staff officer. On July 11, anyhow, Hasley informed his chief admirals, Turner of the amphibious forces and Fitch of the land-based air forces, that this was the proposal and that he was enormously enthusiastic about it. They would leave the thousands of Japanese troops alone on Kolombangara and move right on around them to Vella Lavella. There, they would build airfields from which to attack Rabaul. That was the whole point of the operations, to get up near New Britain Island so that the attacking aircraft would have a milk run.

The Allies did attack Vella Lavella and captured it. They sealed off Kolombangara. At this point, the Japanese realized that the Allies were beating them in the Solomons and that their big stand had to be made at Bougainville. But there was enormous friction between the Japanese army and navy leaders over the method of strategic defense. The navy said the fight must be waged in the Solomons. The army said the fight must be waged in the New Guinea area. The IGH was consulted, and IGH said that both areas must be defended (which was impossible, given the Japanese resources of the moment). On August 13, IGH ordered the central Solomons to hold out until Bougainville could be strengthened. Then, by October, the central Solomons would be evacuated and the defense staged at Bougainville. So General Sasaki on Kolombangara, who was not informed of these plans, prepared his defenses and prepared to fight. But on September 15, he did get the word. At the end of September, all the outposts around New Georgia were abandoned and the Japanese evacuated Kolombangara for a week. It was another of those remarkable Japanese military movements. Air and sea cover kept the Americans at bay, and the Japanese successfully evacuated 12,000 troops from this island and the other islands. In the whole operation, only one destroyer was damaged, twenty-nine small vessels (PT boats and barges) were sunk, and only 66 men were killed. On the morning of October 6, 1943, the Americans landed at Kolombangara Island. They found only forty-nine artillery pieces and a handful of Japanese stragglers who had somehow been left behind. The Allies controlled the central Solomons. The next step in that chain would be Bougainville. But the focus of the battle now shifted back to New Guinea.

CHAPTER TWENTY-ONE

The Huon Peninsula

New Guinea's Huon Peninsula hangs out from the island like the head of a brontosaurus. It faces New Britain Island—at the point furthest away from the Japanese base at Rabaul—as well as Dampier and Vitiaz Straits, which control the approaches to southeastern New Guinea. In the winter of 1943, the Southwest Pacific Command's intent was to capture the Huon Peninsula, which would put them in position above Lae, at the neck of the brontosaurus, and in control of the two straits.

General MacArthur had a serious problem, not shared by Admiral Halsey in the Solomons area. He did not have enough ships to launch a major amphibious campaign. He did not have enough transport aircraft to stage an airborne operation in strength. He had plenty of troops at this point, but little ground transport, and the roads were so few and so primitive that a purely land operation was impossible. So, making a virtue of necessity, MacArthur used every means available—land, sea, and air—to begin the offensive operations.

General Kenney's air force was receiving a comfortingly large number of aircraft that spring and summer. The 348th Fighter Group arrived with P-47s, a new fighter plane for the Pacific area, developed for high-altitude escort work in Europe but discovered to be ideal for strafing and low-level attack. More twin-engined P-38s were coming in, more B-24 bombers, more B-25 medium bombers, and more C-47 troop carrier planes. The goal was fourteen squadrons of C-47s for the 54th Troop Carrier Wing; by the end of August, it had been nearly achieved. The Southwest Pacific had 197 heavy bombers and 598 fighters, although many of them were down for repairs.

The Allies were building new airfields, closer to the scene of action. One was built at Bena Bena. Another was built at Tsili-Tsili. General Kenney thought Tsili-Tsili sounded silly-silly, so he changed the name of the strips to Marilinan, which has the ring of Hollywood starlet to it.

The timing of the operation against the Markham Valley was established by General Kenney because the performance of the air force was all important to the effort. His Australian weathermen told him that September 3 would be the optimum date. On that day, they said, the western end of New Britain Island and Vitiaz and Dampier straits should be fogged in, but the sky above New Guinea should be bright and shining. That would allow the air forces and the airborne troops to operate under optimum conditions, while keeping Japanese fighters away. But the American weathermen disagreed. September 5, they said, was going to be the best day.

General Kenney considered the matter, and chose September 4 as D day.

The change that had been in MacArthur's mind for a long time now came into being. He and his staff did not like the way the Australian ground forces planned their operations. So, Southwest Pacific Command took over, even though the majority of troops employed would be Australian. The Australian 7th and 9th divisions would be employed plus the U.S. 503rd Parachute Infantry Regiment and the 2nd U.S. Engineer Special Brigade. They would be landed by Admiral Barbey's VII Amphibious Force.

Two brigade groups, of about eight thousand men, plus engineers would land at Lae. Meanwhile, the troops already fighting in New Guinea would move up against Salamaua.

In August 1943, the Japanese had about ten thousand men in the Lae–Salamaua area. The Japanese plan had not changed: General Imamura was charged with the recapture of Papua and ultimately the investment of all New Guinea.

The big problems were health and supply. About half the Japanese in New Guinea were sick with malaria, dysentery, and other tropical diseases. They were short of medical supplies and just about everything else. The Japanese had given up trying to supply the troops directly by sea except when submarines could be employed. But by the summer of 1943, only three submarines were assigned to the New Guinea supply system. General Imamura decreed that supply would be carried out by use of big motorized barges that the Japanese had developed and used successfully, most lately in the evacuation of Vella Lavella Island in the Solomons. But there were not enough barges to begin with, and the Allied planes attacked the ones that traveled by day and the PT boats attacked those that traveled by night.

One welcome change had come. General Tōjō, concerned over the reverses in the Southeast Pacific area, as the Japanese called that whole region, had made a trip to Rabaul to see for himself what the problem was. He went home and immediately revamped the Japanese aircraft industry. More planes began to come down the assembly lines and most of them were scheduled for this area. Lt. Gen. Kumaichi Teramoto's 4th Air Army was moved down from Java to Rabaul. There, General Imamura assigned the air army to Wewak for the defense of convoys. The 6th Air Division, 7th Air Division, and 14th Air Brigade were scattered around four Wewak airfields.

During the summer, the Allied forces in the Salamaua area moved slowly forward, supported by the 5th Air Force. Once the Marilinan fields were built, the air force began raiding Wewak to decrease the Japanese air strength build up there. Kenney used a neat trick against the Japanese. For several weeks, his bombers had been moving around the area but never going as far as Wewak. The impression Kenney wanted to give was that the bombers did not have the range. The Japanese were suckered. On August 13, Allied observation-plane photographs showed 199 aircraft on the four airfields at Wewak, out in the open with no revetments or protection. General Teramoto was convinced that the Allies could not reach his planes. Sixty B-24s and more than 50 B-25s struck the four airfields on August 17. In two days, they destroyed about 100 planes, most of them on the ground.

In July and August, three Allied units were operating against Salamaua. The 3rd Australian Division was the prime force. The MacKechnie Force was the American contingent. Then came the 162nd U.S. Infantry Regiment. A new unit called the Coane Force was also organized under Brig. Gen. Ralph Coane, commander of the 43rd Division Artillery. It was no picnic. The Australians and Americans seemed to be fighting each other as much as the enemy. Finally, getting so many conflicting orders from the general commanding the 3rd Australian Division and General Coane, Colonel Mac-Kechnie asked to be relieved of command. He could fight Japanese, but he couldn't take the confusion any more. But in spite of this foolishness, the Allies now had the logistical strength to cover a lot of mistakes, and they kept moving in their erratic way.

By mid-July they had secured the southern end of Tambu Bay. At that point the Coane Force was dissolved and Colonel MacKechnie's blood pressure was down enough for him to take command of the 162nd Infantry contingent again. The Australians by this time had reached a point just south of the Salamaua airfield.

All the way it was hard going. The Japanese had built their usual excellent defense positions. The terrain was marvelous for defense, ridges shot up a thousand feet and then dropped off a thousand to a valley below. The Japanese put in earth and log pillboxes, with trenches and tunnels interlinking, always making sure that they created interconnecting fields of fire.

But on September 1, the handwriting was on the wall. The Allies were moving swiftly against Salamaua Town. They had hoped, by moving against Salamaua overland, to persuade the Japanese that this was the major focus of their attack. The Japanese had believed and had moved about half their troop strength of ten thousand men to the Salamaua area. Thus Lae was open.

On September 1, the 9th Australian Division boarded the ships of Admiral Barbey's 7th Amphibious Force at Milne Bay. The ships steamed up to Buna and Morobe where they picked up the 2nd Engineer Special Brigade in fifty-seven landing craft. At sunrise on September 4, the armada was standing off the landing beaches east of Lae. Just after 6 o'clock, five destroyers began a bombardment on the beaches. They fired for ten minutes. Then the landing craft began to move in. There was virtually no opposition. On one beach, a small group of Japanese saw the Australians coming, watched, and then turned and disappeared into the jungle. The surprise was total. By 8:30 in the morning, all the assault troops had landed. There was a little popping of rifles and machine guns here and there, but no serious fighting developed. By 10:30, the ships had landed fifteen hundred tons of supplies. By the end of the day, the Australians had begun to advance west against Lae.

When the news of the invasion reached Rabaul, General Imamura called for help from the 11th Air Fleet and some eighty planes responded. But Weatherman General Kenney had been proved right. The weather over New Britain was terrible that day, and the fog delayed the Japanese attack. It arrived late in the day, and the Japanese damaged two LSTs (Landing Ships, Tanks) off Cape Ward Hunt and killed about a hundred Australian soldiers and American sailors. That day sporadic small raids did more damage; that night the Japanese bombed the beaches and blew up an ammunition dump, which made something spectacular to talk about back at Rabaul.

It took the Japanese two days to put their defenses together. The Australians moved ahead until they reached the Bunga River. Here, the Japanese had dug in and there was a fight.

The 24th Australian Brigade was advancing along the coast. The 26th Brigade was moving inland to get behind Lae and outflank it.

It was raining again, and the streams were swollen and powerful. The 24th Brigade moved up through the mud and the swamps to the banks of the Buso River. In the dry season, the Buso was not much. But in September 1943, it was five-feet deep and sixty-feet wide, with a current moving at 12 knots and a strong Japanese defense on the west bank. On the morning of September 9, an Australian patrol tried to make it across. The Japanese opened fire and drove the men back through the swift current. But later in the day, four rifle companies staged an assault, using rubber boats and swimmers. They got across. They lost some men to the current and some men to Japanese fire, but they established a beachhead and held it against counterattacks.

For the next sixty hours, the engineers brought up landing craft and moved the 24th Brigade across the swollen stream.

All this while they were under fire from the Japanese infantry and artillery. Fortunately, the weather was terrible and the rain and mist helped hide the movement from the enemy. By the morning of September 14, the engineers had put up a box girder bridge. All this was done under constant Japanese artillery and mortar fire. That night, the 26th Brigade crossed over and both brigades of the Australians were on the west bank of the Busu River. The advance against Lae continued.

While the Australians and Americans were moving against Lae, the airborne troops were moving against Nadzab, which would be the site of an important air base for the investment of New Guinea.

Col. Kenneth H. Kinsler's 503rd Parachute Infantry Regiment was assigned to this task. After they had captured Nadzab, they would prepare the airstrip there to handle C-47 cargo planes, and these planes would bring up the 7th Australian Division from Port Moresby and Marilinan.

Earlier, the American weathermen had picked September 5 as the best day for weather in eastern New Guinea. They were all wet. In fact, so was everybody else that morning for it rained and rained and rained. Takeoff of the airborne troops was scheduled for 6:00 on September 5, but it was delayed by bad weather until nearly 8:30 in the morning. The troops sat around in their parachutes and equipment like stiff dummies, waiting for the weather to clear.

But the men of the 503rd were off the ground at 8:30; the 2nd Battalion of the 4th Australian Field Regiment was waiting. That unit would bring twenty-five-pounder guns to aid the assault. The 54th Troop Carrier Command put up ninety-six C-47s that morning—in about fifteen minutes all were off the ground.

The planes crossed the high Owen Stanley Mountains and then formed up in three groups. An hour later, they were joined over Marilinan by bombers and fighters. By this time, the air armada was substantial—302 planes, the most powerful force that either side had yet put into the air in this Pacific campaign. The planes flew down the Watut River valley, swung right over the Markham River and pointed toward Nadzab. The troop transports began losing altitude, down from three thousand feet to four hundred feet. The paratroopers were standing in the aisles now, formed to hook up and drop at the signal.

First, in went the special B-25s with all those machine guns in their noses. There were six squadrons of them, seventy-two planes, coming in one after the other to strafe the airfield installations, planes on the ground, and to drop parachute-borne fragmentation bombs.

When the B-25s had finished, in came a half-dozen A-20 attack bombers to lay smoke to confuse the Japanese. And then in came the C-47s, cargo doors wide open, with the jumpmaster of each plane standing by and ready.

The jump began at about 10:20 A.M. In four-and-a-half minutes all the men but one of the 503rd were in the air. The one exception fainted in the aisle while waiting to hook up and was left behind.

The jump was a piece of cake. There was no Japanese opposition. Two men were killed when their parachutes failed to open. Since they had packed the parachutes themselves. . . .

One man landed in a tree and his spent parachute then did not save him when he fell sixty feet to smash into the ground. Thirty-three men suffered sprained ankles and other injuries, all from the drop. This was more or less to be expected in any airdrop. It was not the safest way of moving into military action.

But once the men were on the ground, the going was easy, even if they had the kunai grass to contend with.

High above the action was General MacArthur along with General Kenney. They were in a B-17 watching the show. And that is just what it was, just like an air show back in the States. Of course, the participants did not know it was going to be just a show. They had to be ready to get killed and they were.

It was a splendid show, indeed. Five B-17s carrying supplies lazed above the area, dropping fifteen tons of supplies aimed at panels laid out on the ground by the paratroopers. Later in the day, when all was as secure as it could be, the Australian artillery came in. By that time, the paratroopers were already working on the runway. They moved down to the north and east ends of the field and set up perimeters. Planes brought in an Australian Pioneer Battalion and a company of the Papuan Infantry. They worked all night to make the airstrip ready for landings by the transports. On September 6, engineers landed on the field. By September 10, the 7th Division was on the ground and the paratroopers were relieved of responsibility for defense. No one even saw a Japanese soldier until September 15. Then, the 3rd Battalion of the 503rd ran into a Japanese column east of Nadzab; in the fight that followed, eight men were killed and twelve wounded. The Americans did not know it but these were troops following orders and retreating en masse to the coast. The paratroopers were withdrawn on September 17, having participated in an action that was really hardly an action at all. They had been very lucky; the Japanese had opted not to defend here.

But the capture of the Nadzab airstrip was essential to the seizure of Lae and the maintenance of air power over eastern New Guinea. Within two weeks, the engineers had built two parallel airstrips, each six-thousand-feet long. They were working on six other strips.

The Australians did not dilly—or dally. They moved out toward Lae on September 10. The 25th Brigade advanced down the Lae road to Jensen's Plantation. There, they encountered the Japanese and moved on. They captured Heateh's Plantation. After another fight, the 33rd Australian Infantry's 2nd Battalion moved through and pushed forward. They were approaching Lae and they knew it because the Japanese began shelling them with 75-mm guns from the Lae defenses. Lae was now under attack.

The Japanese at Lae had once been ordered to hold at all costs.

At Salamaua, General Nakano announced that they would do just that and began issuing the usual orders, "Even the patients will rise from the hospital beds to fight. No one will be taken prisoner."

But at this point in the war, IGH was not interested in heroics but in preserving troops and territory. Nakano was ordered from Rabaul to hold Salamaua as long as he could but to move out if the Allies threatened him. He did not even have to make the judgment. On September 8, Lieutenant General Adachi ordered him to move out. The seizure of Nadzab and the Australian landing northeast of Lae had convinced the general that the move was necessary. The hospital patients were gotten out of bed, but only to be moved to Lae. On September 11, the withdrawal of the entire Salamaua garrison began.

The ambitious plans of IGH for New Guinea were now sacked. The staff saw that Lae and Salamaua were both goners, and the Allied advance threatened to surround the 51st Division. So, General Adachi issued new orders that involved the defense of the Finisterre Mountains, and Finschhafen. They would also try to hold the Ramu Valley. The troops at Lae were ordered to withdraw to the north coast of the Huon Peninsula and the 20th Division was told to move from Madang to Finschhafen.

So, the Allied troops moving on Salamaua and Lae faced only token resistance. The main body of troops was moving out as swiftly as possible, heading northeast. As the 51st Division moved, it began to be cut down. The Allies harried it, mostly from the air, but the real problem was terrain. The troops began with a ten-day ration of food. But when the ten days ended, they had still not reached their destinations. They were forced to forage for food, and the foraging was very thin, mostly bugs and roots. On the way, the 51st Division lost most of its heavy equipment. The men could not pull the guns up and down the mountains. Ultimately, most of the guns were left behind. The soldiers of this division even did the indescribable: they threw away their rifles. That was not true of all units: the 1st Battalion of the 20th Division was warned by its commander that he would shoot any soldier who abandoned his rifle. That unit arrived very nearly intact, and every man carried his rifle into camp.

The bombing and strafing and an occasional military scuffle were hard on the Japanese. Nine thousand soldiers and sailors had left Lae in September. But only sixty-five hundred arrived on the coast of the Huon Peninsula. Most of the others starved or died from dysentery. For once, malaria was not a problem; nearly everybody had it, but there were plenty of drugs in the columns.

September was the witching month for IGH. Guadalcanal, New Georgia, and Vella Lavella had fallen in the South Pacific campaign. Lae and Salamaua had fallen, after Buna.

There was no longer any question of capturing Port Moresby and threatening Australia. The IGH suddenly realized that the Japanese empire was being carved up. It became time to reassess the whole situation in the southeast.

For a year, the Japanese had been waiting for an invasion of the Gilbert Islands. The Americans had tipped their hand when they sent Lt. Col. Evans Carlson into Makin on a raid with his 2nd Marine Raider Battalion. The raid had accomplished virtually nothing except to point up the importance with which the Americans considered the Gilberts. The real result was a strengthening of the defenses of the Gilberts, with the central defense at the little island of Tarawa. Also, for years the Japanese had been aware of Plan Orange, the U.S. Navy's program for a Pacific War against Japan. If there had ever been any question about it, the *Chicago Tribune* had revealed all just before war broke out in the Pacific, publishing a version of Plan Orange. The scheme had changed a little, but not much; it was the logical, basic plan of attack across the Pacific, moving from one strategically important island complex to another, thus giving the navy bases for warships, submarines, and supply. Every midshipman who went through the U.S. Naval Academy at Annapolis was exposed to the strategy. It would go thus: Gilberts, Marshalls, Marianas. With the capture of the Marianas, the Americans would have a base for their new long-range B-29 bombers, developed specifically for the purpose of striking Japan.

In the fall of 1943, the Japanese knew all this. The progress of the B-29 was carefully chronicled in the American press. A general or two had made specific statements about range and capability. Of course, all this information was immediately transmitted to Buenos Aires, Lisbon, Stockholm, and Geneva, where the Japanese Domei News Agency correspondents scooped it up and sent it home. One did not need so much military intelligence to follow the course of the war and the American plans. All one had to have was access to the American press. For censorship in America was a sometime thing and the most frequent violators were the high military officers. Gen. H. H. Arnold, commander of the army air force, was the man who told the Japanese first about the B-29 in some detail. The information came in an ordinary newspaper interview with an American reporter.

Thus in September 1943, IGH altered its basic defense plan for the empire. The southern defense line would run from western New Guinea to the Caroline Islands and thence to the Marianas. This was the defense line beyond which there would be no passage. This was the line beyond which the Japanese would, indeed, fight to the death. Actually, it worked out a little differently. The Japanese on the wrong side of the line were also told to fight to the death. And they did, although there was no hope for them and no real delay was even accomplished. All that the stout defense of the Gilbert and Marshall islands proved was that a few Japanese could kill and maim a lot of attackers before they died. Rabaul had been the secure headquarters base for operations against New Guinea, and all those little island chains around Australia and New Zealand from which the final assault on Australia could be launched when the time came. Now there would be no assault on Australia, everyone in Tokyo knew that. There would be no campaigns for Samoa or any other islands. Rabaul had moved—the Allies had moved it—straight up to the line of defense for the Japanese empire. The hundred thousand men that General Imamura controlled and the three years of supply in the caves and warehouses were suddenly not very meaningful. The IGH warned General Imamura that he was expected to stand firm at Rabaul. Bougainville must hold. To punctuate the command IGH sent Imamura a new unit, the 17th Division, which had been living high in the fleshpots of Shanghai.

General Imamura began strengthening his defenses at Bougainville. He sent new troops to Madang and Wewak. He told Admiral Kusaka that they must work together to hold Dampier and Vitiaz straits. The Japanese 65th Brigade, reinforced, was moved down to Tuluvu on the north coast of Cape Gloucester. Maj. Gen. Iwao Matsuda, the commander, was told that he also had to defend the coasts of western New Britain. Maj. Gen. Eizo Yamada was sent to Finschhafen. That place had two good anchorages, Finschhafen Harbor and Langemak Bay. It also had an airfield. All this must be maintained, said General Imamura. Yes, said General Adachi. Of course, said Admiral Kusaka.

And the war went on.

CHAPTER TWENTY-TWO

On Towards Rabaul

In the summer of 1943, the great battle of the Pacific War was not that between the Japanese and the Americans but between Gen. Douglas MacArthur, on the one hand, and the Joint Chiefs of Staff and the Navy, on the other.

At the Casablanca Conference, without General MacArthur's consent, the Combined Chiefs of Staff of the United States and Great Britain approved a drive toward Japan through the Central Pacific—basically the old navy Plan Orange. Because there were already so many troops and so much equipment committed to the South and Southwest Pacific, the Joint Chiefs of Staff also decided to maintain a drive up through New Guinea to the Philippines as a secondary effort. That was understood by everyone but General MacArthur. The Central Pacific drive would employ the 1st and 2nd Marine divisions, and most of the assault cargo ships and transports in the south.

When General MacArthur learned of this plan, he began to try to undercut it. He termed the Central Pacific drive, "a diversionary attack." He was quite right. It would divert forces that he had planned to use for his own triumphal return to the Philippines. What the Joint Chiefs of Staff would not understand was that if they would leave MacArthur alone and give him all the men and supplies that he needed, he proposed to win the war for them single-handedly. His big argument was that if the Joint Chiefs withdrew the two marine divisions, then that would cripple his attempts to capture Rabaul.

Ah, yes, said the Joint Chiefs, but they had news for the general. Rabaul was not going to be captured. They had seen the future. Rabaul was going to die on the vine. General

MacArthur did not like what he learned. He fought all the way for the Southwest Pacific drive and he had a powerful ally in Adm. William D. Leahy, military chief of staff to President Roosevelt. But MacArthur was unable to convince either General Marshall or Admiral King that his motive was not primarily the MacArthur ego. General Marshall suggested that MacArthur seize Kavieng on New Ireland Island, Manus in the Admiralties, and capture Wewak. That way Rabaul would be surrounded and could be pelted from every side by air power and shipping and Japanese air strength could be wiped out and kept down. There would be no need for a frontal assault on this enormous base, Rabaul, where General Imamura was keeping thousands of troops, including the fresh 38th Division in reserve.

MacArthur responded that it could not be done. Rabaul would have to be captured, he said, because it had such a nice harbor and that was just what he needed to keep moving up New Guinea toward the Philippines.

In spite of General MacArthur's one-track mind, the Combined Chiefs of Staff decided in the fall of 1943 that it would be as they and the Joint Chiefs said, not as MacArthur would have it. They did throw a sop to his ego: once the bases at Manus, Kavieng, and Wewak were taken, then MacArthur could move west along the north coast of New Guinea to the Vogelkop Peninsula, and after that was taken, he could attack Mindanao in the Philippines.

The general was quiet. He had not stopped his planning. It was his war, he felt, and the Joint Chiefs were all wet. But he was not going to convince them. So, he set about moving on a new level, working with strength. And his strength lay in the White House, not the Pentagon. Meanwhile he followed orders.

The capture of Lae and Salamaua convinced the Japanese that Finschhafen was in imminent danger from Allied attack. General Adachi had been building a road between Madang and Lae, but it was suddenly redundant. There was no Lae any more for the Japanese. It was a very fine road, twenty-feet wide—good for even the rainy season—and it ran along the coast from Madang to Bogadjim, then over the Finisterre Mountains through a pass and into the Ramu Valley. It had reached a point ten miles north of Dumpu.

When the men of the Japanese 20th Division learned of the general's decision to stop construction, they gave three cheers, for they were fighting men and this labor service was appalling to them. The division, less a few troops who were holding the pass through the Finisterre Mountains, marched toward Finschhafen. The division was on the road when the Allies struck.

Despite General MacArthur's tendency to ignore the Australians in the chain of command, the plan for the next move was Australian, offered by General Blamey who was still at least titular commander of the ground forces in the Southwest Pacific. He proposed an amphibious operation against Finschhafen before the Japanese 20th Division could get there. Then the capture of a point midway between Finschhafen and Bogadjim. There were about five thousand Japanese troops in this entire area; that was too many to leave to possibly outflank Finschhafen after it was captured. Finally, Blamey said, they should capture Cape Gloucester on the other side of the straits on New Britain Island and follow that immediately with the capture of Madang.

At a big meeting in September, all was decided. The New Guinea Force would seize Kaiapit in the Markham Valley as well as Dumpu, which was thirty miles south of Bogadjim. The Madang attack was postponed, but the Finschhafen attack was scheduled. So, the Australian troops began to move out of Lae.

By the first of January 1944, the Australians had captured a great deal of territory. They had air bases in the Markham and Ramu valleys, others at Nadzab and at Lae, and one at the junction of the Gujsap and Ramu rivers. Dumpu, having been captured, was now a staging field for Allied fighter planes. The 7th Australian Division was marching right along up the Huon Peninsula. The Japanese rear guard troops of the Finisterre passes were driven out. The Japanese retreated to Madang.

Down at Buna that summer and early fall, Admiral Barbey was getting ready for his amphibious invasion of Finschhafen. It was scheduled for September 2. He did not have much to work with: eight LSTs, sixteen LCIs, ten destroyers, and four big multipurpose transport ships.

On September 21, the Australian 20th Brigade boarded the ships. The Americans supplied special troops, engineers, and medics.

That day the armada sailed. The Australian 22nd Battalion started a march from Lae toward Langemak Bay, making a feint that was to confuse the Japanese about Allied intentions.

For a week, various Allied air units had been employed to work over the landing area and Finschhafen generally. The landing area was six miles north of Finschhafen at the mouth of the Song River. It was nine-hundred-yards long and thirty-feet wide.

The armada lay off the coast on the morning of September 22, and the destroyers bombarded the beach area beginning at 4:00 A.M. It was still dark. It was still dark even when the Australians went ashore at 4:45. Why, no one ever investigated. The result was predictable: the coxswains got lost and most landing craft of the first and the second waves landed in the wrong place, a small cove south of the planned landing beach. Probably, it was just as well. The troops that landed in the cove met very little resistance. Those of the third wave, which went ashore on the right beach, met determined Japanese opposition. But the Japanese had only about four thousand troops at Finschhafen, who were awaiting the arrival of the 20th Division on its overland march. General Yamada had put only a few hundred men on the beaches. The rest were being kept at Hanisch Harbor on the south coast of the peninsula and at Satelberg, a three-thousand-foot mountain that lay six miles west of the beachhead. So, by 9:30 A.M., the Australians had wiped out the Japanese in their beach positions and all troops and supplies were safely ashore. The handful of Japanese survivors retreated to high ground about a half-mile away; when the Australians came up, there was hard fighting. But the outcome was never in doubt.

When the news of the Allied landing reached Rabaul, General Adachi ordered General Yamada to take all his troops to Satelberg, organize and attack to hold the Australians back until the 20th Division could arrive on foot. The 20th Division had reached Gali, a hundred miles from Finschhafen, and had planned to arrive on October 10. General Adachi told General Kitagiri, commander of the 20th, to hurry up.

At the beachhead, the American engineers built dumps. They were harried by Japanese naval aircraft and so was the amphibious command, now heading back to Lae. But the weather was dreadful and the Japanese aircraft had a hard time finding their way down to the ground level without crashing, and so the troops ashore and aboard the ships received relatively little damage.

On September 23, the Australians moved toward Finschhafen proper. They captured Heldsbach, the airfield, and part of the shoreline of the harbor. At the Bumi River, the Japanese had established a defense perimeter and here the fighting stopped the Australians. More troops were brought up and the advance continued. Finschhafen fell to the Allies on October 1. At about this time, the troops of the 22nd Battalion who had advanced up the coast from Lae arrived, and the whole area was consolidated.

Meanwhile, the Japanese were massing at Satelberg for a counterattack.

On September 30, the advance troops of the Japanese 20th Division reached Sio, fifty miles from Finschhafen. Japanese military practice called for General Kitagiri to await the arrival of all his troops and make a concentrated attack. But the word from Rabaul had been frantic; help was needed in a hurry, and so General Kitagiri violated his own rules and sent his forward element of about twenty-five hundred men to make the first attack. The Allies had a stroke of luck. On October 15, they captured an order from Kitagiri to his troops that called for an attack on October 16 by most elements of the 20th Division while another force came around by sea and landed at the back of the beachhead.

In the darkness of early morning, the Japanese landing barges came up toward the Australians and overhead Japanese planes bombed and strafed the beach. But they were not a lot more accurate than the Allies had been when they worked in the darkness here, and the Allies began firing on the landing craft. Two barges were sunk and only one of the four actually landed its troops. About 150 Japanese got ashore and attacked. But they were stopped quickly by the Allies and a handful of Americans, one of whom, Pvt. Nathan Van Noy, Jr., of the 532nd U.S. Engineer Boat and Shore Regiment, won the Medal of Honor for killing about 30 Japanese with his machine gun. As was so often the case, the award was posthumous.

General Kitagiri continued his attacks, but they were piecemeal and the Australians had sufficient troops to fend them off. What would have happened if General Kitagiri and General Yamada had put all the troops of the Finschhafen defense force and the 20th Division together for one great attack will never be known. Suffice it to say that they did not, and because they did not, the Japanese attacks were dealt with one after the other.

By October 25, General Kitagiri was running out of food and ammunition. To investigate and plan a new defense, General Adachi came down from Madang and sat up on the mountain trying to figure out how to turn stalemate into victory. But while he and Kitagiri talked, the Australians brought up the 4th Brigade. The PT boats from Milne Bay had now moved up to Finschhafen; their presence and harassment of supply barges meant that the Japanese were getting very little in the way of supply. November, and more Allied power came to the area. On November 17, the 9th Australian Division fought a major engagement with the Japanese 20th Division, and won. On December 8, the Australians captured the three-thousand-foot Satelberg peak. The Japanese began retreating up the coast to Sio.

The Japanese story was almost a carbon copy of the tales of Buna, Lae, and Salamaua. On September 12, the 20th Division numbered 12,500 men. By December the number was down to 7,000 men. Disease and starvation were again taking more of a toll than the enemy. The Japanese high command could contemplate that problem while the men retreated to Sio, and beyond.

With the capture of Sio, the Allies achieved their main objectives at this stage. They held the airfields and towns on the coast of Vitiaz Strait.

The invasion of Bougainville by Admiral Halsey's South Pacific forces was a part of the overall strategy for the isolation of Rabaul. It was a hard and wearing fight, beginning in November when the Americans moved into Empress Augusta Bay.*

The next step for the Allies in New Guinea was to secure control of the Vitiaz and Dampier straits and, irrevocably, with the capture of the island and capes of the New Britain shore.

As the planning for the next stage of operations in New Guinea was being done, MacArthur was still thinking about attacking Rabaul. To attack Rabaul it would be best to have air bases on the western end of New Britain Island and PT boat bases on the south shore.

Operation Dexterity was assigned to General Krueger's 6th Army, which was also the Alamo Force, in the MacArthur plan to take control of ground forces away from the Australians. The operation was designed to seize Cape Gloucester on New Britain Island by airborne and amphibious assault, to knock out the Japanese forward base at Gasmata, and to capture Vitu Island and Long Island. General Blamey's New Guinea Force would continue its land operations on the Huon Peninsula above Finschhafen. After Gasmata, General Krueger was to plan for the invasion of Rabaul. The final date for the attack on Cape Gloucester was set for December 26.

The fact was, however, that the Cape Gloucester operation was a waste of time, as General Kenney pointed out well before the fact. He knew of the Joint Chiefs of Staff's decision to bypass Rabaul. That being so, there was no need to take Cape Gloucester. It would take too long to develop it into a useful air base, he said. He already had enough air bases to support invasions as far away as Kavieng. But MacArthur was not a man to be moved from his own ideas by anything less than a direct order from above. So Cape Gloucester was on.

That fall the Japanese knew what was coming and they strengthened their bases in western New Britain. All the more

*The battle for Bougainville was a part of Southwest Pacific operations only insofar as Admiral Halsey, for administrative purposes, was subject to the orders of General MacArthur. In fact, Halsey fought the battle himself. I have dealt with this battle in *The Glory of the Solomons* (Military Book Club, 1983).

reason for forgetting about Cape Gloucester said the dissidents. Let the Japanese put more troops in western New Britain, and then let them sit there and wither on the vine. But as usual, MacArthur was not listening.

MacArthur's planning went forward in a very confused fashion. The 503rd Parachute Infantry Regiment was to make an airdrop, simply because the 503rd was a parachute regiment and should be employed. As for the air drop, nobody wanted it, and Maj. Gen. William Rupertus, the commander of the 1st Marine Division, was especially opposed to this way of trying to take Cape Gloucester. The marines, who had experience in Guadalcanal, had many objections to the MacArthur plans. Finally, the airdrop was canceled out but the planning went on.

At Rabaul, General Imamura was prepared to see the Allies jump one of two ways. They might either attack Cape Gloucester, preparing for an attack on Rabaul, or they might try to isolate Rabaul by attacking the Admiralty islands and Kavieng. Knowing MacArthur, he bet on the Cape Gloucester operation and sent his reinforcements there. He did not have the troops to spare to reinforce Cape Gloucester and the Admiralties and Kavieng. So, he made the wise decision. He fully expected the Allies to attack Rabaul in February or March 1944, as MacArthur was planning to do.

The 17th Division, which came down from China, was sent to western New Britain. The commander of the 17th Division was given control of all troops in the area, which included the 65th Brigade and several smaller special units. The 17th Division put its headquarters at Gavutu, which was east of the Willaumez Peninsula and a long way from where the fighting was going to take place.

The Southwest Pacific Command was now fat. In November, General Kenney began almost daily air strikes against some targets that would be important in the invasion. He had all the planes he could use. During December, his planes flew nearly nineteen hundred sorties over Cape Gloucester, dropping four thousand tons of bombs. The Tuluvu airfield, one of the chief targets, was knocked out and stayed out. Japanese air power, so enormous at the beginning of the Guadalcanal campaign, was now very weak. The 7th Air Division had lost almost all its planes in the neat trick General Kenney had played on them at Wewak, and in December that disorganized unit was sent up to Java for rehabilitation.

Before Cape Gloucester was attacked, the Allies would take a toehold on New Britain.

The 112th Cavalry Regiment was assigned to make landings at Arawe Island. Arawe, as it was called for short, was really a complex, consisting of Arawe Island, Pilelo Island, and a long boomerang of a peninsula jutting down from New Britain below Umtingalu. Here was a harbor suitable for oceangoing vessels, one that had been a regular port of call before the war for trading ships. The Amalut Plantation ran up one side of the peninsula. The best landing beaches were House Fireman near the plantation and the one just down from Umtingalu. Much of the rest of the area was stone cliff and mangrove swamp.

The 112th cavalry moved up the Goodenough Island, part of the Buna complex, and trained there for ten days. Principal items in their training were two new weapons: a much-improved flamethrower and the 2.36-inch rocket launcher known as the bazooka. They made two simulated landings, which were a dreadful mess. It was the usual problem: the confusion of command and the incomplete training of junior officers and noncoms. There was no time to do much about it, the deficiencies would have to be remedied in combat, which had a way of hardening the survivors in a few hours.

On December 14, all Admiral Barbey's ships were at sea. The landing at Arawe began just before 5:00 A.M. The Japanese were surprised because General Kenney's air forces, while plastering Cape Gloucester with bombs, had left this little area untouched in the hope that the Japanese would suspect nothing. Thirty-nine amphibious tractors were launched, carrying the assault waves of troops. They were guarded going in by two amphibious DUKW tractors armed with rockets.

A Troop of the 112th was assigned to hit the beach at Umtingalu. They went in fifteen rubber boats to make a "surprise landing" and block the coastal trail so the Japanese could not escape from the Arawe area and reinforcements could not come from the east.

But the Japanese knew what the good beaches were as well as the Americans, and machine gunners were waiting.

It was a nice bright night and the Japanese could see the rubber boats coming in from a long way off. When the boats came close enough they began firing and within a few minutes sank twelve of the boats. They then began shooting at the survivors struggling in the water. Not until the destroyer *Shaw* moved in and opened up with its 5-inch guns did the Japanese fire from the beach slow down. Boats went in to pick up the survivors and took them to House Fireman Beach later. Twelve men were killed, four were missing, and seventeen were wounded. The landing at Umtingalu had been a failure.

B Troop was to land on Pilelo Island, surprise the Japanese, and capture a radio station there. The troop left its transport in fifteen rubber boats. But there was no surprise. The Japanese opened fire as soon as they saw the Americans. That was a mistake because the rubber boats changed course and landed on the other side of Pilelo rather than at Paligmete Village where they were assigned. They got ashore safely and began moving overland toward their objective. Just after 6:00 A.M., the soldiers reached Winguru where they came under fire from two caves in the rising ground. They left a squad with flamethrowers and bazookas to deal with the caves and moved out to Paligmete, but there was no radio station and no Japanese. They returned to Winguru and found the squad still working on the Japanese. One cave was closed up by a bazooka. The other was barricaded with logs and cement. A flamethrower came up and let loose a blast of fire. Then soldiers tossed in grenades and the cave was silent. One American was killed in this action. Seven dead Japanese were found in the unsealed cave.

The main landing was on House Fireman Beach. It consisted of five waves supposed to be landing at five-minute intervals. But when the first wave was boated, it headed immediately for shore. Radio communication failed, so it was hard to stop them. Finally, a subchaser went in and rounded up the strays and brought them back to the starting point before a disaster could occur. Obviously, if there had been any hope of surprise, the confusion had alerted the enemy.

Fortunately for the invaders, it did not make much difference. The Japanese force here was very slight. The landing parties made just about every mistake possible. On the way in, the Japanese ashore began firing, but the fire was silenced by the rocket fire from the control boats and the two rocket DUKWs. That quieted the Japanese.

The first wave got ashore. But the second wave, which was supposed to follow in five minutes and help the first, did not get ashore for twenty-five minutes. Had there been many Japanese about the first wave would have been wiped out by that time. Then, fifteen more minutes went by and all the other waves came in together. There were about 30 Japanese in this area; within a couple of hours, they had been routed out of their caves or their palm trees. Altogether there had been only two companies (about 250 men) of Japanese soldiers in the area, and all but the rear guard had retreated before the Americans landed.

It was a very quiet invasion, punctuated only by a mid-morning air raid from the 11th Air Fleet at Rabaul. About thirty planes attacked, bombing and strafing the beaches and the landing craft. Most of the fleet had either returned to New Guinea or had sought cover in the overcast. The Japanese scored a few hits on landing craft, but there were no casualties. They left with P-38 fighters chasing them. For the next two weeks, the Japanese airmen from Rabaul attacked the area almost every day, sinking some supply ships and harrying the troops. But by late December, General Kenney's air forces plus those of the South Pacific Command had played hob with the Rabaul air forces of the Japanese. Admiral Halsey's planes were working over Rabaul nearly every day, and blasting many Japanese planes on the ground. So, by the end of December, the Japanese decided that their remaining air forces must be used to defend Rabaul and Wewak. The western end of New Britain was ignored.

The Japanese did make several attempts to knock the Americans out at Arawe. Maj. Masamitsu Komori was in command of a small force that tried hard. On December 18, two Japanese bargeloads of troops landed at the Pulie River east of Arawe and began advancing west. On December 26, the Japanese attacked in battalion strength; later, they were joined by another battalion. The idea was to crush the Americans in a vise. But it did not work. General Krueger sent in reinforcements from the 158th Infantry, and these saved the day. The Japanese dug in around the airstrip. But they did not know that the Americans did not want or need the airstrip anyhow (indicating the puerility of the whole Arawe operation). By the end of the first week in January, the Americans had about 5,000 men in the Arawe front line. The Japanese had about 100 men in foxholes and shallow trenches. The Americans brought up tanks and General Kenney sent planes, and they attacked. They drove the Japanese back to the airstrip and they remained there until February when Rabaul ordered them to withdraw. In the fighting, the Japanese gave a good account of themselves. In spite of the vastly superior American strength, the Americans lost 118 dead, 352 wounded, and 4 men missing.

And for all that, after the fighting was over, it was decided not to build the PT base for which it had all been done. So, General Kenney was right about Arawe.

The main event was at Cape Gloucester, which Kenney also had said was an unnecessary attack.

This was bigger business. The 1st Marine Division, which made the landing, was escorted to the scene by the cruisers *Phoenix* and *Nashville*, the HMAS *Australia*, the HMASSD *Shropshire*, and eight destroyers.

The troops landed on the morning of December 26.

Once again, lack of knowledge of the landing area and the general terrain created enormous difficulties. The 7th Marines landed on narrow beaches and then faced immediate thick jungle. Behind the beach was a shelf of dry ground. But behind the shelf was a swamp. Men floundered in up to their armpits. And the giant trees toppled as the men disturbed their shallow root structure. The first fatality on Cape Gloucester was a marine killed by a falling tree.

There was no opposition on the beaches. There were Japanese around and one detachment missed the proper beach and landed three hundred yards to the west. It ran into Japanese fire.

The Japanese Rabaul air force was very active this day. The bombers and fighters were over the invasion force in strength. They sank a destroyer, damaged two more destroyers badly, and hit two others. They also damaged two LSTs.

But by the end of D day, the beachhead was secure. The 1st Marines came up to pass through the 7th Marines and advanced west toward that valuable airfield General MacArthur coveted. There were about three thousand Japanese in the area. They counterattacked the first night in the miserable rain. They failed to dislodge the 7th Marines.

The marines moved toward the airfield supported by tanks. They moved three miles that day. On December 28, the marines encountered a Japanese strong point. With tanks, flamethrowers, bazookas, .50-caliber machine guns and the ubiquitous riflemen, they reduced the strong point at the end of the day. The reinforced 5th Marines came up on December 29 and the advance proceeded. Within hours, the airfield was captured, and the Japanese retreated from the Cape Gloucester region. By the end of February, they had retreated all the way to Rabaul, for General Imamura was convinced that the Americans and Australians would move there next.

As General Kenney had predicted, there was really no use for this whole operation. The airstrip was repaired and the construction of another started. But the second strip was never completed. The first was totally unnecessary: by March, when it was ready to handle planes, the advance had gone so far that Rabaul was neutralized. Thus, Cape Gloucester was virtually unused, except to remain as a monument to General MacArthur's ego. In the official army history of the period, this is the only justification that could be found:

> In the light of hindsight [Arawe and Cape Gloucester] were probably not essential to the reduction of Rabaul or the approach to the Philippines. Yet they were neither completely fruitless nor excessively high in casualties. The 1st Marine Division [which did not need the practice] scored a striking tactical success at the cost of 310 killed, 1,083 wounded. And the Allied forces of the Southwest Pacific area, had by means of these operations, broken out through the narrow straits.

Which, as General Kenney had said long before the action, with excellent foresight, was not necessary either.

CHAPTER TWENTY-THREE

The Admiralties

February 1944.

In the South Pacific campaign, the battle for Bougainville had settled down to a slogging match. The Japanese knew that they were losing the campaign, although they would not give up. General Imamura began reinforcing the 6th Division, which was entrusted with the defense of the island. The navy did what it could to try to stem the Allied tide. It was not nearly enough. The Americans, in particular, were now able to put dozens of warships into the area. They had learned a great deal in the past two years. One of the most distinguished performances afloat in this period was that of Capt. Arleigh Burke's destroyer squadron, which proved to be anathema to the Japanese.

There was more hard fighting ahead, including a major Japanese counterattack on Bougainville that would come the next month.

But for practical purposes, the isolation of Rabaul was now almost complete. Even General MacArthur had accepted the Joint Chiefs of Staff's order that the attack on Rabaul be called off. He was now excited by the prospect of moving up the coast of New Guinea and then undertaking the invasion of the Philippines, as the Joint Chiefs had promised him he would be able to do.

To assemble the enormous forces needed for an invasion of the Philippines, the Allies needed a very large harbor. Such existed, Seeadler Bay of Manus Island in the Admiralty chain, named for the ship of that legendary German naval fighter of World War I, Count Felix von Luckner. Here in the South Pacific that German raider had finally reached the end of her career.

Seeadler Harbor was six-miles wide, almost twenty-miles long. Its water was deep, about twenty fathoms, which would accommodate the battleships and aircraft carriers very nicely.

Manus Island, the focus of the attack, lies two hundred miles northeast of New Guinea on the road to Manila. It is forty-nine-miles long and sixteen-miles wide, and it is bisected along its length by a mountain range three-thousand-feet high. The shoreline is largely mangrove swamp. At one end of Manus lies Los Negros Island, which is separated only by a narrow canal-like passage. It then had several coconut plantations in the flat central portion of the island.

The invasion of the Admiralties was to be the largest amphibious operation yet undertaken in the Southwest Pacific. It would involve three naval units: Adm. Thomas Kinkaid's 7th Fleet, Admiral Halsey's 3rd Fleet, and additional ships lent for this particular purpose by Admiral Nimitz's Pacific Fleet. Admiral Halsey would be in charge of the entire operation as long as it was in the amphibious stage. Once the ground units got ashore and were established in their beachhead, command of the ground would pass to General Krueger of the 6th Army. Forty-five thousand men would be involved.

The Japanese had built two excellent airfields, one at Lorengau on the north shore of Manus Island and the other near Momote Point on Los Negros.

Toward the end of 1943, General Imamura at Rabaul had decided to reinforce the Admiralties and had ordered the 66th Infantry Regiment from New Guinea to move up to the Palau Islands and there wait for replacements and equipment to rebuild the losses of the New Guinea campaign. The regiment reached Palau, but its replacements did not.

By the end of 1943, the submarines of Admiral Kinkaid's 7th Fleet and those of Adm. Charles Lockwood's Pacific Fleet submarine force had created a very effective blockade of the Japanese empire. The Japanese responded by sending ever-larger convoys southward, but the result was that more Japanese ships were sunk by the growing force of U.S. submarines. In January, Tokyo organized two sets of convoys, one called the Matsu Convoys, which were to reinforce the Marianas, and the other called the Take Convoys, which were to move to Palau and thence down to the New Guinea area to reinforce General Imamura.

But none of these convoys got through intact. Near the Marianas, the first Matsu Convoy encountered the U.S. submarine *Trout*, which sank one transport carrying four thousand men. Half of them were drowned. That same fate was in store for the transport carrying the replacements for the 66th Infantry. When General Imamura learned of this bad news, he ordered the remaining troops at Palau, remnants of several abortive convoys, to reorganize with the 66th Infantry and come down to Manus. The convoy set out, but was so harried by American submarines and planes that it turned back to Palau and unloaded. Imamura finally achieved some reinforcement by sending two battalions (or about two thousand men) who were brought in by destroyer transports. In February, Col. Yoshio Ezaki, the commander of the Admiralties garrison, had those two battalions, a regiment of transport service troops, and several small naval detachments. The Japanese defense was built around Seeadler Harbor.

Early in February, the Allied air forces began the softening up campaign against the Admiralties. By the end of the first week in February, both Japanese airfields were knocked out. No planes were left intact and the runways and facilities were unserviceable. A few days later, destroyers sank a Japanese transport a hundred miles east of Manus. Survivors said they were part of the ground force detachment of the airfields in the Admiralties, that the fields had been abandoned and that they were being transferred to bases farther north. So, the fact was becoming clear that the Japanese had, indeed, changed their perimeter of defense and that New Guinea had, in fact, been written off as well as Rabaul, Truk, and everything south of the Mariana Islands. Truk was almost deserted by this time. Even Palau, the newly designated base of the Combined Fleet, was about to be deserted. Allied submarines were wreaking such a toll on Japanese tankers that fuel was in short supply everywhere, and the Japanese were splitting up their Combined Fleet, moving parts of it to the Dutch Indies where they would be on top of their fuel supply. By February 1944, the Southwest Pacific campaign, as such, had ended in triumph for the Allies. This invasion of the Admiralties, over which MacArthur and his commanders worried so much, was not going to be nearly so difficult nor nearly so important as they expected.

Adm. Raymond Spruance's U.S. 5th Fleet staged a gigantic air raid on Truk just after the middle of February and found only a handful of remnants of the Combined Fleet, a sort of naval rear guard that had been caught by surprise. Thereafter, Truk was not even important as an air center. Its value to the Japanese as a naval base, ''the Gibraltar of the Pacific,'' had been completely expended.

General Kenney, who had been watching the development of Allied power and the decline of the Japanese, suggested that it would be possible to send in a small force of men to seize Morote Airfield. His pilots, flying low over the field, had not been encountering any antiaircraft fire, nor had they seen any Japanese or any serviceable aircraft or vehicles. There was a reason for this, one General Kenney did not know. Colonel Ezaki had decided to conserve his strength. His men were committed to defense of Manus to the last, and they did not want to reveal their positions until the actual time of invasion. So they hid out.

Kenney suggested that a small force of men might take and hold the airfield for the Allies pending the real invasion.

When General Kenney proposed this plan to MacArthur and his staff at Brisbane, General Willoughby, the intelligence officer, jibbed. He said the Japanese garrison at Los Negros was strong, about four thousand fighting men. But MacArthur went with Kenney. He ordered General Krueger to send in a reconnaissance force of eight hundred men of the 1st Cavalry Division. They would be taken in fast by destroyer transport.

In sharp comparison with the past, the Allies now had plenty of transport and plenty of support. Rear Adm. Russell S. Berkey was assigned this task. He had the cruiser *Nashville*, the cruiser *Phoenix*, and four destroyers to cover the landing force. Rear Adm. William M. Fechteler had eight destroyers and three transport destroyers to deliver the men. The cruisers were not really a part of the plan, they were added because General MacArthur decided to go along and take Admiral Kinkaid to watch the show. The official reason was to judge from firsthand observation whether to evacuate or hold the position once it was attacked. Admiral Kinkaid added two cruisers and four destroyers to the force. It was a tribute to the people back home who were producing so many ships by the winter of 1944 that they could be employed in this fashion, an enormous change from those days in 1942 when Admiral Carpender would not even commit a single destroyer to the eastern shore of New Guinea for fear that he might lose it.

The whole matter of strength was further complicated by the rules that had been set up to govern MacArthur's navy. MacArthur needed a cruiser because there was no place aboard a destroyer, including the captain's cabin, big enough to give honor to General MacArthur. A cruiser had better accommodations. But a cruiser could not travel alone, under Kinkaid's rules, so two cruisers had to be added, and that meant four more destroyers. Thus, the Manus mission consisted of six destroyers escorting three transport destroyers. And the MacArthur mission, launched simultaneously, consisted of two cruisers and four destroyers carrying General MacArthur. Why should not a commander come along to watch the results of his genius?

General Willoughby sat at Brisbane and worried. Brig. Gen. Ennis C. Whitehead, the deputy commander of the 5th Air Force, had an entirely different picture of Japanese strength. He said that there were probably three hundred Japanese on the island. The intelligence officer of the 1st Cavalry Division said there were probably five thousand Japanese over there. On February 27, a PBY flying boat delivered a six-man scouting party to a point off the Los Negros southern shore when an air bombardment was going on and the Japanese, if there, could be expected to keep their heads down. The scouts went in by rubber boat and reported by radio that the place was "lousy with Japs."

Willoughby shook his head in assent. Kenney shook his head in disbelief. To a scouting party, he said, twenty-five Japanese in the woods at night would look like the entire Imperial Army.

The net result was that the scouting party report proved nothing. The plan for the reconnaissance mission went ahead.

The commander was Maj. Gen. Inis P. Swift, commander of the 1st Cavalry Division.

The eight-hundred-man force would land and see what happened. If it held on, then two days later the Brewer Reconnaissance Force would come in, under Col. Hugh T. Hoffman. If all went well, then a whole succession of troop units would follow shortly.

On February 27, General MacArthur and Admiral Kinkaid flew from Brisbane to Milne Bay and boarded their cruiser, the *Phoenix*. That same day, at Oro Bay, the Brewer Force loaded up aboard Admiral Fechteler's ships. On the morning of February 29 (it was leap year), the ships came up to Hyane Harbor on Los Negros. There was absolutely no Japanese opposition on the sea, under the sea, or in the air.

The action began at 7:23 in the morning when Admiral Fechteler's ships began decanting men into a landing craft, from a point two miles off the beach. The ships began to fire a naval barrage against the apparent Japanese position on Los Negros. The first sign of the enemy came when the landing craft approached the entrance to Hyane Harbor. Machine guns on both points opened fire. So did 75-mm guns on the shore, shooting at the warships. But the warships soon had the big guns silenced and then the destroyers shot up the 20-mm machine gun sites on the points. The sky was overcast and an expected Allied air strike did not materialize until very late, but by a few minutes after 8:00 A.M. the troops were landing and there was no firing. When the first Americans landed, a Japanese machine-gun crew nearby scuttled for cover. There were no American casualties. Several Japanese were shot down as they ran. Then in came the second, third, and fourth waves to land. Only the fourth wave received any enemy fire. There was virtually no damage.

At 9 o'clock Gen. William C. Chase, commander of the 1st Cavalry Brigade, whose troops were ashore, radioed General Krueger that a perimeter had been established three hundred yards inland. He did not then know where his enemy was or how many he faced. An hour later, the Americans had captured Momote Airfield. They found it covered with debris and weeds. The whole area was marred by bomb craters full of water.

The Japanese ashore were occupying their time by firing

at the ships offshore and firing at the landing craft. They damaged four of them. By noon, however, the whole reconnaissance force had gotten ashore with antiaircraft guns and 75-mm pack howitzers. Two cavalrymen had been killed and three wounded. Two U.S. sailors were killed and three wounded. And five dead Japanese had been counted.

By midafternoon the Americans had advanced across every foot of the airfield. They found a warehouse full of food. At 4 o'clock, General MacArthur came ashore to have his picture taken awarding 2nd Lt. Marvin J. Henshaw the Distinguished Service Cross. Henshaw had been the first man ashore in the invasion. The general was hard put to find people to pin medals on because the whole action had been so quiet, so far. It was not a very nice day. The general's raincoat was soaked and so was Lieutenant Henshaw's poncho.

The general made a little speech, instructing General Chase "to remain here and hold the airstrip at any cost."

Since the cost so far had been minimal, it seemed a fair guess. And then, heroically, "having ignored sniper fire [of which there was virtually none] and wet, cold, and dirty with mud up to the ears," the general moved back to the warmth and comfort and clean sheets of the cruiser *Phoenix*. Lieutenant Henshaw remained out in the rain.

The general then sent orders back to Brisbane to send up all the reinforcements that were available to the Admiralties, and he went to dinner.

General Chase, ashore in the rain, was inclined to believe General Willoughby's estimate of the number of Japanese on the island. He decided to abandon the airstrip because it would be too hard to defend it, and he established a perimeter to the east.

Late in the afternoon, the soldiers organized their perimeter. The .50-caliber machine guns were set up. Outposts were established on the other side of the airstrip. All this took time because the ground was coral and the digging was arduous. That afternoon General Chase asked for an airdrop of barbed wire. He was very uneasy. General Willoughby's estimate of the number of Japanese on Manus and Los Negros islands was more nearly correct than that of the 5th Air Force. There were several thousand troops, most of them on Los Negros, and they were preparing an attack. At Rabaul,

General Imamura had told Colonel Ezaki to attack this first night with all strength.

So as darkness fell, he issued his orders. This was not to be a delaying action, he told the commander of the 1st Battalion of the 229th Infantry. It was an annihilation fight and all his men were to be prepared to die, particularly if they were in danger of being captured.

Darkness came quickly, as it does in that part of the world. The sound of rifles firing began at dusk and increased as night came on. The American outposts were withdrawn and the men brought back within the perimeter.

The Japanese attacked on all sides, usually in small groups. Some swam around behind the Americans and approached from the beach. The Americans stayed in their foxholes and fired at everything that moved.

Late in the evening, two Japanese penetrated almost to General Chase's command post before they were stopped by Maj. Julio Chiaramonte, the force intelligence officer, who had a submachine gun. One was killed and the other captured, wounded.

When morning came, seven Americans were dead and fifteen wounded, but there were sixty-six Japanese bodies inside the perimeter.

General Chase reconsidered his defenses. He sent out patrols, and they encountered the enemy four hundred yards from the perimeter. Another attack was imminent obviously, and the support force would not arrive until the third day.

But on this second day, he, at least, received airdrops of ammunition, medical supplies, mines, and grenades. The planes did not bring any barbed wire.

Colonel Ezaki's force was very strong around the airfield. In the dispersal area where the Americans had first set up outposts, the Japanese had built fortifications. That afternoon, General Chase asked for an air strike on this area and began firing thereabouts with his two 75-mm pack howitzers. The air force came in beginning at 4:00 P.M. and attacked until dark. The planes were fired on by Japanese antiaircraft guns, which had kept silent until now. The destroyers *Bush* and *Stockton* came up to about a half-mile off the beach and opened fire on the airfield. From Wewak several Japanese 4th Air army planes arrived, but they were driven off by American fighters without doing any damage. The air and naval bombardment caused about a hundred Japanese to flee from the dispersal area, and they came right into the field of fire of the American machine guns. Most of the Japanese were killed.

That afternoon, the Japanese organized a special attack force of noncommissioned officers, who were led personally by Captain Baba, the commander of the 229th Battalion. The ostensible purpose was to wipe out General Chase's command post. It was a truly desperate attempt. Do or die, said Captain Baba, remembering the words of General Imamura. And so, he came forth to succeed or die in one gallant gesture.

The Japanese managed to approach within thirty-five yards of the command post, when the attackers were sighted. Before they could organize for a *banzai* charge, Major Chiaramonte and several enlisted men opened fire with automatic weapons. Baba was killed and so were several others. The rest, facing automatic fire and without cover, killed themselves with grenades and short *samurai* swords.

That afternoon, the Japanese hit the perimeter at 5:00 P.M. That was a mistake; the American weapons were excellent and the attack was turned back. During the night Japanese infiltrators tried to get inside the lines and succeeded in most places because of the lack of barbed wire. About fifty of them swam across the harbor entrance to attack. That night, the artillerymen fired three hundred rounds from the two 75-mm guns. They also fired their rifles continually. In the morning, nearly fifty Japanese bodies were found around the artillery position.

Colonel Ezaki had made a glaring mistake. He had not followed General Imamura's orders, thus his force was being chewed up piecemeal.

On the morning of March 2, the third day, the support force of about two thousand men arrived from New Guinea. They were supported by more destroyers. One destroyer led two minesweepers to the entrance to Seeadler Harbor, hoping to go in and establish the harbor. But the Japanese had field guns on the islands of Hauwei and Ndrilo and more guns on the shore of Los Negros Island. So, the fire was heavy, and the sweeping job could not be accomplished. The ships retired outside. More destroyers were brought up to give support fire and another attempt was made; again, the Japanese guns prevented the minesweeping.

When the support forces landed, at Hyane Harbor, they were brought under fire by Japanese mortars and machine guns. It was nothing like that first day when it almost seemed as if there were no enemy on the island. But the landings were successful, made under the cover of B-29 bombing and strafing attacks. Within a matter of minutes, the five hundred Seabees in the augmenting force were ashore with their bulldozers, building ramps for the other vehicles. Unloading of men, supplies, and equipment was finished by 5:00 P.M., and most of the ships returned to New Guinea. Four destroyers remained off Los Negros to support the ground troops and to prevent any Japanese attacks from the sea.

That morning, with another two thousand men coming in, the American perimeter threatened to get pretty crowded, so General Chase organized an attack to broaden his base. After a bombing attack early in the afternoon, the troops of the 5th Cavalry began to attack the airfield. By 3 o'clock that afternoon, they had captured it, Colonel Ezaki had sacrificed too many men and did not have the resources just then to defend very well. The Americans had taken the airfield with a total of six casualties—two dead, four wounded—all caused by an American bomb that had fallen in the wrong place.

Now the Americans captured some Japanese documents that indicated the strength of Colonel Ezaki's force—or the strength as it had been four days earlier. There were about two thousand Japanese troops in the west half of Los Negros Island.

The perimeter was prepared for more attacks that night. An outer perimeter around the aircraft dispersal area of the airfield was established by the infantry. The antiaircraft troops were put down at the beach. The Seabees held an interior defense line on two sides of General Chase's command post. The field pieces now numbered three, and they were put into revetments with overlapping fields of fire to the south and west. There was still no barbed wire.

Colonel Ezaki was preparing his major attack, two days late. General Imamura had told him to consolidate his forces on that first day; on the third he did so. Troops were called from Manus and the outer islands. They came up to see the Americans using bulldozers to clear fields of fire. One bulldozer dug a three-hundred-foot trench for the Americans. It beat using an entrenching tool all the way. Colonel Ezaki postponed the attack for twenty-four hours. So, the Americans had another day to strengthen their defenses. They spent March 3 clearing fields of fire with the bulldozers, laying mine fields, and setting up their own warning devices. They used bits of field wire (the Japanese had effectively cut the telephone lines that first night, giving the Americans plenty of scrap) and empty C ration cans with coral lumps inside to provide warning bells. These were strung where possible. And where not possible, they were scattered about so that a Japanese shoe striking a can would produce a very clear rattle. The 60-mm mortars were massed in front of the field artillery. The 81-mm mortars were dispersed to fire deeper.

At sea, the destroyers fired on Japanese positions. They discovered several barges beached behind mossy mangrove trees and shot them up.

Dusk came and turned to darkness. A single Japanese plane came over and dropped eight bombs. One of them cut the telephone line between the 5th Cavalry command post and the 1st Squadron. Not long after 9:00 P.M., the Japanese launched another infantry attack against the southwest part of the perimeter held by the 1st Squadron.

This was beaten off by the cavalrymen. But this attack was a feint, the main attack was to be against the north and east. It started not long afterward, but in a thoroughly ragged and disorganized fashion.

The Japanese came up noisily, shouting and singing, apparently to distract the defenders. They began firing before they were in range and wasted a lot of grenades. They entered the minefields and the mines began popping. They did not stop but drove forward into the interlocking fields of fire of the .50-caliber machine guns. They did make some infiltration and did cut communications lines. G troop of the 2nd Squadron was out of touch. But the men stayed in their foxholes, hurling grenades and firing at movement, and they held. Just before morning, some Japanese penetrated within the G troop perimeter and Capt. Frank G. Mayfield led an attack that drove them out again. G troop began to run out of ammunition and the Japanese attacked again. H troops heavy machine guns came to the rescue.

It was a night of ferocious fighting, particularly in the G troop positions. Sgt. Troy McGill was holding one captured Japanese revetment with his squad of eight men. One by one the men were cut down until only he and one other were unwounded. He ordered all the wounded survivors out of the position and then began firing his rifle furiously. It jammed. The Japanese came on. He used the rifle as a club and fought until he was shot down. His relatives received his posthumous Medal of Honor.

Some of the Japanese had been studying English. Late in the night, a column of men came marching up the road from Porlaka, singing "Deep in the Heart of Texas," a popular American song of the 1940s. Americans? No. Japanese. They marched up, singing. But there is a line in the song that does not say, "the moon shines on the one I rove." That was the tipoff. American machine guns, mortars, and rifles spoke up and the column fell down.*

Other English-speaking Japanese moved around shouting fake orders. One such was received by the weapons squad of the 2nd Squadron. The squad believed the order was real and moved back, thus depriving the 2nd Squadron of its 81-mm mortar support.

Individually, the Japanese effort was sometimes fantastically courageous.

One Japanese squad with a knee mortar moved up onto the roof of the dugout used by Col. William Lobit as command post for the 2nd Squadron. Capt. Bruce Merrit, crouched in a foxhole, picked them off one by one.

Other Japanese in squad strength moved among the artillery and into the Seabee line of defense. The Seabees fought with rifles and grenades as hard as the cavalry did.

The Japanese squads did their job, but their officers failed them. The attack was so badly coordinated that it could not succeed. At daybreak, the Japanese pulled back, although

*The official U.S. Army history of the battle suggests that this tale was apocryphal because the song was a favorite of the 1st Cavalry Division. The author prefers to believe that the story was true.

their mortars and field pieces continued to fire on the American perimeter.

The Japanese had attacked in so many places and the corpses were strewn around so broadly that no body count was made that morning except in the G troop sector, which had borne the brunt of the heaviest attack. There, 168 enemy bodies were counted. No prisoners were taken. That is an indication of the desperation with which the Japanese fought. Not even a wounded man would let himself be captured.

Colonel Ezaki brought his battered remnants together again, but it was too late. The chance was lost. Within two days, the Allies began bringing in thousands of more reinforcements: the 7th and 12th Cavalry regiments as well as special troops. Soon enough, they seized all of Los Negros. The Japanese resisted fiercely, but it was hopeless and had been since the failure on the first and second nights to dislodge the Americans.

More warships came, and more planes, and they blasted the defenses around Seeadler Harbor, which had been seriously weakened anyhow by the call of Colonel Ezaki for all the available men to come to the airfield on March 3. On March 5, all the harbor defenses were knocked out and American vessels began entering freely. On the morning of March 9, six LSTs and a big cargo ship came into Seeadler harbor to land the 2nd Cavalry Brigade.

An attack was made against Lorengau and the rest of Manus Island. There was heavy fighting all the way. One advance patrol was sent to Hauwei, an island just offshore, to look for good artillery positions. The platoon left Salami aboard an LCV and a PT boat. The men landed on the western part of the island. But inland, they ran into well-prepared Japanese positions that caught them from front and both sides. The Americans made a fighting withdrawal to the beach, supported by fire from the LCV and the PT boat. But the PT boat skipper was wounded and the crew took the boat back to its tender. Five of the cavalrymen got aboard the LCV, but the rest of the platoon was pinned down on the shore by the enemy. The Japanese were using mortars and machine guns. Then the LCV, in trying to maneuver, struck a submerged reef two hundred yards offshore and sank. The survivors were now afloat in the water. A half-dozen Japanese brought a machine gun down to the beach to work them over, but the cavalrymen on the beach used their submachine guns to wipe out the Japanese squad and then took to the water with the others. They were out there for three hours in the sun and wind. Then reinforcements came in the form of a destroyer, which stood off and shelled the island while another PT boat picked up the eighteen survivors of the LCV and the cavalry platoon. Every survivor had been wounded.

Most of the 2nd Squadron was then assigned to the capture of Hauwei with tanks. They came, and the fighting was ferocious. The Japanese had well-prepared bunkers and other defenses. The Americans landed on the afternoon of March 12 and were reinforced that evening. The 61st Field Artillery fired a thousand rounds into the Japanese sector. With tanks, 75-mm guns, machine guns, and mortars, the squadron took the island in two days. Eight Americans were killed and forty-six were wounded. They counted the bodies of the dead garrison, all Imperial Japanese Navy sailors. There were forty-three of them. This handful of men had held up a thousand men with warships, air power, and every other weapon for three days. It was quite an accomplishment, but bound to be unheralded in the story of the war.

Los Negros was finally cleared of all Japanese by the end of March; shortly afterward, the Americans captured Lorengau Airfield and cleaned up most of the Admiralties. Yet it took two squadrons of cavalry, a number of tanks, many air strikes, and thousands of rounds of artillery fire to do so.

In April, the Americans were mopping up in the outer islands. When the battle ended, and this was not until May, the Americans counted the cost. The 1st Cavalry Division had lost 326 men killed, 1,189 wounded, and 4 missing. They had killed 3,280 Japanese defenders and captured 75; they estimated that the Japanese had buried or burned another thousand of their own dead. So, General Willoughby had been right about the defenses, although not even he knew how desperately these Japanese would defend. A new pattern had been set, which would be followed throughout the rest of the Pacific War. The Japanese at Buna and beyond had been the victims of starvation, and their commanders tried desperately to save them for further action. But now, the Japanese attitude had changed. Every man was a hero. Every man was expected to die for the emperor. There would be no quarter in this new war. That was the story of the Admiralties. The enormous power of the Americans was making itself felt. In spite of Imperial General Headquarters' (IGHs') new claim that the Japanese would still win, through tenacity and high purpose, the handwriting was on the wall. There was no way that *Bushido* spirit could stand up against overwhelming air, naval, and army strength when it was vigorously applied. By the spring of 1944, the Americans were seasoned fighters. They had begun to know their enemy, taught in the steaming jungles of Guadalcanal and New Guinea, and they were preparing for the movement to the Vogelkop (now Doberai), to Hollandia (now Djajajsura), and beyond. There was power aplenty. Out of the old raider battalions, the marines had created the new 4th Marine Regiment. It captured Emirau Island only to discover that there were no Japanese ashore. The isolation of Rabaul was now complete. The next step would be movement up the Vogelkop and the capture of Hollandia.

This would be the beginning of an entirely new campaign and the return of General MacArthur to the Philippines. Through events that occurred in the Marianas and at Pearl Harbor in the summer of 1944, the impetus for the attack of the Allies would be taken away from the navy and its Central Pacific campaign and would be put into MacArthur's hands. But that is another story.

NOTES

1 Retreat Down Under

The material about the fall of the Philippines in the early pages of this chapter comes from Louis Morton's *The Fall of the Philippines*. General Homma's remarks about the possibility of an American counterattack come from his testimony at his war crimes trial in Tokyo. Homma was a much maligned man, by the Americans and by his own military contemporaries. Before the fall of the Philippines, Imperial General Headquarters (IGH) sent one of its bright young colonels to the islands, Colonel Tsuji. He was a very tough fellow: he had pulled his pistol during the Bataan Death March and shot dead an American straggler. He also returned to Tokyo and reported that Homma was soft on the Americans. So, Homma was brought back to Tokyo and forcibly retired from the service. He spent the rest of the war writing articles for the newspapers. Then, after the war, this man who was soft on the Americans was tried as a war criminal, proving once more that victor's justice is hardly justice at all.

The decision of the Roosevelt administration to prosecute the war in Europe at the expense of the war in the Pacific seems to have been well known to everyone but the American people and the American servicemen in the Pacific. All the servicemen knew was that they were not getting the materials that would let them win. They did not know why. The Germans knew, so did the Japanese. There was a lot of brave talk, some of it from President Roosevelt, about sending aid to Bataan. But there was never any real intention of doing so. The original Plan Orange, the navy's war plan for the Pacific, had indicated that the Philippines would have to be sacrificed and won back. So, that was the course that was followed without much regard for events. Morton discusses this in some detail, and he quotes former Secretary of War Patrick J. Hurley on the matter of MacArthur's extrication from the

Philippines. Hurley was one of MacArthur's major supporters, and he had a pipeline to President Roosevelt's office.

The speed with which the Japanese rolled up the western colonies surprised everyone, including the Japanese. They had claimed that the Westerners were effete, sloppy, and lazy, but they did not know how right they were. The surrender of the British at Singapore to a Japanese force only one-third the British size was an indication of the Western soldiers' inability to fight. It was not the fault of the men but, as usual in such cases, of their officers, who had grown rotten in the colonial service. The Americans were not immune to the disease. The years between the wars had softened the American military in every sense of the word. It was only toward the end of the Bataan campaign that the officers began to pull themselves together.

The Quezon–MacArthur–Washington interchange comes from Morton. President Roosevelt's various messages about defending the Philippines "to the death" come from Morton as well. There was some pretty murky thinking going on in Washington. The truth was that the U.S. Army and some of the U.S. Navy wanted to fight the Pacific War. This could have been done, but at the expense of giving to the Pacific the weapons and supplies that Britain also wanted. Prime Minister Churchill persuaded President Roosevelt that without this material, Britain would fall. The evidence indicates that this claim was truthful. The summer and fall of 1941 were desperate days for Britain, beset by the U-boats and at bay in the Mediterranean. Had the United States sent the aid to the Philippines, and used its Pacific Fleet submarines, probably the islands could have been held, but at the cost of adding Britain to Hitler's *Festung Europa*.

As Morton discusses, a major problem for the American high command in Washington was an almost total lack of information about what was happening in the Pacific. It is a bit puzzling that the American communications system was so poor. The technical equipment existed. The organization did not. But this was to be expected of a military system that had watched the U-boat depredations against Britain for more than two years but had not bothered to build up an antisubmarine force of its own.

MacArthur's heroic message to Washington about his safe

arrival in Australia is from Morton. It was a typical MacArthur message, written for the grandstand, as always. As Morton indicates, MacArthur really did believe the government in Washington was going to support an immediate drive back to the Philippines. It was some time before he was given the true word and a long time before he accepted it.

The development of the strange and really rather inefficient duality of command in the Southern Pacific was the ultimate responsibility of President Roosevelt. In the political sphere, he had always surrounded himself with men of divergent views and picked and chose the advice he wanted to take. Admiral King and General Marshall both wanted to lead the show in the Pacific. Admiral Leahy, the president's military aide, favored MacArthur, but privately Roosevelt, a former assistant secretary of the navy, had a soft spot for his old service. Thus the dichotomy, which infuriated MacArthur, but also was probably responsible for the victory in the Solomon Islands. MacArthur was very much opposed to the marine landings on Guadalcanal and predicted to Washington that they would fail. As was so often the case, MacArthur was dead wrong.

2 Japan's Drive South

Much of the material for this chapter comes from various studies I have made over the years of Pacific affairs. The material about the development of Japanese military policy against the United States comes from my own book on the Russo-Japanese War and from my own *Pacific Destiny*. Theodore Roosevelt's refusal to grant the Japanese monetary reparations at the Treaty of Portsmouth was a blunder, since such reparations were common at the time. He did not know that the Japanese army, just beginning to stir in its ambitions, was counting on that money to build up its forces. Then, Roosevelt's dispatch of the Great White Fleet around the world was another blunder. He is famous for his quotation, "Talk softly but carry a big stick." In this White Fleet maneuver, he did neither. He talked loudly, and the Great White Fleet was neither great nor a fleet. It was a motley concatenation of warships, many of them superannuated, some of them built up with fake armor and structures that were intended to impress the Japanese, which it did—badly. Out of this maneuver came the change in Japanese policy, designating the United States as Japan's number one enemy.

The development of that Japanese policy is shown in the series of books issued by the Japanese government in the postwar period, giving in great detail the history of the Pacific War. *Nanto Homen Kaigun Sakusen* (*Naval Operations in the Southeast Area*, 3 vols.) tells of the Japanese build up. Another source for this material was my research for *Japan's War* and Samuel Milner's *Victory in Papua*. The *Nankai Shitai*, the shock-troop force employed by the Japanese in Papua, was a very effective fighting unit. But the Japanese had been persuaded by their series of early victories that one Japanese soldier was worth three Western Soldiers. It was not true, at least not after the beginning of the New Guinea campaign.

The capture of Rabaul was described by the Japanese in the operational reports of the *Nankai Shitai* and the 18th Army. I used the Japanese Defense Agency's volumes on army operations in New Guinea.

The Japanese were not very much aware of the difficulties they would face in conducting military operations in the rain forest of New Guinea. They did not supply enough medicines to their troops in the beginning, and these quickly ran out. They, like the Allies, did not fully appreciate the natural dangers. Thus throughout the campaign, the Japanese, like the Allies, suffered dreadfully from malaria and dysentery.

A serious deficiency in the Japanese scheme of conquest for New Guinea was the inability of the army and navy to cooperate fully. This deficiency was built into the Japanese military system. It had existed since the earliest days of the Meiji restoration when the Satsuma clan took over the navy and the clan took over the navy. In modern years, the clans had lost their control, and in Japan, the navy always regarded itself as the more respectable service. The army was far more democratic and plebeian. General Tōjō, for example, was the son of an impoverished *samurai* who joined the army and worked his way up. Many generals of World War II came from peasant stock. The growing army offered opportunity to the poor.

The story of early American naval operations in the South Pacific comes from my long interview in 1974 with Adm. Aubrey W. Fitch. The story of the Japanese invasion of Lae and Salamaua comes from the Boei volumes, from my own *Japan's War,* and from my own *Blue Skies and Blood,* the story of the battle of the Coral Sea.

The remarks about the early problems of the B-17s come largely from Japanese sources. In the first days of the war, American bombing techniques were not very well developed, but as will be seen, they improved mightily.

3 Port Moresby

The material about General MacArthur's reactions and plans on reaching Australia is from Milner's *Victory in Papua,* Lida Mayo's *Bloody Buna,* and William Manchester's biography of General MacArthur, *American Caesar.* MacArthur's correspondence with General Marshall gives his views of the command problems and indicates his shock at having been told he would be the kingpin of American forces in the Pacific and then having the plum pulled away from him.

The table of organization was included in MacArthur's General Order No. 1 as Commander-in-Chief of the Southwest Pacific Area.

Samuel Milner stated that one of the great pluses for the Allies in the New Guinea campaign was plenty of shipping. But by the time the campaign began, that coastal shipping surplus had been whittled away to nothing by the Japanese. The greatest problem of the Allies during the first half of the campaign was supply, and they saw a small fleet of trawlers converted to cargo vessels go down one by one before the Japanese air force from Rabaul.

MacArthur's high hopes of the spring of 1942 are delineated in his correspondence with Washington. He expected to have a real naval force. Instead, he got an admiral, a handful of destroyers, such ships as Australia had (although Admiral Halsey had equal designs on them), and a flock of submarines, most of them (at first) of the old S-boat class. MacArthur also wanted three American divisions. He got two National Guard divisions, neither of them fully trained for combat, although one of them, the 32nd, was thrown into the fight very soon. He struggled against the inevitable, trying all sorts of ploys that confused the military and political situations. Only once did he come up against that old bear, Winston Churchill, and from that encounter even MacArthur emerged with his tail feathers badly burned. His correspondence with General Marshall on the subject tells the tale.

One of the interesting aspects of the New Guinea planning was the paucity of information about anything to do with New Guinea that existed in the MacArthur headquarters. There is no indication of any particular effort by MacArthur's staff to discover the facts of New Guinea's topography and ambience. The people who knew, the district officers of the Australian government, could have given some very intelligent briefings. Instead, MacArthur's headquarters went into the campaign flying blind and with considerable distrust of the Australians.

4 The Battle of the Coral Sea—I

This account of the Battle of the Coral Sea comes from my own book on that battle, *Blue Skies and Blood;* and from the Boei Series; Volume 1 of the Japanese *Southeast Area Naval Operations* volumes; and from materials for my forthcoming biography of Admiral Yamamoto. The reassessment of a number of the naval leaders of this period of the war is most interesting. Admiral Yamamoto had not had any hand in the selection of Admiral Nagumo to head the Japanese carrier striking force. He had never liked Nagumo very much. He considered Nagumo to be a timid flower; by the time of the battle of the Coral Sea, he was furious with Nagumo who was off in the Indian Ocean. From Yamamoto's point of view, Nagumo had botched the Pearl Harbor operation and the Trincomalee attack. Admiral Frank Jack Fletcher, the senior American naval officer at the Battle of the Coral Sea, was Nagumo's kind of admiral. He, too, was very, very cautious. Had Admiral Fitch been in total command from the beginning, the Americans might not have lost the *Lexington* and the Japanese might have lost the *Shokaku* and the *Zuikaku* as well as the carrier *Shoho*.

Admiral Yamamoto was not particularly worried about the

coming MO Operation. His control of that landing was more theoretical than real. It was Admiral Inoue's show. Yamamoto's flagship was still up in Japanese waters. In fact, there was no intent to bring it to the Southern Pacific. His next move would be to accompany the fleet in its attack on Midway and the Aleutians in June. He would do that for two reasons: (1) he expected to draw the American fleet out from Pearl Harbor and fight a decisive fleet battle and (2) he did not trust Admiral Nagumo, who otherwise would be in charge.

In the late days of April and early May, the Americans had two task forces in the Southern Pacific waters, and they were doing absolutely nothing. Admiral Fletcher was maundering about, spending most of his time worrying about the weather and refueling. Admiral Fitch was shuttled from pillar to post. Had either force stepped in and made a strong attack on Rabaul at this point, the battle of the Coral Sea might never have been fought. Later, in the days of Bougainville, Admiral Halsey would clobber Rabaul harbor and its naval contingent; from that battering, Rabaul would never recover.

5 The Battle of the Coral Sea—II

This account of the second stage of the Battle of the Coral Sea is from my own book on that subject. American and Japanese pilots both performed admirably in these carrier attacks. Admiral Fitch had a hunch about the Japanese location—a very educated hunch as it turned out—and although the American search got fouled up, the strike force he sent off and kept out there found the enemy. The American combat air patrols above the two carriers were extremely effective and the Japanese did not really get a very good shot at the *Lexington*. But they were lucky, she was an old carrier and her damage-control mechanisms left a good deal to be desired. The *Shokaku* was so badly damaged by the American attack that when Admiral Hara, the commander of the carrier force, came steaming out of a squall in the *Zuikaku* and saw the *Shokaku*, she was listing so badly and burning so fiercely that he thought she was going to sink. But, although she lost a hundred men and many aircraft, she was saved from the fate of the *Lexington* by her crew, just as the men of the *Yorktown* saved their ship after she took an armor-piercing bomb below decks.

6 New Defenses

The material about the Rabaul air defenses throughout this chapter comes from several sources. *Rabauru*, a Japanese naval aviator's account of the 11th Air Fleet, is one of them. Another is the Boei volumes on naval operations in the Southeast. Milner's *Victory in Papua* is the major source for the running account of Allied military operations. *Double-Edged Secrets* is the source for material about the American intercepts of Japanese coded messages. Mayo's *Bloody Buna* is also a source here.

What Admiral Yamamoto had feared happened at Midway. Admiral Nagumo allowed himself to be surprised and outmaneuvered. The result was a disaster for the Japanese fleet, the loss of four fleet-class carriers could not easily be remedied with Japan's slender resources. The Midway defeat sent reverberations throughout the Japanese military machinery and was a major reason for the inability of the Japanese to carry out their ambitious plans in the South and Southwest Pacific.

The material about the genesis of the American invasion of Guadalcanal comes from my own *Guadalcanal*. The distaste and opposition of General MacArthur and Admiral Ghormley for the whole operation are thoroughly explored therein. They were dead wrong, of course, and Admiral King was dead right. Had the Japanese succeeded in building up the airfield that we know as Henderson Field, they would have had such complete control of the air over Australia and New Guinea that General MacArthur's Papua campaign would never have gotten started. But MacArthur's objections were not so much to the operation as to the fact that he was not going to control it. Throughout the Southwest Pacific campaign and the South Pacific campaign, he was angry because the Joint Chiefs of Staff, who had promised him control, would not give it to him. The successful Japanese landings at Buna and Lae indicated the Japanese superiority in the air and on the sea. They came at a time when MacArthur was just beginning to get organized. Had not the Guadalcanal invasion materialized, New Guinea would have been lost in August 1942.

7 Overland Attack

The reports of the South Seas Detachment and the Japanese Volume 1 on Southeast naval operations are the major sources for the activities of General Horii's force. The whole Japanese attack plan was changed by the Midway defeat. The army was now expected to do what the navy had done before, move to take Port Moresby. The accounts of the fighting along the Kokoda trail from the Allied point of view come from Milner's *Victory in Papua* and Mayo's *Bloody Buna*. The material about the Guadalcanal invasion is from my own book on that subject.

The Allied air build up in the Southwest Pacific was much more forceful and speedier than the ground force build up. From the day that the Japanese landed at Buna, they were in trouble because of the Allied air interdiction of their supply ships. Half a dozen transports were sunk in that operation, and the army transportation system was badly damaged. From that point on, the army had to depend on the navy for supply and the navy was busy with Guadalcanal.

The Japanese in New Guinea, as their accounts show, had no difficulties about manpower and very little about ammunition. Their real problem was getting food and medicines to the troops. The authorities at Rabaul had seriously underestimated that problem; ultimately, the men on New Guinea paid for it. But in the beginning, the Japanese were very effective. They had about 12,000 men in the Buna–Gona area and on the Kokoda Track, far more than the Allies could put into New Guinea at the time.

8 The Japanese Attack

The building of the Allied airfields on New Guinea, a prime factor in their defense, is delineated in Milner's *Victory in Papua*. The material about Japanese military training is from my own studies of the Japanese army and my *Japan's War*. The account of Japanese operations is from the army and navy Boei volumes on New Guinea.

As is shown in this chapter, one of the constant nagging problems in the New Guinea campaign was the lack of coordination between MacArthur's headquarters and the Australians, who knew the country of New Guinea far better. A prime example of this failure is the tale of the Ropuana Falls operation, a disaster that could easily have been prevented if General McNider and the MacArthur staff had listened to the Australians, who tried to tell them the route was impracticable. This is clearly shown in Milner. For an official army history, in fact, the Milner book is quite frank about many of the failings of the command structure.

9 The Allied Offensive

The material about the Japanese operations is from the army and navy Boei volumes. The material about MacArthur and his planning comes from Milner and from Mayo's *Bloody Buna*. By October, the battle for Guadalcanal was having serious repercussions on the New Guinea campaign, as can be seen in this chapter. There was another factor (not explored in this book): the growing success of American submarine operations out of Brisbane and Fremantle. The submarines were working around the Dutch East Indies, and they were sinking Japanese supply ships before they could get to Rabaul.

10 The Japanese Stand

For the discussion of Buna and the Americans fighting there, I am much indebted to George Weller, war correspondent for the *Chicago Daily News,* who covered the Buna campaign for his newspaper. He described in detail the Japanese defense techniques that confused the Americans for so long. The Japanese defenses were very strong and very ingeniously planned and used. The bunkers and blockhouses were built of coconut logs and concrete, some with metal reinforcement. The key was a remarkable system of communications, with outposts all around the central position; the outposts were further protected by scouts who were mostly in coconut trees. Weller described in detail how the Japanese would entice the Americans to attack, letting them come up to within a few feet of the bunker, and then begin picking them off from behind while the main force unleashed a hail of fire. It worked time and again; at Gona, it worked against the Australians. Correspondent Weller also told me about the conditions under which the Americans and Australians lived. Similar material is to be found in Milner. The accounts of the Japanese situation are from the Boei series.

The difficulties of General Harding and the men of the 32nd Infantry, well-documented in the Milner book, are an indication of the disastrous results of throwing untrained men into battle. It was not just a question of the enlisted men's lack of training. The whole division was completely unready for combat, particularly for combat in tropical conditions. A prime example of the errors that were made, was the dying of khaki uniforms with camouflage colors for use in the field. The liquids used produced a nonporous cotton that retained the heat and moisture and caused virtually every man to suffer from jungle rot and other skin irritations, some so serious that men had to be taken out of the field. And when they came up against the Japanese enemy, the men of the 32nd Division were thoroughly inept and confused. This was the fault of the training system, period.

11 Buna

The major sources for this chapter are the Milner book, the reminiscences of George Weller, the Boei volumes on New Guinea operations, and Mayo's *Bloody Buna*. Major David Parker, who is quoted in this chapter, made a report on his observations of the fighting.

At Buna, the men of the U.S. 32nd Division came up

against the Japanese knee mortars for the first time. These rifle grenade launchers were one of the most effective infantry weapons of the early stages of the Pacific War. They were miniature mortars, and the Japanese were expert in their use. Colonel Miller's battalion was one of those observed by Correspondent Weller. Its attack on the bridge was completely stymied by superior Japanese defense tactics. And, in assessing the fighting of this period, it should be remembered that the Japanese enemy was superior in numbers, its defensive positions were well established, and the Japanese knew the terrain where the Americans did not.

The most serious single problem of General Harding and the 32nd Division was inadequate training. Because of it, General Harding did not have a great deal of confidence in his officers. But he understood why they failed when they did and he tended to forgive and hope that they would learn from experience. At the top, Generals MacArthur and Eichelberger, who knew nothing of the problems up front and did not even realize their own responsibility for sending untrained men into action, were extremely critical. Their criticism was leveled against the Australians as well as the Americans. General Blamey and his Australian officers understood far more of what was happening and why than did the American high command. The fact was that as of 1942 the American army was not much of an army, at home or abroad. At home, troops were training and learning. But at home, the untrained were being pushed into battle and the impression they gave was of ineptitude and sometimes of cowardice. This would be true that autumn in North Africa as well as in the Pacific.

12 The Buna Blues

Every source I consulted, with the exception of the MacArthur headquarters reports, indicates the total inadequacy of General MacArthur's staff planning and operations offices. At Brisbane, the high command simply did not understand what was happening at Gona and Buna. Although men up front tried to tell the brass something about the strength of the Japanese defenses, General MacArthur preferred to believe that both Americans and Australians were lagging, and he attributed their reverses to cowardice and lack of effort. As events showed and as General Eichelberger later admitted, back at Brisbane and later at Port Moresby, the brass was dead wrong. They had sent men into the jungle to fight, without adequate training, equipment or food supply. (The Americans at Buna were down to one-third of a C ration a day.) They remained unable to supply the troops at the front with adequate food or medicines. And they criticized endlessly.

The story of General Eichelberger's involvement in the Buna campaign is one of the most telling of this early period of the war in showing just how inept and overbearing the American high command could be. MacArthur's draconian order to Eichelberger to come back with his shield or on it, was only the beginning. It set the stage for what was to happen next.

13   Buna Shock

After General MacArthur sent General Eichelberger up front to fire General Harding, the pressure was on. In a way it was an indication of the futility of sending to the front a man like General Sutherland, MacArthur's chief of staff, who knew nothing of the problems involved and did not know the people involved except through his own spit-and-polish prejudices. One of the problems of the Southwest Pacific Command as far as fighting was concerned was that the staff represented the peacetime army more than did the staff of any other command. It was a transplant from the Manila Army Navy Club.

The first victim was General Harding and the text here and in subsequent chapters shows that his relief was unnecessary, unconscionable, and a great error. General Eichelberger's delusions that he was not only a corps commander, but an infantry line officer took a long time to vanish. Before they did, a lot of Americans died because of Eichelberger's totally unnecessary low-echelon interference and mistakes. The fact was that the plan General Harding was following was the plan the Americans eventually employed and that the new officers who replaced Harding's battalion commanders did not do any better than the old ones had until they learned how to fight the Japanese. The replacements, in fact, set the war effort back a couple of notches.

The sources for the material in this chapter are again the Weller interview and Milner's official army history.

14 The Fall of Buna—I

The material for this chapter comes largely from the Boei narrative of the war in New Guinea. Also, Milner was the basic source for the story of American army operations.

General Eichelberger had the good grace to admit at the end of the Buna operation that he had been dead wrong in his assessments of the enemy, of the American and Australian troops, and of the responsibility of the high command. General MacArthur exhibited no such compassion. The great ego could not admit to having been wrong.

15 Buna Mission

After the fall of Buna Village it was only a matter of time for the Japanese, and they knew it. The Boei volumes indicate the determination of the Japanese command to hold, but there was no way it could be done without adequate reinforcement and supply. By this time, General Kenney's air forces were doing a very good job of interdicting the Japanese supply. The 11th Air Fleet was more occupied in the Solomons area just at this time, trying very hard to be of as much help as possible to the beleagured two divisions of Japanese troops cast ashore there without reinforcement or supply.

Until this point of the New Guinea campaign, the fighting had been done with very primitive weapons. Rifles, grenades, mortars, and machine guns were the most common. The Japanese had more artillery than the Americans and Australians, although their ammunition was limited. But at Buna Mission and beyond, the Australians began to use tanks and brought in more field guns. These made the difference. It was a lot easier to attack a coconut log fortress with a tank or a field gun than to try to subdue the occupants with grenades and satchel charges. The Japanese had some tanks, too. They had used them at Milne Bay. But they did not have many tanks, and most of theirs were bogged down and lost at Milne Bay. Rabaul did not try to send them any more.

Even after General Eichelberger saw the Japanese defenses at Buna Village and realized how wrong he had been, he found it impossible to divest himself of his proclivity to interfere in battalion operations. He alone has to bear the responsibility for the disaster at Entrance Creek because he refused Colonel Grose permission to do what Grose knew should be done. And when it was all over, Grose was proved right and Eichelberger wrong. It would have been much simpler if General Eichelberger had followed the pattern of America's very best World War II general, Omar Bradley, whose standard advice to his commanders was, "Do what I tell you, do it any way you want, but do it."

16 The Fall of Buna—II

Again, a major source for this chapter was Correspondent George Weller's reminiscences of the Buna campaign. *Bloody Buna* has some interesting information about the fighting. Milner carries the narrative from the American point of view. The Boei army Volume 2 on New Guinea operations tells the Japanese story.

This chapter is another indication of the futility of meddling by high officers in infantry battalion maneuvers. General Eichelberger ran the show again here and, as usual, the result was a mess. In spite of the meddling, not because of it, the Allies did take Buna, and then General Eichelberger's eyes were open to what the American and Australian troops had faced in assaulting this stronghold. He had the good grace to admit he had been wrong about the troops. Not General MacArthur, who had called his own men of the 32nd Division "cowards." He now blamed the outside world (read Joint Chiefs of Staff) for criticizing the failure of the Southwest Pacific forces to take the eastern coast of New Guinea earlier. It was a typical MacArthur maneuver.

17 End of the Papua Battle

The fall of Buna coincided with major changes in the logistics of the Southwest Pacific command. More troops, more tanks, more aircraft, more everything became available in the winter of 1943. The pipeline from America was opening up a little now that the troops and supplies had been delivered to North Africa. General MacArthur, however, once more proved that he did not really know what was happening in New Guinea when he interfered in General Blamey's operations, only to have his fingers burned.

Throughout, Milner has detailed the heroic actions of the men of the 126th U.S. Infantry Regiment, thrown into battle with inadequate equipment and ill trained by their superiors. They had gone into battle 1,400 strong, and they emerged 165 strong. That means the regiment suffered casualties of about 88 per cent during the Buna campaign. No one ever saw the public apology that General MacArthur owed this unit, which had saved his reputation in spite of his blunders.

The Japanese, who by January had no hopes of victory in New Guinea, continued to resist with every fiber. Colonel Yamamoto and Captain Yasuda had gone to their maker voluntarily, suicides apologizing to the emperor for their failures. But the failures were not theirs, goodness knows. They fought to the end; the failure lay at Rabaul and Truk where the high commands for the area were unable to mount the resupply missions necessary to save the Japanese position. Ultimately, the failure lay at the door of Imperial General Headquarters (IGH), which had failed to anticipate the violent American reaction to the attempt to cut Australia off from the United States. It could have been done in 1942, but only if the Japanese had been willing to move major troop elements down to the Solomons and New Guinea before the Americans could manage their logistics. Japanese intelligence, so remarkable at the tactical level, was marked by major failures at the command level.

18   Against Rabaul

With the fall of Buna, Colonel Tsuji of the Imperial General Headquarters (IGH) went back to Tokyo from Rabaul to report on the total failures of the Solomons and New Guinea campaigns. At this point the Japanese had not written off New Guinea or the Northern Solomons. Tokyo was confident that a little more effort would turn the tide and put the Japanese juggernaut back on track. So General Imamura and Admiral Yamamoto were ordered to concentrate on New Guinea, while holding in the Solomons, until the strong points of Lae and Salamaua could be used as a fulcrum to take Port Moresby. Despite the constant failure of supply missions to New Guinea, the Japanese continued to believe that they were but inches from their goal.

General MacArthur was still talking about capturing Rabaul, but the Joint Chiefs had already decided that Rabaul was to be isolated and left to wither, while the Allies went on around it, through the Central Pacific and up to the Philippines.

Once again the Japanese plan for New Guinea was bound to fail because Imperial General Headquarters underestimated the American forces involved and the determination of Americans and Australians to drive the Japanese from this area. It was no good asking General Imamura to "reinforce the garrisons of Lae and Salamaua." What was needed was to bring in three or four divisions, and this was not even considered. The troops were available, in the Dutch East Indies, in the Philippines, in China. But each month it became harder to move them because of the growing Allied submarine menace. And now, in the New Guinea area the Allied air power was making itself felt. The fate of that January convoy to Lae, which sank two transports bearing half the supplies for the 102nd Japanese Regiment, is an indication of the way the wind was blowing. The ease with which the Australians repelled the Japanese overland attack on Wau should have warned General Imamura that his hope of attacking through the mountains with limited forces was doomed to failure.

19 The Battle of the Bismarck Sea

At the end of February, Admiral Yamamoto could have told the Imperial General Staff what was wrong. It was what was wrong from the beginning of the Pacific War, the underestimation of the U.S. potential. Admiral Yamamoto had known for many years that the only possible way for Japan to defeat the Americans was by striking a lightning blow that would paralyze their fleet and so discourage them that they would come to the peace table and accept Japanese conquests in the Pacific. Yamamoto believed this was possible, based on his own studies of the American character during his terms as naval attaché in Washington. He might have been right; had the Pearl Harbor striking force done its job and had all the American carriers in the Pacific been wiped out in December 1941, American gloom could have been pretty serious. But the destruction would have had to be complete.

As it was, the Japanese attack had aroused American fury, and by the beginning of 1943 the results were showing in the Solomons and New Guinea. The complete destruction of the Bismarck Sea convoy by Allied air power alone had to be a lesson to Imperial General Headquarters (IGH), and it was. The Japanese air forces in the South Pacific waters were ordered to destroy the Allied air forces, thus making the seas again safe for Japanese vessels. This program was ordered. Admiral Yamamoto was in charge of it. But Yamamoto did not want to risk his entire naval air force in this manner. He launched several major assaults on Guadalcanal and on New Guinea, and when they produced virtually no results, he leaped to the conclusion that the Allied air power in the area was really not much. The effort to destroy the Allied air forces was to be declared to be successful and abandoned, although it would do virtually nothing to slow down the Allies. The fact was that by this point the naval airmen in the South Pacific area were well aware of the growing strength of Allied air and the diminished power of their own. They were not getting the new aircraft and the trained pilots they needed to win an air war but, the Japanese military system being what it was, there was no use to complain.

20 Spring Offensive 1943

Operation I was launched and failed. Tokyo was told that it was a great success.

While the Japanese spoke of regaining all the old ground in New Guinea and the Solomons, the Allies were confidently moving forward to isolate Rabaul. General MacArthur was still talking about capturing it. Operation I and the death of Yamamoto really brought an end to Japanese offensive operations in the South Pacific and Southwest Pacific. From now on, they would be almost completely on the defensive.

21 The Huon Peninsula

The major sources for this chapter are the Japanese Boei volumes on naval and army operations in the New Guinea area, Milner, and Samuel Eliot Morison's *Victory in the South Pacific*. Also, an interview with Admiral Barbey in 1947 was useful for dealing with the amphibious landing material. The Boei volume dealing with defense of the Japanese homeland has a long section on the development of the B-29, as watched from Tokyo, through neutral sources. Actually, the capture of Lae and Salamaua were more or less anticlimactic. The Japanese had really lost the New Guinea campaign already.

22 On Towards Rabaul

The whole of the New Guinea campaign now became anticlimactic. There was really only one more move to be taken, and that was to capture the Admiralty Islands. Even the need for the taking of the Vogelkop was questionable, although from there the Japanese could do considerable harassment of the Allied build up for attack on the Philippines. But for several reasons—including the ignorance of the Joint Chiefs of Staff of local conditions and the stubborn insistence by General MacArthur that Rabaul was still significant and must be captured—the preparations for the assault on Rabaul continued. MacArthur's complaints and activities are well documented in Milner.

The attack on Arawe was strictly overkill against an unneeded objective. The Cape Gloucester airfields were never used for anything except casual flights.

The same could almost be said of Finschhafen, although the Japanese 20th Division would have had to be dealt with anyhow. The Satelberg attacks were expensive, but the Australians did a remarkable job here, as they did throughout the campaign.

23 The Admiralties

This operation against the Admiralties was so casually approached that many people did not know the enormous importance of these islands for the future of the Pacific campaign. Seeadler Harbor would become the staging point for the American fleet from this point until the capture of Guam in the summer of 1944, when it would begin to build up and would ultimately become Admiral Nimitz's forward Pacific Fleet base. In the interim, for the carrier raids against the Central Pacific islands and for the invasion of the Marianas and then the Philippines, Manus would be invaluable. It would also be known to the sailors as the most uninviting leave port they had ever seen. From time to time, ships would come in for replenishment and the men would be landed with cases of beer to swim, play football and softball, and try to amuse themselves in the sand. The harbor was beautiful, one of the finest in the world. And that is why it was so important.

As noted in the text, the Japanese defense of the Admiralties was very weak. Major air and sea attacks never materialized because the Japanese did not have the resources to launch them. The Los Negros and Manus garrisons fought valiantly but without real hopes of victory.

The fighting at Hauwei on Manus Island was the fiercest of all. In this fighting, the Japanese defenders gave a preview of what was going to happen all the rest of the way across the Pacific. Outnumbered, without a chance to escape or save themselves, forty-five Japanese navy sailors set up defenses that stalled the Americans for days. Every one of the defenders was killed but not before they had exacted a very large price in American blood.

The Japanese were under no illusions about the importance

of the Admiralties to the Allies. Even during the Okinawa campaign, they continued to try to attack at Seeadler Harbor. Several *kaiten* suicide submarines were launched with Manus as their objective. The Japanese inside hoped to sink aircraft carriers, but all they ever sank there was one merchant ship. Even to the end, they never stopped trying and had more plans on the boards.

BIBLIOGRAPHY

U.S. Sources

Hoyt, Edwin P. *Blue Skies and Blood: The Battle of the Coral Sea*. New York: Paul Eriksson, 1975.
———*Guadalcanal*. New York: Stein & Day, 1982.
———*The Glory of the Solomons*. New York: Stein & Day, 1983.
Ito, Masanori. *The End of the Imperial Japanese Navy*. New York: W. W. Norton, 1962.
Johnston, George E. *The Toughest Fighting in the World*. New York: Duell, Sloan & Pearce, 1943.
Kahn, E. J., Jr. *GI Jungle*. New York: Simon & Schuster, 1943.
Mayo, Lida. *Bloody Buna*. New York: Doubleday, 1974.
Miller, John, Jr. *Cartwheel, the Reduction of Rabaul*. Washington, D.C.: Office of the Chief of Military History, 1959.
———*Guadalcanal: The First Offensive*. Washington, D.C.: Historical Division, Department of the Army, 1949.
Milner, Samuel. *Victory in Papua*. Washington, D.C.: Office of the Chief of Military History, 1957.
Morison, Samuel Eliot. *History of United States Naval Operations in World War II*. Boston: Atlantic-Little, Brown, 1948–1959.
Morton, Louis. *The Fall of the Philippines*. Washington, D.C.: Office of the Chief of Military History, 1953.
Paull, Raymond. *Retreat from Kokoda*. London: Heinemann, 1958.
Shaw, Henry I. Jr., and Maj. Douglas T. Kane, USMC. *Isolation of Rabaul*. Washington D.C.: Historical Branch, G-3 Division, Headquarters U.S. Marine Corps, 1963.
U.S. Strategic Bombing Survey. *The Allied Campaign Against Rabaul*. Washington, D.C.: U.S. GPO, 1946.
Willoughby, Maj. Gen. Charles A. *MacArthur, 1941–1951*. New York: McGraw Hill, 1954.

Japanese Sources

Near the end of World War II, the Japanese Self Defense Agency began the publication of 101 volumes of historical records and narrative to tell the Japanese people the facts of the Pacific War. Since so many Japanese records were lost in the battles, many of the accounts depend heavily on American sources, but the Japanese were careful to check against survivor stories and existing reports. For this book, I used the three volumes concerning Japanese naval operations in the South and Southwest Pacific and three volumes concerning Japanese army and army air force operations in the same areas. Also, the reports of the South Seas Detachment and accounts of the 17th Army and 18th Army operations prepared by Japanese sources.

Unpublished sources include materials for my forthcoming biography of Admiral Yamamoto and my forthcoming biography of General Tōjō.

INDEX